Myriads of Chinese Culture:
A Comparative Reading and Thinking

比较视野中的
中国文化

曾新　褚颖　主编

李海燕　钱雅欣　副主编

上海三联书店

序　言

　　2019 年，中共中央颁布《爱国主义教育实施纲要》，明确提出"要进行中华民族优秀传统文化教育"。新中国成立以来，我国出版发行的中国文化史方面的教材多达数十本，其中有些经典教材都已再版甚至三版，然而美中不足的是，其中大多数中国文化教材都以中文撰写，以简述的形式介绍中国文化。更重要的是，这些教材都是单向度的，仅仅站在中国人的角度认识和介绍中国文化，这与当今的世界形势以及中国的全球地位不免有些脱节之处。本教材的几位编者都是长期在第一线担任语言文化课程的教师，在多年的教学经历中，我们也发现，了解中国传统文化、能够使用地道的英语、又具有一定文化思辨能力，能够有效阐释和传播中华优秀传统文化的学生实在不多，这无疑是当今语言文化教学需要关注的现象。因此编纂一套双语中国文化教材是我们几位同道中人由来已久的愿望，也符合《爱国主义教育实施纲要》的要求。在编写过教材《文化万象：英语视听说》的《西方篇》和《中国篇》之后，我们又推出了这本以阅读材料为主的中国文化教材。

　　本教材涉及两个核心词汇，一为"中国"，二为"文化"。费孝通先生曾言："生活在一定文化中的人，对其文化要有自知之明，明白它的来历、形成的过程、所具有的特色和它的发展趋势，自知之明是为了加强文化转型的自主能力，取得适应新环境、新时代文化选择的自主地位。"因此，编一本中国文化教材，首先需要梳理其中这两个核心术语的来龙去脉。由于教材的体例问题，编者难以将这两个核心术语的沿革涵盖进某一章节，特此在序言中加以说明。

　　历史上的"中国"与现代的"中国"在含义上有很大不同。"中国"一词最晚在周初就出现了,古代"国"、"或"相通,意指城邑,因此当时的"中国"指的是周王直接统治的都城。后来其含义渐渐扩展为中央政权直接统治的地区或中原地区,并且具有了区别于夷狄、四方的文化内涵,贯穿着"中央之国","宗主之国"的含义。由于这一原因,很多学者到清朝仍对这一国名不以为然,章太炎说:"中国之名,别于四裔而为言。印度亦称摩伽陀为中国,日本亦称山阳为中国,此本非汉土所独有者。就汉土言汉土,则中国之名,以先汉郡县为界。然印度、日本之言中国者,举中土以对边郡;汉土之言中国者,举领域以对异邦,此其名实相殊之处",直接指明它名实不副。黄遵宪甚至说:"吾人所最惭愧者,莫如我国无国名之一事。寻常通称,或曰诸夏,或曰汉人,或曰唐人,皆朝名也;外人所称,或曰震旦,或曰支那,皆非我所自命之名也。"

　　然而,"中国"这一国名仍然流传并沿用至今,其中民国时期孙中山先生和其他革命党人对这一术语的发展提倡之功不可小觑。孙中山先生倡导"五族共和"思想,提出"对于满洲,不以复仇为事,而务与之平等共处于中国之内","国家(中国)之本,在于人民合汉、满、蒙、回、藏诸地为一国,即和汉、满、蒙、回、藏诸族为一人"。"中国"由此不再仅仅指中央政权统治的地区及其代表的正统文化,完成了其由古代至近代意义上的转变,逐渐具备了我们现在提到这一术语所有的地理、历史、民族和文化等多重含义。

　　较之于"中国","文化"一词更难界定。据不完全统计,文化的定义有将近两百种。英语中的"culture"来自拉丁语,意为"栽培"。因其农业和园艺学内涵,在二十世纪之前,"culture"这一术语大多都用来表达个人修养的提高和改善之意,尤其是以教育为途径的提高和改善。十九世纪中期,有些科学家用其来表达人类普世的能力。到二十世纪起,这一术语成为了人类学的一个核心概念,其范畴几乎涵盖了遗传之外的所有人类现象。"culture"这一术语的演变过程使得其难以界定,但亦更加激发了学界的研究热情。

中文中的"文化"一词古已有之。古代辞书中的"文"乃"纹身、纹理"之意,由此引申出文物典籍、装饰和美德等义。"化"为"改易、生成、造化"之意。因此古代中文的"文化"是以文教改易,教化的意思,与武力征服相对。但现代意义上的"文化"是从日语转译而来,已极具西方"culture"之内涵。

梳理这两个核心术语的过程使我们明白,全球化时代的人们虽然都在谈论"文化",但中西文化却各有其来路和特色,要实现费孝通所倡导的文化自觉,我们需要了解中国文化,也需要了解世界,更需要了解世界如何看待中国文化。倘不如此,适应当今环境,进行有效的文化传播和交流可能将会是一场空对空的言说。

循此思路和理念,我们策划了这本《比较视野中的中国文化》教材。与以往的同类教材相比,本教材的特色在于:

一、本教材以双语撰写,兼顾了英语和中国文化教学,更符合当今全球化要求以及党和国家"中国文化走出去"的战略构想。

二、本教材采用主流媒体报道以及名人著作的形式介绍中国文化,让材料自己说话,较之简述形式,这些材料也更具代表性和经典性。

三、本教材中的材料既有中国人的观点,也有西方人的看法;既有事实陈述,也有观点争鸣。这样的编排有助于培养学生的逻辑和思辨能力,让他们多角度全方位认识中国文化,认识他者,这样的编排更符合当今文化交流与传播"双向度"的需求,更具比较意识和全球视野。

四、比较视野是本教材最大的特色。每个单元核心术语的中西方词源梳理,焦点集中却中西视角兼备的材料,传统和现代的相互映照,都是编者苦心经营,希望能启发学生思考和洞见的"比较"的出发点。

具体到每个章节的设计,本教材的编排形式如下

1. 每个单元第一部分为"词源梳理",强调"追本溯源":引导学生认识中国文化的核心概念与西方的同和异。

2. 每个单元的第二部分为"引导阅读",基本都选取中西方主流媒体的报道,让学生倾听主流媒体声音。明瞭其立场和视角。

3. 在第二部分基础上,第三部分的"阅读与比较"选取中西方学者对于

同一本著作的不同译本,或者关于同一论题的学者的研究成果,中西对照,相映成趣,让学生在比较阅读中了解中西方观点,形成自己的见解。

4. 第四部分的"拓展阅读"是对第三部分的拓展和延伸,有助于学有余力的学生从更深层次上理解和思考第三部分的内容。

5. 各个单元都最终落脚于"现代回声"。教材中介绍传统文化,但更强调中国文化的延续性和生命力。这样的编排更容易引起当代学生的共鸣,让他们明白中国文化从不僵化,始终在与时俱进,因此才能源远流长,千年不绝,生机勃发。

最后,编者建议学生阅读梁漱溟所撰写的《中国文化要义》之绪论,如前所述,"文化"本身就非常复杂、庞杂,中国文化又绵延数千年,其复杂性更是不言而喻。梁漱溟的《中国文化要义》贵在其问题意识,在学习了前面的章节之后,编者希望学生由此能够再次思考中国文化的前世今生,精华与糟粕,问题与出路,而这才是每一个了解和热爱本国文化的中国人最重要的觉知和责任。

本教材编者深知,中国文化博大精深,研究成果浩如烟海,我们选取的板块和材料亦不免挂一漏万,管窥天地。我们虽殚精竭虑,如履薄冰,亦难免见笑方家。祈望同道鼓励和指教,我们将锱铢汲取,如获至宝,今后再版,本教材必能更上层楼。

曾　新

2019 年 10 月

目　录

第一章　历　　史

一、词源梳理

　　"历史"在中文里最初仅用"史"一字代表。甲骨文中"史"字与"事"相似，指事件。许慎《说文解字》说："史，记事者也；从又持中，中，正也。"可见"史"的本意即记事者，也就是"史官"。由此引申，"史"代表被史官被记录的事，也即文字记录的过去。

　　汉代有"史记"一词，先是用于指先秦史官所记而成的史书，东汉恒帝以后成为司马迁所写史书的专有名字，这是当时史书甚少、史学不发达的反映。魏晋南北朝时期，史书数量增多，"历代史"、"历史"、"史学"等新词应运而生。《三国志·吴书·吴主传》注引《吴书》，吴主孙权"博览书传历史，藉采奇异"。

　　这里的"历史"虽与上述"诸史"、"历代史"同样泛指各种史书，但含义要更宽泛，这是我国第一次出现"历史"一词。"历"字是指经历、历法，也就是人类经历的一段时间，在事件中加入时间的概念，"历史"一词就具有了当今的含义。

　　在西方，多数语言"历史"一词源出自希腊语ιστορία（Historia），原义为"探究，通过调查而得来的（关于过去的）知识"（a learning or knowing by inquiry；an account of one's inquiries；knowledge，account，historical account，record，narrative），可追溯到原始印欧语词根 weid-"to see"派生出 to know 之意。英语 history 经由古法语 estoire，histoire"story；chronicle， history"而来。在中世纪英语中 history 可能与 story 同义,因为通俗拉丁语中的字母 h 发音非常弱,法语、西班牙语、意大利语等现代罗曼语中都没有 h 这个音,法语中的 estoire 和 histoire 存在变体的可能性。

二、引导阅读
➢ 背景知识

近代以前,中国西部的葱岭、西南的喜马拉雅山脉、西北的阿尔泰山脉和昆仑山脉,东北的内外兴安岭,以及东面大海所构筑的天然屏障,极大阻碍了中华文明与外界的交往。而西方文明的演化,则自始至终处于不同核心区的激烈碰撞和深度交融中,很大程度上从两河流域、尼罗河流域等其他文明核心区移植而来,同时也将欧洲文明传入其他核心区。古代东西方文明以不同方式各自独立演进,其文明的内在特质及其在现代的发展轨迹有着显著差异。中西方文明的关键差异是什么,如何相互交流,取长补短,这是中外不断探讨的一个问题。

伯兰特·罗素(Bertrand Russell),英国人,20 世纪著名哲学家、数学家。著述丰富,广涉哲学、数学、科学、伦理、社会、教育、历史、宗教、政治等领域。作为一位关注并拥护人类进步事业的学者,罗素一直对中国人民怀有特殊的真诚而友好的感情。上世纪 20 年代初,对西方文明和苏俄体制深感失望的罗素收到访华邀请,欣然前往。他在京沪等地巡回演讲,也对所到之处进行了实地考察,返回英国后就此行感受写成《中国问题》一书。

全书共 15 章,作者以深刻的历史观和全球意识全面阐述了他对中国问题的见解,集中讨论了中国的历史和当下,西方列强,尤其是日本与中国的关系。此外,罗素也指出了中国经济、交通、工业等的发展前景,呼吁中国重视教育。同时,他又代表有良知的西方现代知识分子,从比较角度谈中国的历史、文化和民族性格,书中对中西文明的对比以及对中国人性格特质的分析引发了持久的讨论,也得到了广泛的认可。因为《中国问题》这本书,孙中山先生称罗素为"唯一理解中国的西方人"。本文摘自其中第 11 章"中西文明对比"。

Chinese and Western Civilization Contrasted

(Bertrand Russell, *The Problem of China*,

George Allen and Unwin, 1966.)

There is at present in China a close contact between our civilization and that which is native to the Celestial Empire. It is still a doubtful question whether this contact will breed a new civilization better than either of its parents, or whether it will merely destroy the native culture and replace it by that of America. Contacts between different civilizations have often in the past proved to be landmarks in human progress.

With the exception of Spain and America in the sixteenth century, I cannot think of any instance of two civilizations coming into contact after such a long period of separate development as has marked those of China and Europe. Considering this extraordinary separateness, it is surprising that mutual understanding between Europeans and Chinese is not more difficult. In order to make this point clear, it will be worthwhile to dwell for a moment on the historical origins of the two civilizations.

Western Europe and America have a practically homogeneous mental life, which I should trace to three sources: (1) Greek culture; (2) Jewish religion and ethics; (3) modern industrialism, which itself is an outcome of modern science. We may take Plato, the Old Testament, and Galileo as representing these three elements.

China belongs, in the dawn of its history, to the great river empires, so the original civilization of China was rendered possible by the Yellow River. Lao-Tze and Confucius, who both belong to the sixth century B. C. , have already the characteristics which we should regard as distinctive of the modern Chinese.

The oldest known Chinese sage is Lao-Tze, the founder of Taoism. He held that every person, every animal, and everything has a certain way or manner of behaving which is natural to him, or her, or it, and that we ought to conform to this way ourselves and encourage others to conform to it. "Tao" means "way". His ideas were developed by his disciple Chuang-Tze, who is more interesting. The philosophy which both advocated was one of freedom. They thought ill of government, and of all interferences with Nature. They complained of the hurry of modern life, which they contrasted with the calm existence of those whom they called "the pure men of old."

However, the Taoists were entirely ousted from the favour of the educated classes by Confucianism. I must confess that I am unable to appreciate the merits of Confucius. His writings are largely occupied with trivial points of etiquette, and his main concern is to teach people how to behave correctly on various occasions. His system is one of pure ethics, without religious dogma; it has not given rise to a powerful priesthood, and it has not led to persecution. It certainly has succeeded in producing a whole nation possessed of exquisite manners and perfect courtesy. Europeans often regard this as weakness, but it is really strength, the strength by which the Chinese have hitherto conquered all their conquerors.

There is one, and only one, important foreign element in the traditional civilization of China, and that is Buddhism. Buddhism came to China from India in the early centuries of the Christian era, and acquired a definite place in the religion of the country. A man may be both a Buddhist and a Confucian, because nothing in either is incompatible with the other. Buddhism has a message to the world intended to cure the despair which it regards as natural to those who have no religious faith. It assumes an instinctive pessimism only to be cured by some gospel. Confucianism has nothing of all this. It assumes people fundamentally at peace with the world, wanting only instruction as to how to live, not encouragement to live at all. The result of the co-existence of these two religions in China has been that the more religious and contemplative natures turned to Buddhism, while the active administrative type was content with Confucianism, which was always the official teaching, in which candidates for the civil service were examined.

Comparing the civilization of China with that of Europe, one finds in China most of what was to be found in Greece, but nothing of the other two elements of our civilization, namely Judaism and science. China is practically destitute of religion, not only in the upper classes, but throughout the population. What will be the outcome of the contact of this ancient civilization with the West?

The distinctive merit of our civilization, I should say, is the scientific method; the distinctive merit of the Chinese is a just conception of the ends of life. It is these two that one must hope to see gradually uniting. But, it will be said, you have been comparing Western practice with Chinese theory; if you had compared Western theory with Chinese practice, the balance would have come out quite differently. There is, of course, a great deal of truth in this. Possession is certainly dear to the heart of the average Chinaman. Their politics are corrupt, and their powerful men make money in disgraceful ways. All this it is impossible to deny.

Nevertheless, as regards the other two evils, self-assertion and domination, I notice a definite superiority to ourselves in Chinese practice. There is much less desire than among the white races to tyrannize over other people. If any nation in the world could ever be "too proud to fight," that nation would be China. Although there have been many wars in China, the natural outlook of the Chinese is very pacifistic.

It is interesting to contrast what the Chinese have sought in the West with what the West has sought in China. The Chinese in the West seek knowledge, in the hope that knowledge may prove a gateway to wisdom. White men have gone to China with three motives: to fight, to make money, and to convert the Chinese to our religion. The last of these motives has the merit of being idealistic, and has inspired many heroic lives. But the soldier, the merchant, and the missionary are alike concerned to stamp our civilization upon the world.

Contact between East and West is likely to be fruitful to both parties. They may learn from us the indispensable minimum of practical efficiency, and we may learn from them something of that contemplative wisdom which has enabled them to persist while all the other nations of antiquity have perished.

➢ 注释

the Celestial Empire　天朝

dwell on　详述；老是想着

homogeneous　adj. 由相同(或同类型)事物(或人)组成的；同种类的

disciple　n. 信徒，门徒，弟子

oust　vt. (～ sb. from sth.)剥夺，罢免，革职

etiquette　n. 礼仪，礼数

dogma　n. 教义，信条

hitherto　adv. 到目前为止，迄今

incompatible　adj. 不相容的，矛盾的

destitute　adj. 极度缺乏，赤贫的

➢ 练习

1. What are the three common sources of European and American civ-

ilizations?

2. What are the characteristics of traditional Chinese civilization? What elements distinguish the civilization of China from that of Europe and America?

3. According to the author, what do China and the West seek in each other? Does the author have a positive attitude towards their contact, and why?

三、阅读与比较:司马迁和他的《史记》

➤ 背景知识

中华文明源远流长,史家的贡献不容忽略。与其他古老文明相比,中华文明在起始阶段就十分重视历史记载,司马迁的《史记》被列为"正史"后,受后人效法,更是代代修史,以致"二十四史"。

《史记》被誉为"史家之绝唱,无韵之离骚",其史学价值与文学审美吸引着无数研究者,尤其20世纪的《史记》历史学研究取得了突破性进展,从繁复的史料考证上升到系统深入的史学理论研究。

李长之(1910—1978)是盛名卓著的中国古典文学评论家,他在代表作《司马迁之人格与风格》中精辟地指出,"单篇文章看,他(司马迁)所尽的乃是一个艺术家的责任,只有就他整部的《史记》说,他才是尽的历史家的责任。"作为我国第一部全面评介司马迁和《史记》的专著,《司马迁之人格与风格》重视创作主体、主张整体分析,而不是无穷无尽地沉迷于细枝末节,这一研究策略后来逐渐成为了《史记》研究的主旋律,后世研究司马迁及《史记》所牵涉到的重大问题几乎在这部书中都有洞彻和阐释。

美国汉学家格兰特·哈代(Grant Hardy)和史蒂文·W·达兰特(Stephen W Durrant)对《史记》的整体性研究正是海外汉学界受中国《史记》研究趋势变化影响的体现。前者聚焦《史记》独特的编撰体例,对比司马迁与西方主流史学家选择叙事主体时的不同史学观;后者则从《太史公自序》与《报任安书》中司马迁的矛盾形象出发,层层剖析立志效法孔子编史的司马迁,在面对孔子不曾面对的两难处境时是如何自处的。

➤ 素材 1.《史记》一书的个性

(李长之《司马迁的人格及风格》,商务印书馆,2011 年。)

凡是读一部书,就像认识一个朋友一样,如果不晓得他的个性,则无论说短论长,全无是处,在论《史记》时,我觉得至少这下面的几个前提是必须注意到的:

第一,要知道司马迁是拿整个的《史记》与人相见的,并非单篇分开给我们(虽然在汉朝似乎是各篇单行,但那是流传的情形,并非著述的情形),因此他对于每一问题的看法,我们不能单就篇名的外形去找。例如管仲、晏婴的贡献或历史地位,如果我们只看《管晏列传》当然要责备司马迁所记太略的,然而在《齐世家》中却仍有详细的记载。又如信陵君的真相,单看《信陵列传》也不够,而在《范雎蔡泽列传》中才能看出来。原来他没有像《信陵列传》中人格那样完整,在急人之难上也有时很犹豫。再则他在魏国的关系之重要,单看《信陵列传》也仍是不足,那就又要看《魏世家》。再如子产本见于《循吏列传》,但《循吏列传》中的子产太平凡了,不够一个大政治家,可是在《郑世家》中却便又见出他的真正的设施来。原来司马迁在一个历史家之外,兼是一个艺术家,他晓得每一篇传记一定有一个中心,为求艺术上的完整起见,便把次要的论点(在艺术上次要)放在别处了。这是前人所发见的"互见法"。我们可以这样说,就他单篇文章看,他所尽的乃是一个艺术家的责任,只有就他整部的《史记》说,他才是尽的历史家的责任。倘就单篇而责备之,他就太冤枉了。

第二,就原则上说,司马迁对自己的主观见解和客观描写是分开去处理的。大概在传记中的叙述往往是纯粹客观的,而主观的评衡则见之于《自序》中说到所以做各传之故处。所以我觉得要真正看司马迁的见解时,《自序》最重要。其次便是每篇的赞。但多数的赞是处在客观与主观之间的。所以就是有些评衡,也是个人的意味(personal)居多,如叙到个人的经验或与传中的人物的关系等,有时则是传中的补充而已。我觉得司马迁这个办法也很好,让人假若要看客观的描写,就看他的传记。假若要看他的通体的看法,就看他的序。假若对他的自己的个人的印象发生兴趣,就看他的赞。他的体例如此(但只是疏而不失的体例),清清爽爽,免得有人执此而求彼,反而加以责难。至于司马迁在事实上是否绝对在描述中维持客观的限度呢,那是另一个问题,他之选择描写的材料,也无疑是经过了主观的决定的,但无论如何,他这体例是我们在论《史记》时必须考虑到的。

第三,我们又必须了解司马迁的反面文章。他是一个巧于讽刺的人,他善达难言之隐。所以他的本意,必须就全书推求而得,决不能专看表面文章,例如书中的最大的讽刺,是对付汉代,尤其集中在武帝。他的方法却是指秦骂汉。这个秘密,自明清以来的学者,都已经窥破了。同时,他能以褒作贬,笔下是酸酸辣辣的,那要完全从他的语气中看出来。《史记》一书的难读,这也是一个大原因。必须靠我们对他的表现方式的熟悉,才能得其真正命意所在。

第四,我们又当晓得《史记》中虽然有些得自他父亲的旧稿,但各篇已大体上经过了他的润色。所以纵然看出某一篇可能成自他的父亲之手,而仍然可以由之而见司马迁的见解——至少是他同意的见解。再则《史记》固有补缺,但全文中也往往有他原来的几段书稿,我们也都须分别援用,不能因为业已认定某篇为后人补改,就全然不加信任了。

第五,我们更必须注意《史记》在是一部历史书之外,又是一部文艺创作,从来的史书没有像它这样具有作者个人的色彩的。其中有他自己的生活经验、生活背境,有他自己的情感作用,有他自己的肺腑和心肠。所以这不但是一部包括古今上下的史书,而且是司马迁自己的一部绝好传记。因此,我们必须能把握《史记》中司马迁之主观的用意,才能理解这部书,才能欣赏这部书。

➤ 素材 2. Sima Qian：Representing The World

(Hardy, Grant. *Worlds of Bronze and Bamboo* , Columbia University Press, 1999.)

Historical writing in the West begins with the inquiries (*historia*) of

Herodotus, who set the basic pattern of historiography that continues to this day. A historian, as Herodotus invented the role, is someone who, through a combination of curiosity, intelligence, and questioning, has managed to discover something of the past and then offers the results of these researches to the public in his or her own voice. As we read his *Histories*, we are constantly aware of the presence of the author at our elbow, telling stories, pointing out this or that, offering judgments, and generally exhibiting the wit, sensibility and chattiness that make Herodotus a memorable guide through the past. A history is not a representation of the past itself; it is a representation of the author's conception of the past. There is no history without a historian, just as there is no memory without a rememberer. English speakers are constantly reminded of these intimate connection by the somewhat confusing dual function of the word *history*, which refers to both writings about the past and the past itself.

The role of a historian has been refined since Herodotus's day—more emphasis is not given to the critical reading of sources, to the documentation in the public reporting of research, to the identification of causes, and to the recognition of the historian's own biases—but the central issue remains that of Herodotus. Historians are still saying, "You can trust me. I know what I'm talking about. I am using my sources responsibly." Historical rhetoric in the West is a mode of persuasion, the object of which is to convince the reader that the historian's account of history reflects the truth, that her reconstruction accurately represents what actually happened.

It is possible to fit Sima Qian's history in this general framework, and early Western sinologists were eager to do so. Trying to convince their audience not only of their own credibility but also of the worth of their subject matter, they naturally stressed those elements of the *Shiji* that seemed to cast Sima Qian in the expected role. He turned out, not surprisingly, to be a tireless researcher and traveler, an archivist, a critical user of sources, and an "objective" reporter. He was also blessed with the hallmarks of a great historian: he was a fine storyteller, an innovator, and a compassionate observer of human behavior. There is evidence in the *Shiji* for each of these characteristics, but taken together they do not fully account for Sima Qian's work, for the *Shiji* is a very different type of historical text.

The *Shiji* offers a multiplicity of voices and perspectives, and to read the text is to enter a confusing world of narratives and counter-narratives, differing explanations and corrections, and a variety of literary styles and historiographical approaches. It represents neither a unified view of the past nor a consistent interpretation of what history means. This might not be surprising in a *Shiji* that is a compendium of disparate materials gathered together with a minimum of editorial oversight, and in fact, many scholars have seen the *Shiji* in this light—the creation of an ambitious editor with too much material and too little time. Yet Sima Qian works hard to create an identity for himself in the last chapter of the *Shiji*, which should give us pause. By revealing something of his own biography and motivations, he invites readers to speculate on the connections between his text and his life. By providing a comprehensive overview, chapter by chapter, with comments on why he chose to include each, he suggests that there is, despite appearances, an overarching plan to his method. Finally, by concluding with a few brief but suggestive remarks about the organization of the *Shiji*, he intimates that there is meaning in the arrangement of his history. In trying to determine exactly how the *Shiji* handles history, it is useful to begin with its most distinctive feature—its structure. The structure of the *Shiji* is complex and it deliberately calls attention to itself in the way that contrasts with the most straightforward narrations of early Western histories.

When Sima Qian set out to write a history of the world, he found the traditional historical forms inadequate. The collection of speeches in the *Classic of Documents* , the year-by-year chronicles in the *Spring and Autumn Annals* and its commentaries, and the anecdotes arranged by states in the *Intrigues of the Warring States* all were insufficient to convey his conception of what history should be. So he invented a new method of organizing historical data that divided his account of the past into five major sections: basic annals, chronological tables, treatises, hereditary houses, and categorized biographies.

In the *Shiji* Sima has presented a history of the entire world as he knew it from its legendary beginnings to his own day. His account focuses on China, but it also includes chapters on the barbarian tribes at the peripheries of the Chinese cultural sphere. Within China itself, the focus is on the political and military elite, but Sima expands his account to include chapters on other individuals who possess different types of authority. In addition to portraying the human world, Sima also reserves space in his history for the natural world. The comprehensive topics that Sima takes off in the *Shiji* is marched by the exhaustive range of his sources. He names more than eighty texts that he consulted in composing the *Shiji*, in addition to numerous memorials, edicts and stone inscriptions.

Another striking feature of the *Shiji* is the degree to which the vast amount of information has been systematized, organized and coordinated. We see Sima struggling with problems of historical evidence of attempting to develop a critical methodology. He carefully identified sources, both written and oral, and evaluated his documents by comparing them with texts of known authenticity. In addition, he tried to verify accounts by travelling extensively, personally examining important sites and artifacts, and when possible, interviewing eyewitnesses and reputable local experts. Sima made it a rule not to guess on matters for which he had insufficient evidence and he deliberately omitted details of doubtful authenticity. He argued that facts could be properly interpreted only in context and insisted that analyses take into consideration both the beginnings and the ends of historical processes. When he did discover that generally auepted accounts were false, he tried to point out and correct those errors in direct comments. He also cultivated a critical attitude that acknowledged deficiencies in the Confucian classics, and he remained skeptical even have his own impressions. All in all, the *Shiji* represents an impressive performance for a pioneering ancient historian.

But unfortunately it does not add up to a unified, credible account of the past. The *Shiji* is fragmented and sprawling. Indeed reading the *Shiji* can be a frustrating experience, especially if one has been previously informed of its standing as one of the greatest Chinese histories, because its format breaks at least for critical requirements of traditional Western historical representation.

First there is no unity of narrative voice. The personal comments clearly belong to Sima, but elsewhere there is doubt due to his habit of copying early accounts directly into his own history. To make things worse, Sima often fails to fully explain or interpret his narratives. For example, over the course of the *Shiji*, some thirteen people (including Sima himself) offer various explanations for Xiang Yu's defeat at the hands of Gaozu, an event critical to the founding of the Han dynasty in 202 B. C. E. He simply reports what was said without comments. Even when he does offer personal remarks in his own voice on the subject, these interpretations are not always consistent.

The second way in which the *Shiji* thwarts Western expectations is that its accounts do not display a consistent level of coherence. Whereas much of the biographies and hereditary houses consists of stories with beginnings, middles, and ends with explanatory details, other *Shiji* sections lack a clear narrative structure. Events frequently occur with no explicit causes and little effect, and odd, unexplained incidents abound. In fact, some of the events briefly mentioned in the tables are never referrdd to again.

Third, the *Shiji* does not recount events within a unified narrative. There is considerable overlapping among the sections. Different biographies may include separate accounts of the same event and the same person may show up in several biographies, a couple of hereditary houses, a table and an annal. For example, information about the rivalry between Gaozu and Xiang Yu is scattered over more than twenty-five nonconsecutive chapters. Incidents that are only mentioned in some chapters are fully narrated in the others. For the most part readers must either consult modern indexes or read the entire text several times through to gain a comprehensive picture of events.

Fourth, *Shiji* accounts sometimes lack consistency Sima's fragmented organization allows him to tell the same story more than once, but these multiple narrations do not always agreed. Sima occasionally tells strikingly different versions of the same event that are not strictly compatible. We meet these problems early in the *Shiji* when the Shang and Zhou annals relate to the traditional miraculous tales of the birth of the ancestors of these dynasties—the mother of one became pregnant from eating an egg, and the other's mother conceived after stepping in a mysterious footprint—whereas the"Table by Generations of the Three Dynasties"assigns ordinary fathers to these two legendary ancestors and trace their lineages back to the Yellow Emperor.

What are we then to make of this text? Perhaps Sima really was more of a compiler than a historian. This was the solution adopted by earlier generations of Western commentators, who saw Sima Qian's extensive copying as a strength—he presented earlier accounts "objectively" and kept his own interpretations separate. Perhaps the inconsistent aspects of the *Shiji* reflect Sima's own contradictory inclinations. Or maybe the kind of unity we expect in a historical account was impossible for Sima to imagine, given his own experiences with historical records. Alternatively, perhaps he was developing a critical methodology and working toward a notion of history similar to our own but simply ran out of time. Or he might have been overwhelmed by the task.

All these solutions are plausible to some degree, but let me further confuse an already complicated question by proposing yet another resolution. My assumptions. The fragmented and overlapping accounts that we find in the *Shiji* are deliberate and serve a well-thought-out historiographical purpose. His ideas and judgements can be discerned in the arrangement of his material, as well as in specific statements. My solution is that the *Shiji* is a "reconstruction of the past" much more literal than that usually denoted by the phrase. When we hold this in our hands, we are holding a model of the past itself, which intentionally replicates the confusing inconsistencies, the lack of interpretive closure, and the bewildering details of raw historical data.

➤ 素材 3. The Frustration of the Second Confucius

(Durrant, Stephen W. *The Cloudy Mirror: Tension and Conflict in the Writings of Sima Qian*, State University of New York Press, 1995.)

I transmit and do not create.

—Analects, 7. 1.

I grieve that my heart has that which it has not completely expressed, and that I might die and my writing not be known to later ages.

— Sima Qian.

What we know of Sima Qian derives almost exclusively from his own hand; he creates himself, much as he creates China's past, through his written word.

Sima Qian speaks extensively of himself in two documents: the "Self-Narration of the Gentleman Grand Astrologer" ("Tai shi gong zixu"); and "Letter in Response to Ren An" ("Bao Ren An shu"). The first of these is a formal document in which Sima Qian establishes his credentials as a historian, explains why he wrote his monumental history, and summarizes his text's overall structure. The second document is a long letter written to Ren An, a friend who was in prison under a death sentence and was subsequently cut in two at the waist. From these two documents, quite different in purpose and in form, emerges a picture of a profound tension within Sima Qian between a "classical" demand to contain and transmit tradition and a need to vent an enormous creative energy nurtured by deep personal frustration.

Two figures dominate Sima Qian's Self-Narration": his father, Sima Tan, and Confucius, both as conservative voices, voices of ritual (Li) and duty (*yi*) that constrain Sima Qian and require him to construct the broad tradition of the past according to a pre-established blueprint.

On his deathbed, Sima Tan declaims to his son: "Will it end with me? ... When I die, you must become Grand Astrologer...do not forget what I have desired to evaluate and to write!" He also quotes Classic of Filial Piety to reinforce the plea, "To raise one's name in later generations and thereby glorify one's parents, this is the greatest expression of filial piety." These words hardly remind us of the Sima Tan who advocates a path that is neither harsh nor troublesome in his essay entitled "the Essential Meaning of the Six Schools" ("Liu jia yaozhi"). The deathbed Sima Tan bestowed upon his son the mission to be the second Confucius.

How do we explain the apparent discrepancy between the Taoist author and the stern voice of Confucian responsibility? Part of the explanation may be sought in a critical feature of Sima Qian's style as a compiler of the past. *Records of the Historian* is a vast collection of diverse texts and conflicting voices. Sima Qian sometimes adapts older texts to ensure full compliance with his own language and narrative style, while other texts are edited in a cursory fashion, and still others are quoted verbatim.

Sima Tan's treatise on the Six Schools is accurately reproduced by his son, but his deathbed words are quite another matter. Standing between the death of his father and his own record of that death is the crucial event of Sima Qian's tragic involvement in the Li Ling affair and his subsequent imprisonment and castration. Faced by such overwhelming shame and disgrace, Sima Qian must present a compelling justification for rejecting suicide and continuing to live. Such a justification is found in the dying voice of his father.

Another reason leads us toward Confucius, the second dominating figure of the "Self-Narration." To Sima Qian, Confucius is clearly the ultimate authority but such a lofty ambition is not without dangers. First, it can hardly be considered modest. Second, it is to imply a correspondence between his own time and the politically chaotic time of the Sage, which arrogant Emperor Wu would hardly find pleasing.

In addition, Sima Qian's own theory of literary creativity was certain to subvert the model of restraint and economy presented by *Spring and Autumn Annals*. According to Sima Qian, literary power springs from an enormous frustrated energy that makes constraint and control all but impossible. In one of his most important passages, Sima Qian explains the origin of creative energy in the following words:

> Confucius was in distress in the region of Chen and Cai and created *Spring and Autumn Annals*. Qu Yuan was banished and wrote *"Encountering Sorrow"* ("Li sao"). Zuo Qiuming lost his sight, and then there was *Discourses of the States* (*Guo yu*). Master Sun had his legs cut off at the knees and stated *Military Tactics* [*Bing fa*]. Buwei was removed to Shu and generations have passed down his "Overviews of Lü" ("Lü lan"). Hanfei was imprisoned in Qin and we have "The Difficulties of Persuasion" ("Shuo nan") and "The Frustrations of Standing Alone" ("Ku fen"). The three hundred pieces of *Poetry* were, for the most part, written as a result of worthies and sages expressing frustration. In all these cases, men had ideas that were stifled. They could not manage to communicate their doctrines [in their generation]. Therefore, they narrated past events and thought of people to come.

Sima Qian's theory of literary production, evokes one of the fundamental contradictions of his life. Confucius, the representative of restraint and economy, stands before him. But his frustration, validated and enhanced by physical damage that left him "a remnant of saw and blade" fights against containment. Confucius was not without his own frustrations. But the Sage's response to political failure is one of restraint. He never falls into the extremes of frenzy and self-destruction typical of so many other characters portrayed in *Records of the Historian*.

Sima Qian's comprehensive and fervent treatment of the past inevitably leads the historian to a profound and self-tortured questioning of all boundaries. This questioning is illustrated most directly in the "Traditions of Bo Yi" (chapter 61), an extremely important chapter that stands at the head of the "Traditions" section, the longest and most literarily significant section.

This one chapter alone concerns a figure from a significantly earlier period, the last years of the Yin and the earliest years of the Zhou. It is stylistically unique with Sima Qian's direct evaluation and discussion of the story occupying two thirds of the text.

The chapter begins by stating a principle that guides much of Sima Qian's "formal" thought: "Now, the writings recorded by scholars are extremely vast, but one still tests reliability on the basis of the Six Arts." But he questions it as soon as he quotes it:

> Confucius ranks the humane, intelligent and worthy men of antiquity, and such people as Wu Taibo and Bo Yi are discussed in great detail. From what I have heard, [Xu] You and [Wu] Guang were men of the highest dutifulness. But not even a small number of words concerning them appears [in the classics]; why is that?

Sima Qian implies here that the standard of reliability provided by the Six Arts, which in his time had become identified with the Six Classics, might not be complete, that preservation of one's name within the canon might be partly a matter of chance and not the result of the Sage's thorough sifting of the historical record.

To indicate precisely what it is that he finds "unusual", Sima Qian must retell the story of Bo Yi and Shu Qi:

Bo Yi and Shu Qi were the two sons of the Ruler of Gu Zhu. Their father wished to establish Shu Qi as successor, but when the father died, Shu Qi yielded the throne to Bo Yi. Bo Yi said, "It was father's command," and thereupon fled. Shu Qi also was unwilling to ascend the throne and fled the state. The people of the state established a middle brother as successor.

Thereupon, Bo Yi and Shu Qi heard that Chang, the Earl of the West, was fond of nourishing the old. "Why not go over to him?" When they arrived, the Earl of the West had died. King Wu was carrying the wooden ancestral tablet, had given [the Earl of the West] the posthumous name "King Wen" and was attacking King Zhou to the east. Bo Yi and Shu Qi detained his horse and rebuked King Wu, saying, "When your father is dead but not buried, can it be called filial to take up shield and spear? Can it be called humane for a minister to kill a ruler? [King Wu's] retainers wished to put them to the sword, but Duke Tai said, "These are dutiful men, So, helping them along, they sent them away.

When King Wu had pacified the disorder of Yin, the empire was united in Zhou. But Bo Yi and Shu Qi were ashamed of this and by principle would not eat the grain of Zhou. They hid at Shou Yang Mountain, picked ferns and ate them. When they were starving and about to die, they wrote a song. Its words are,

"We ascend this western mountain and eat its ferns.

With violence he replaces violence and does not know it is wrong.

Shen Nong, Yu, and Xia have suddenly departed, where can we go?

Alas, it is over; the mandate has been lost."

This story raises some very troublesome political problems. However, the troubling political implications are not Sima Qian's primary concern. Instead, he pursues another problem: "When we examine this story, are they (i. e. , Bo Yi and Shu Qi) resentful or are they not resentful?" How could Confucius have said that the two Yin loyalists died without resentment? Thus, Sima Qian implies, not only are the Six Arts incomplete, but Confucius himself is fallible. But instead of pursuing this issue further, the historian turns quite suddenly to a much larger problem.

Confucius illumined Bo Yi, Shu Qi, and Yan Yuan. By praising them, he guaranteed their immortality. The historian thereby becomes the savior, those attached to him are saved, living on through the power of his writing brush. Unfortunately, Sima Qian's reading of the facts of history does not support heaven's fairness, for paragons of morality, like Bo Yi and Shu Qi, starved to death, and Yan Yuan, the only disciple Confucius could heartily recommend, died young, while the evil Robber Zhi lived to a ripe and happy old age. Faced with such distressing examples, Sima Qian becomes increasingly troubled: " I am extremely confused by this. If this is what we call 'the way of heaven', then is it right or is it wrong?"

Thus, Sima Qian knows his work, like that of Confucius, will be imperfect—injustice will remain. The historian must try to make up for the unfairness of heaven, but he, like heaven, will fail... The energies of history cannot be bound up into a neat new synthesis. Sima Qian has found too many margins of doubt, too many loose ends, that defy containment.

Confucius was the transmitter of the distilled truth from the past. But the "unified" tradition continued to break down despite Confucius' efforts, and the Warring States period witnessed a proliferation of literary culture such as had never occurred in China before. The hundred schools contended, mid a vast assortment of new texts appeared. The past had become too large. Sima Qian's attempt to organize the tradition into a clean Confucian unity fails, and his later readers, as they try to comprehend his brilliant text, frequently fall into befuddlement, perhaps the same type that Sima Qian sometimes felt as he himself tried to make sense of the accounts before him.

➤ 注释

historiography   n. 历史的编撰

archivist   n. 档案保管员

intrigue   n. 密谋策划,阴谋

annal   n. 记录

chronological   adj. 按时间排列的,编年的

treatise   n. 论文,专著

edict   n. 法令,告示

thwart   vt. 阻挠,使受挫

coherence   n. 一致性,连贯性

analects   n. 论文,选集

astrologer   n. 占星家,星座研究者

discrepancy   n. 差异,不符合,不一致

cursory   adj. 粗略的;仓促的

verbatim   adj. &adv. 一字不差的/地

castration   n. 割除(男子或雄性动物的)睾丸,阉割

remnant   n. 剩余部分,残余,零头

fallible   adj. 容易犯错的

illumine   vt. 阐明,解释

proliferation   n. (不可数,单数)激增,涌现,大量的事物

➤ 练习

1. Please translated the five characteristics of the book *Records of the*

Grand Historian summarized by Mr. Li Changzhi in the first passage.

2. Reading *Shiji* might be a frustrating experience for a Westerner，because its format breaks traditional Western historiography. Can you point out four critical requirements of Western historical representation that *Shiji* does not adhere to?

3. Why is the author of the third passage nickname Sima Qian "the second Confucius"? And why is the second Confucius frustrated?

四、拓展阅读：《太史公自序》及英译节选
➤ 背景知识

《史记》独特的体例特点，丰富的文化内涵，体大思精的艺术高度，都对译介工作形成巨大挑战。《史记》英译起步很早，始于 19 世纪末，从最初零星章节的译介，到后来华兹生、杨宪益夫妇等人具有一定规模的选译，再到倪豪士带领大型团队尚在运作中的《史记》全译工程，已绵延百年之久。

美国学者华兹生 20 世纪 50 年代启动《史记》英译项目，其译本可谓是开疆破土之作，被公认为同类译本中覆盖面最大的英文译本。他选择了《史记》中 66 个文学性较强的文本，对其中的 57 篇做了全译，9 篇做了节译。华兹生的英译侧重《史记》的文学特质，读者定位为普通人群，尽量不做注释，追求语言流畅自然，因而可读性很强，承载了很高的文学价值。

本处节选的《太史公自序》完成于 1960 年，与《报任安书》、《三代世表》序言以及《大宛列传》等一起，被《亚洲文明导论》丛书收录于其中的《中国传统之本源》。

➤ 素材 1. 太史公自序（节选）
（司马迁.《史记》,中华书局,2019.）

是岁天子始建汉家之封，而太史公留滞周南，不得与从事，故发愤且卒。而子迁适使反，见父于河洛之间。太史公执迁手而泣曰："余先周室之太史也。自上世尝显功名于虞夏，典天官事。后世中衰，绝于予乎？汝

复为太史,则续吾祖矣。今天子接千岁之统,封泰山,而余不得从行,是命也夫,命也夫!余死,汝必为太史;为太史,无忘吾所欲论著矣。且夫孝始于事亲,中于事君,终于立身。扬名于后世,以显父母,此孝之大者。夫天下称诵周公,言其能论歌文武之德,宣周邵之风,达太王王季之思虑,爰及公刘,以尊后稷也。幽厉之后,王道缺,礼乐衰,孔子修旧起废,论诗书,作春秋,则学者至今则之。自获麟以来四百有余岁,而诸侯相兼,史记放绝。今汉兴,海内一统,明主贤君忠臣死义之士,余为太史而弗论载,废天下之史文,余甚惧焉,汝其念哉!"迁俯首流涕曰:"小子不敏,请悉论先人所次旧闻,弗敢阙。"……

维我汉继五帝末流,接三代业。周道废,秦拨去古文,焚灭诗书,故明堂石室金匮玉版图籍散乱。于是汉兴,萧何次律令,韩信申军法,张苍为章程,叔孙通定礼仪,则文学彬彬稍进,诗书往往间出矣。自曹参荐盖公言黄老,而贾生、晁错明申、商,公孙弘以儒显,百年之间,天下遗文古事靡不毕集太史公。太史公仍父子相续纂其职。……罔罗天下放失旧闻,王迹所兴,原始察终,见盛观衰,论考之行事,略推三代,录秦汉,上记轩辕,下至于兹,着十二本纪,既科条之矣。并时异世,年差不明,作十表。礼乐损益,律历改易,兵权山川鬼神,天人之际,承敝通变,作八书。二十八宿环北辰,三十辐共一毂,运行无穷,辅拂股肱之臣配焉,忠信行道,以奉主上,作三十世家。扶义俶傥,不令己失时,立功名于天下,作七十列传。凡百三十篇,五十二万六千五百字,为太史公书。序略,以拾遗补艺,成一家之言,厥协六经异传,整齐百家杂语,藏之名山,副在京师,俟后世圣人君子。第七十。

➤ 素材 2. The Sacred Duty of the Historian

Sources of Chinese Tradition (Volume 1) compiled by WM. Theodore de Bary, Wing-Tsit Chan, and Burton Watson, Columbia University Press, 1960.

The following excerpt from the autobiography of Ssu-ma Ch'ien relates the words of Sima Tan to his son as he lay dying. [From Shiji 130：8a-b, 30b-32a])

The Grand Historian [Ssu-ma T'an] grasped my hand and said weeping："Our ancestors were Grand Historians for the House of Chou. From the most ancient times they were eminent and renowned when in the days of Yü and Hsia they were in charge of astronomical affairs. In later ages our family declined. Will this tradition end with me? If you in turn become Grand Historian, you must continue the work of our ancestors. ... When you become Grand Historian, you must not forget what I have desired to expound and write. Now filial piety begins the serving of your parents; next you must serve your sovereign; and finally you must make something of yourself, that your name may go down through the ages to the glory of your father and mother. This is the most important part of filial piety. Everyone praises the Duke of Chou, saying that he was able to expound in word and song the virtues of King Wen and King Wu, publishing abroad the Odes of Chou and Shao; he set forth the thoughts and ideals of T'ai-wang and Wang Chi, extending his words back to King Liu and paying honor to Hou Chi [ancestors of the Chou dynasty]. After the reigns of Yu and Li the way of the ancient kings fell into disuse and rites and music declined. Confucius revived the old ways and restored what had been abandoned, expounding the *Odes* and *History* and making the *Spring and Autumn Annals*. From that time until today men of learning have taken these as their models. It has now been over four hundred years since the capture of the unicorn [481 B. C., end of the Spring and Autumn period]. The various feudal states have merged together, and the old records and chronicles have become scattered and lost. Now the House of Han has arisen and all the world is united under one rule. I have been Grand Historian, and yet I have failed to make a record of all the enlightened rulers and wise lords, the faithful ministers and gentlemen who were ready to die for duty. I am fearful that the historical materials will be neglected and lost. You must remember and think of this!"

I bowed my head and wept, saying: "I, your son, am ignorant and unworthy, but I shall endeavor to set forth in full the reports of antiquity which have come down from our ancestors. I shall not dare to be remiss!" [130: 8a-b]

This our house of Han has succeeded the descendants of the Five Emperors and carried on the task of unification of the Three Dynasties. The ways of Chou fell into disuse of the Ch'in scattered and discarded the old writings and burned and destroyed the *Odes* and the *History*. Therefore the plans and records of the Illustrious Hall and the stone rooms, of the the metal caskets and jade tablets, became lost or confused.

Then the Han arose and Hsiao Ho put in order the laws and commandments; Han Hsin set forth the rules of warfare; Chang Ts'ang made the regulations and standards; and Shu-sun T'ung settled questions of rites and ceremonies. At this time the art of letters began again to flourish and advance and the *Odes* and *History* gradually reappeared. From the time when Ts'ao Ts'an put into practice Master Kai's teachings of the Yellow Emperor and Lao Tzu, when Chia Shen and Ch'ao Ts'o expounded the doctrines of the Legalist philosophers Shen and Shang, and Kung-sun Hung achieved Eminence for his Confucian learning, a period of some one hundred years, the books that survived and records of past affairs were all without exception gathered together by the Grand Historian. The Grand Historians, father and son, each in turn held and carried on the position. ...

I have sought out and gathered together the ancient traditions of the empire which were scattered and lost. Of the great deeds of kings I have searched the beginnings and examined the ends; I have seen their times of prosperity and observed their decline. Of the affairs that I have discussed and examined, I have made a general survey of the Three Dynasties and a record of the Ch'in and Han, extending in all back as far as Hsien Yüan [the Yellow Emperor] and coming down to the present, set forth in twelve Basic Annals. After this had been put in order and completed, because there were differences in chronology for the same periods and the dates were not always clear, I made the ten Chronological Tables. Of the changes of rites and music, the improvements and revisions of the pitch-pipes and calendar, military power, mountains and rivers, spirits and gods, the relationships between heaven and man, the economic practices handed down and changed age by age, I have made the eight Treatises. As the twenty-eight constellations revolve about the North Star, as the thirty spokes of a wheel come together at the hub, revolving endlessly without stop, so the ministers, assisting like arms and legs, faithful and trustworthy, in true moral spirit serve their lord and ruler: of them I made the thirty Hereditary Houses. Upholding duty, masterful and sure, not allowing themselves to miss their opportunities, they made a name for themselves in the world: of such men I made the seventy Memoirs. In all one hundred and thirty chapters, 526,500 words, this is the book of the Grand Historian, compiled in order to repair omissions and amplify the Six Disciplines. It is the work of one family, designed to supplement the various interpretations of the Six Classics and to put into order the miscellaneous sayings of the hundred schools. [30b-32a]

> **注释**

　　expound　vt. 详细讲解

　　ode　n. 颂诗, 颂歌

remiss　adj. 玩忽职守的，马虎的

illustrious　adj. 著名的，杰出的

commandment　n. 戒条

constellation　n. 一系列（相关的想法、事物），一群（相关的人）；星座

miscellaneous　adj. 五花八门的，各种各样的

> 练习

Please find the corresponding original Chinese texts of the following expressions.

1. The Grand Historian

2. in charge of astronomical affairs

3. Filial piety begins the serving of your parents; next you must serve your sovereign; and finally you must make something of yourself.

4. From that time until today men of learning have taken these as their models.

5. A period of some one hundred years, the books that survived and records of past affairs were all without exception gathered together by the Grand Historian.

6. It is the work of one family, designed to supplement the various interpretations of the Six Classics and to put into order the miscellaneous sayings of the hundred schools.

五、现代回声

> 背景知识

"以史为镜，可以知兴替"。后疫情时代，面对按下暂停键的全球化和被永远撤销的富布莱特项目，我们有必要回顾战后中美关系如何从封闭对峙走向开放合作，以及如何影响了两国及世界的发展进程。说到这个话题，就不得不提被到被誉为"头号中国通"的美国著名历史学家费正清。他深入研

究,著书立说,教书育人和组织工作齐头并进,并积极推动学术影响现实决策,可以说以一己之力改变了中西文化交流的整个过程。费正清于 1991 年去世时,《纽约日报》专门发布了讣告,用不足千字的文章勾勒出他浓墨重彩的一生。

John K. Fairbank,China Scholar of Wide Influence,Is Dead at 84

By David Gonzalez,Sept. 16,1991

(https://www. nytimes. com/1991/09/16/nyregion/john-k-fairbank-
china-scholar-of-wide-influence-is-dead-at-84. html)

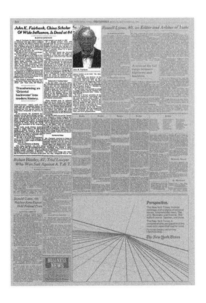

John K. Fairbank, the Harvard history professor who was widely credited with creating the field of modern Chinese studies in the United States and was a leading advocate of diplomatic recognition of the People's Republic of China,died Saturday in Cambridge,Massachusetts. He was 84 years old.

He died of a heart attack,said Roderick MacFarquhar,a colleague.

A towering figure in the field of Chinese studies, Mr. Fairbank left an indelible mark on scholarship and policy. He wrote and edited more than two dozen books, including "The United States and China," first published in 1948 by Harvard University Press, which many consider to be the best short introduction to Chinese history, culture and civilization.

As a mentor to fledgling scholars and an organizer of academic programs, he helped pioneer Chinese and Asian studies at many universities, government agencies and private institutions in the United States and abroad.

With Edwin O. Reischauer, Mr. Fairbank wrote "East Asia, The Great Tradition" and "East Asia, the Modern Transformation," widely used textbooks that are considered classics in their field. He and Mr. Reischauer introduced the first survey course on East Asian civilization at Harvard in 1939.

In his lectures, Mr. Fairbank displayed a dry wit and a formal, courtly manner, but he was also known for his close, even paternal ties with his students. He influenced scores of future China scholars and authors, including Theodore H. White, whom Mr. Fairbank once described as his brightest student.

"He really made Chinese modern history a major field in the general study of modern history," said Mr. MacFarquhar, the Leroy B. Williams Professor of History at Harvard and director of the John K. Fairbank Center for East Asian Research.

"He took it out of the Oriental backwater it was in before 1945, making it accessible to a wider range of students who could go on. "

From South Dakota to Beijing

John King Fairbank was born in Huron, S. D. , in 1907. He attended public schools in Sioux Falls and went on to Phillips Exeter Academy. Originally enrolling at the University of Wisconsin, he transferred to Harvard, graduating summa cum laude in 1929.

As a Rhodes Scholar from 1929 through 1932, Mr. Fairbank traveled to Beijing and served as a lecturer at Qinghua University. Over the next two years as a Rockefeller Foundation Fellow, he traveled widely in a dozen Chinese provinces.

Mr. Fairbank joined the Harvard faculty in 1936, where he began to transform a field that until then had been largely concerned with Chinese antiquity.

During World War II, Mr. Fairbank took a leave from Harvard and served with the Coordinator of Information and the Office of Strategic Services in Washington. Later in the war, he was special assistant to the American Ambassador and director of the American Publications Service in Chongqing. He returned to Washington and the Office of War Information in 1944, leaving again for China the following year, where he served as Director of the United States Information Service until 1946.

Debate Over "Losing China"

In the late 1940's and early 1950's, Mr. Fairbank became caughtin the debate over who was responsible for "losing China" to the Communists, becoming a target for the anger of Senator Joseph R. McCarthy. One former student said that period made a deep imprint on his thinking, leaving him infuriated with the American right wing and somewhat sympathetic with the Chinese Communists.

Three decades later he acknowledged his earlier belief that Communism was "bad in America but good in China." That opinion had also reflected his view that Chinese issues should be evaluated in the context of that country's history and culture. But some critics charged that he had ignored the repressive excesses of the Communist government.

During the 1950's, he and Mr. Reischauer designed a master's degree program in regional studies of China, Japan and later Korea which would train scholars, businessmen and journalists.

Mr. Fairbank entered a prolific period in the 1960s, with his extensive writings and active lecture schedule focused on urging the United States to recognize the People's Republic of China and to bring it into the United Nations and replace Taiwan on the Security Council.

Invited to China

Mr. Fairbank returned to China in 1972, after President Richard M. Nixon restored relations with the Asian superpower. Seen as an enormously influential figure who helped form America's perceptions of Communist China, Mr. Fairbank was among a select group of scholars who were invited by Premier Zhou Enlai.

"He often wrote things they didn't like, but they recognized him as the master builder in the field," Mr. MacFarquhar said.

Mr. Fairbank was director of the East Asian Research Center at Harvard from 1955 until 1973. He was named Francis Lee Higginson Professor of History at Harvard in 1959, retiring in 1977. In 1979, he accompanied Vice President Walter F. Mondale on an official visit to China.

Mr. Fairbank was recalled as being a tireless worker, and he recently finished editing his latest book, "China: A New History."

➢ **注释**

indelible   adj. 无法忘记的;不可磨灭的

fledgling   n. (刚会飞的)幼鸟;(通常置于另一名词前)初出茅庐的人;

无经验的组织；新体系

Edwin O. Reischauer 埃德温·赖肖尔，又译作赖世和。美国历史学家和外交家，1961 年至 1966 年任美国驻日本大使，是美国公认的日本问题专家。

dry adj. 机敏的；不形于色的；不露声色的

backwater n. 与世隔绝的(或缺乏生气的、落后的)地区

summa cum laude adj. & adv. (源自拉丁语)(美国)以优异成绩(三等优异成绩的第一等)

➤ 练习

1. Mr. Fairbank is credited as the founder of modern Chinese studies in the United States. What examples are used in the first part to prove this attribution?

2. On his course of academic growth, when did Mr. Fairbank begin to transform to the field of Chinese studies?

第二章 汉 字

一、词源梳理

  关于汉字起源问题的学术著作自古至今可谓汗牛充栋,车载斗量。然而关于"汉字"这一称谓的词源问题,却鲜有专题论述。或许是韩国学者陈泰夏教授对这个盲区的发现触发了学术界的热烈反响,关于"汉字"一词的生成和流变迅速成了汉字学新的重要议题。

  《辞海》(语词卷)对"汉字"的定义为:"记录汉语的文字。世界上最古老的文字之一,已有六千年左右的历史。现存最古可识的是三千多年前殷商的甲骨文和稍后的金文。现用是从甲骨文、金文演变而来的。在形体上逐渐由图形变为笔画,象形变为象征,复杂变为简单;在造字原则上从表形、表意到形声。除极个别的例子外,一般一个字一个音节,绝大多数是形声字。现代汉字已实现部分简化,更具实用价值。收在《康熙字典》里的汉字有四万七千多,收在《汉语大字典》里的有五万四千左右,通用的大约有五千到八千。在中国悠久的文化历史中积有大量的汉文典籍。"

  《辞海》(语言学卷)的"汉字"字条内容为:"汉字具有一定的超时空性,通过汉字记录的上古和中古文献,后代一般文化水平的人也大体能看懂;同一个汉字有不同的方言读音,但是不同方言区的人对同一个汉字字义的理解却是相同的。几千年来,汉字在维护民族和国家统一,记录和保存文化遗产等方面发挥了巨大作用;同时对于中国其他民族的文字(如西夏文、契丹文、女真文等)以及周边国家的文字(如日文、朝鲜文、越南文等),也曾经产生巨大的影响,以至在东亚地区形成了一个汉字文化圈。现代汉字已实现部分简化,更具实用价值,目前是中国各民族和国际社会通用的正式文字之一。"

其它权威辞书对"汉字"的解释大同小异,这些辞书中的条目包含了对"汉字"这一概念认识的不同角度。它既是一个语言学概念,也是一个文化传播概念,其中既有历史要素,也有地理和政治要素,甚至技术要素。但是,关于"汉字"一词的词源均无一言涉及。

汉字一词中的"汉"字,在不同语境中可以分别指代中国,汉代,汉族,汉语,汉文化,汉文化圈等多重义项。

相比之下,对"字"的理解相对集中,主要是在语言学范畴内进行的讨论。根据人们的常识理解,"字"即"文字"。然而在先秦,"文"和"字"是分开使用的。

《左传》称文字为"文",例如《宣公十二年》在解释"武"时这个字时说:"夫文,止戈为武。"晋·杜预注:"文,字。"

《仪礼》称文字为"名",例如《聘礼》:"百名以上书于策,不及百名书于方。""策"和"方"都是形状不同的竹木简,汉·郑玄注:"名,书文也,今谓之字。"

《荀子》称文字为"书",例如《解蔽》:"好书者众矣,而仓颉独传者,壹也。"《韩非子·五蠹》:"古者仓颉之作书也,自环谓之私,背私谓之公。"《易·系辞下》:"上古结绳而治,后世圣人易之以书契。"都把文字称为"书"。

《吕氏春秋·序》称文字为"字":"暴之咸阳市门,悬千金其上,有能增损一字者与千金。"

第一次对"文字"做出解释的人是东汉的学者许慎。《说文解字·序》中说:"仓颉之初作书,盖依类象形,故谓之文;其后形声相益,故谓之字。"

"文"字本来指刻在人胸口上的花纹。《说文》释为"错画也"。古代汉语中名词可以当作动词用,因此画花纹或者刺花纹也叫做纹。《庄子·逍遥游》中有"越人断发文身"的句子,句子中的"文",就是指在身体上绘制花纹。

先民绘制花纹通常要摹拟某些客观物体,而最早产生的文字——象形字也是描摹客观事物,因而象形文字被许慎称之为"文"。

"字"字本来指女人分娩或者蛋中孵出幼雏。《说文》释为"乳也。"《易·屯》:"女子贞不字",这里的"字"就是说分娩;王充《论衡·论死》中说:"鸡卵之未字",就是说鸡蛋还未孵出小鸡来。人们把象形字作为声符,可以生产出更多的新字。这些新产生的字,对于象形字而言就像是母体分娩出的婴儿或者是蛋中孵出的幼雏一样,所以被称为字。"文"为母,"字"为子,总称为文字。

汉字的"字"一般在英语里译作"character"或者"script"。"Script"的原始印欧语词根是"Skribh-",意思是"to cut, separate",对应的动作是"carve marks in tone, wood, etc(在石头,木头上刻下印记)";后来的拉丁文"scriptum"意思逐渐扩大,包括了"a writing, book, law, etc. 书写,书,成文法律"等义。到 14 世纪末,"script"的英文释义明确为"something written(书写)"。"Character"一词溯自希腊语"kharakter",意为"a defining quality, individual feature",即鲜明的个体特征。英语从古法语借来 caratere 一词,15 世纪恢复该词的拉丁文拼法"character",释义为"alphabetic letter, graphic symbol standing for a sound or syllable(字母,表示一个音或音节的图形符号)"。

二、引导阅读

➤ 背景知识

汉字是中国语言独特的文化标志。在西方人的印象里,汉字是深奥难懂的,所以常常有外国人汉语已经说得非常流利了,却仍目不识字。与此同时,汉语罗马化以取代汉字的尝试屡见不绝。在浩瀚的汉语研究英文学术论著中,以西方语言学理论框架来解释汉字书写体系的不少,但是深入探讨汉字内在逻辑的并不多。本部分节选自大卫·R·奥尔森(David R. Olson)在《大英百科全书》(Encyclopedia Britannica)的 "Chinese writing(中文书写)"条目。作者试图解释汉字作为一种书写系统延用至今的系统构造和发展逻辑。

Chinese writing, basically logographic writing system, one of the world's great writing systems.

Like Semitic writing in the West, Chinese script was fundamental to the writing systems in the East. Until relatively recently, Chinese writing was more widely in use than alphabetic writing systems, and until the 18th century more than half of the world's books were written in Chinese, including works of speculative thought, historical writings of a kind, and novels, along with writings on government and law.

It is not known when Chinese writing originated, but it apparently began to develop in the early 2nd millennium bc. The earliest known inscriptions, each of which contains between 10 and 60 characters incised on pieces of bone and tortoiseshell that were used for oracular divination, date from the Shang(or Yin)dynasty(18th—12th century bc), but, by then it was already a highly developed system, essentially similar to its present form. By 1400 bc the script included some 2,500 to 3,000 characters, most of which can be read to this day. Later stages in the development of Chinese writing include the guwen("ancient figures")found in inscriptions from the late Shang dynasty(c. 1123 bc)and the early years of the Zhou dynasty that followed. The major script of the Zhou dynasty, which ruled from 1046 to 256 bc, was the dazhuan("great seal"), also called the Zhou wen("Zhou script"). By the end of the Zhou dynasty the dazhuan had degenerated to some extent.

The script was fixed in its present form during the Qin period(221—207 bc). The earliest graphs were schematic pictures of what they represented; the graph for man resembled a standing figure, that for woman depicted a kneeling figure.

Because basic characters or graphs were "motivated"—that is, the graph was made to resemble the object it represented—it was once thought that Chinese writing is ideographic, representing ideas rather than the structures of a language. It is now recognized that the system represents the Chinese language by means of a logographic script. Each graph or character corresponds to one meaningful unit of the language, not directly to a unit of thought.

Although it was possible to make up simple signs to represent common objects, many words were not readily picturable. To represent such words the phonographic principle was adopted. A graph that pictured some object was borrowed to write a different word that happened to sound similar. With this invention the Chinese approached the form of writing invented by the Sumerians. However, because of the enormous number of Chinese words that sound the same, to have carried through the phonographic principle would have resulted in a writing system in which many of the words could be read in more than one way. That is, a written character would be extremely ambiguous.

The solution to the problem of character ambiguity, adopted about 213 bc(during the reign of the first Qin emperor, Shihuangdi), was to distinguish two words having the same sound and represented by the same graph by adding another graph to give a clue to the meaning of the particular word intended. Such complex graphs or characters consist of two parts, one part suggesting the sound, the other part the meaning. The system was then standardized so as to approach the ideal of one distinctive graph representing each morpheme, or unit of meaning, in the language. The limitation is that a language that has thousands of morphemes would require thousands of characters, and, as the characters are formed from simple lines in various orientations and arrangements, they came to possess great complexity.

The relation between the written Chinese language and its oral form is very different from the analogous relation between written and spoken English. In Chinese many different words are expressed by the identical sound pattern—188 different words are expressed by the syllable/yi/— while each of those words is expressed by a distinctive visual pattern. A piece of written text read orally is often quite incomprehensible to a listener because of the large number of homophones. In conversation, literate Chinese speakers frequently draw characters in the air to distinguish between homophones. Written text, on the other hand, is completely unambiguous. In English, by contrast, writing is often thought of as a reflection, albeit imperfect, of speech.

The Chinese traditionally divide the characters into six types(called liu shu, "six scripts"), the most common of which is xingsheng, a type of character that combines a semantic element(called a radical)with a phonetic element intended to remind the reader of the word's pronunciation. The phonetic element is usually a contracted form of another character with the same pronunciation as that of the word intended. For example, the character for he"river"is composed of the radical shui"water"plus the phonetic ke, the meaning of which("able")is irrelevant; the combined shui-ke suggests the word he meaning"river. " Seventy-five percent of all Chinese characters are of this type.

The other types of characters are xiangxing, characters that were originally pictographs (these have a semantic element originally expressed by a picture; for example, the character for tian"field"represents a field by means of a square divided into quarters); zhishi, characters intended to symbolize logical or abstract terms(e. g. , er"two"is indicated by two horizontal lines); huiyi, characters formed by a combination of elements thought to be logically associated(e. g. , the symbols for"man"and"word" are combined to represent the word meaning"true, sincere, truth"); zhuanzhu, modifications or distortions of characters to form new characters, usually of somewhat related meaning(e. g. , the character for shan"mountain"turned on its side means fou"tableland"); and jiajie, characters borrowed from(or sometimes originally mistaken for)others, usually words of different meaning but similar pronunciation(e. g. , the character for zu "foot"is used for zu"to be sufficient").

Chinese script, as mentioned above, is logographic; it differs from phonographic writing systems—whose characters or graphs represent units of sound—in using one character or graph to represent a morpheme. Chinese, like any other language, has thousands of morphemes, and, as one character is used for each morpheme, the writing system has thousands of characters. Two morphemes that sound the same would, in English, have at least some similarity of spelling; in Chinese they are represented by completely different characters. The Chinese words for"parboil"and for "leap"are pronounced identically. Yet there is no similarity in the way they are written.

The Chinese language has clearly distinguished syllables that are easily recognized in speech and hence easily represented by a sign. These syllables correspond to morphemes; each morpheme is one syllable long. In English one morpheme is often expressed by two syllables(e. g. , balloon), and two morphemes may be contained in one syllable(e. g. , boys). In Chinese, with a general correspondence between morpheme and syllable, each morpheme is easily represented by a sign for the corresponding syllable. Moreover, one morpheme in Chinese is more or less equivalent to a word. Unlike English, in which morphemes combine to make new words(e. g. , make + past = made, can also form making, makes, and so on), Chinese is an isolating language, in which elements of meaning are strung together as a series of isolated morphemes. Similarly, the pronunciation of a syllable is relatively uninfluenced by adjacent syllables, which, therefore, remain relatively invariant. It is these invariant units of sound and meaning that are represented by distinctive logographs.

The process of combining simple graphs to make complex ones is enormously prolific and has generated thousands of unique characters capable of representing the morphemes of the language. With some 40,000 graphs, the system comes close to the ideal of a fully explicit writing system that represents each distinctive unit of meaning with a distinctive unit of writing. But, of course, such a large number of graphs imposes a major obstacle to learning to read and write. The problem is intensified by the fact that neither the sound property nor the semantic property of the characters is of much help in the recognition of a character. Because of changes in pronunciation of the language, the complex signs no longer reflect the sound pattern that they originally grew out of. Similarly, the semantic relations represented by the graph are no longer so clear. Consequently, as the relations between the characters and what they represent are largely unknown to readers and writers of the language, the graphs are seen as groups of lines and angles that make up repeated visual units, just as readers of English recognize whole words without analyzing them into their constituent letters.

A literate Chinese person knows perhaps 4,000 of the most important characters. Chinese characters are arranged in dictionaries according to the radicals of which they are composed or with which they are traditionally associated. The 214 radicals are arranged in modern dictionaries according to the number of strokes used in writing them.

Most scholars now believe that neither the logographic Chinese writing system nor the alphabetic Indo-European writing system possesses any overall advantage. The Chinese writing system requires more memorization, while the Latin alphabet requires more analysis and synthesis; both appear to be relatively optimal devices for the transcription of their respective, very different, languages.

For the Chinese, a single logographic system is particularly useful because it is capable of representing very different spoken forms, just as the numerals 1, 2, and 3 are understandable across many regions though they represent different words in different languages. In this manner Chinese logographs form a common medium of communication for a vast country because they can be read by people who speak mutually incomprehensible dialects or languages.

(——adapted from *Chinese writing* , by David R. Olson, *Encyclopedia Britannica*.)

> **注释**

logographic   adj. 语标的,字符的,语素的

Semitic   adj. 闪族语系的

alphabetic   adj. 字母的,按字母顺序的

speculative   adj. 推测的

millennium   n. 千年,千禧年

inscription   n. 印刻,铭文,题字

incise   v. 雕刻

oracular   adj. 神谕的,谜似的

degenerate   v. 使退化,恶化,堕落

schematic   adj. 图解的,概要的

ideographic   adj. 表意的,表意字构成的

picturable   adj. 图像的,可以用图片表示的

phonographic   adj. 标音的,记音的

Sumerian   adj. 苏美尔语的

morpheme　n. 语素

analogous　adj. 类似的, 可比拟的

unambiguous　adj. 明确的, 不含糊的

albeit　conj. 尽管, 虽然

semantic　adj. 语义的, 语义学的

contract　v. 收缩, 缩短

pictograph　n. 象形文字, 图画文字

distort　v. 扭曲, 变形, 失真

parboil　v. 快速煮半熟, 飞水

isolating　adj. 孤立的, 隔断的

adjacent　adj. 邻近的, 毗连的

invariant　adj. 不变的

constituent　adj. 构成的, 组成的

radical　n. 自由基, 部首

medium　n. 媒介

➢ **练习**

1. What is a logograph? Why is the Chinese characters system now recognized as logographic, not ideographic or pictographic?

2. What are the six common ways of constructing Chinese characters? Which amongst the six ways is most prolific. Give some examples.

3. How does Chinese differ from English in meaning-makings of morphemes and syllables?

4. What's the amount of characters expected to be qualify for literacy in Chinese language?

5. What role does the Chinese characters play in communication between various dialects and regional languages.

三、阅读与比较:汉字的解析

➤ 背景知识

　　为了"解谬误,晓学者,达神恉",东汉许慎撰著《说文解字》,成为中国第一部按照偏旁部首编排的字典,也是世界上最早的字书之一。它首立部首排列法,运用六书理论分析汉字的形体构造,因形说义,因声求源,是人们认识、掌握上古语音、词汇和读通先秦两汉古籍的重要工具书,在中国语言学史上有极其重要的地位。许慎是汉代有名的经学家、文字学家、语言学家,是中国文字学的开拓者,被称为"字圣"。

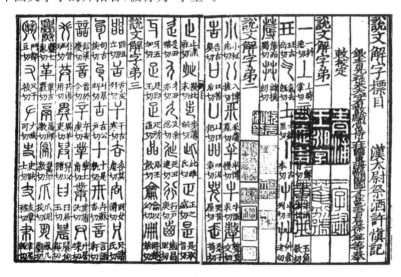

上图为《说文解字》所列部首列表

Examples from the Shuowen Jiezi

1.　　　　　　　　　一 or 弌

【一】惟初太始道立於一。造分天地,化成萬物。凡一之屬皆從一。(於悉切。)【弌】古文一。

　　一［Unity, one］is where the start of the Great Beginning of the Way is based upon. In unity, Heaven and Earth are separated from each other [unity or one thus becoming two] and then transformed into the ten thousand creations. All things related to "one" are written with the radical 一 (Pronounced/ʔ-iět/). 弌 is an old-script character variant for 一.

2. 天

【天】顛也。至高無上。從一、大。（他前切。）

天 [Heaven] is the summit (/tien/ [Note: puns were very popular during the Han period]), or the highest point which nothing can surpass. The character is composed of "one" and "great". (Pronounced/tʰ-ien/.)

3. ⊥ or ᅩ

【⊥】高也。此古文上。指事也。凡上之屬皆從上。（時掌切。）【上】篆文上。

⊥ [Above, ontop] means high. It is the old-style character for 上, character type "pointing to situation". All things related to "above" are written with the radical ⊥(Pronounced/z-iaŋ/.)上 is the Small Seal script character for ⊥.

4. 帝 or 帝

【帝】諦也。王天下之號也。從上、朿聲。（都計切。）【帝】古文帝。古文諸上字皆從一，篆文皆從二。【二】古文上字。辛、示、辰、龍、童、音、章，皆從古文上。

帝 [Emperor] Denomination for the true ruler of the earth. The character is composed of 上 "above" and the phonetic 朿 (ce or qi). (Pronounced/ti-ei/.)帝 is an old-style character for 帝. All old-style characters with the radical 上 are written with a simple stroke 一, and the Small Seal style characters with a double stroke 二. 二 is an old-style character for 上. The following characters are written with the old-style 上：xin 辛 (one of the Celestial Stems)，shi 示 "to display"，chen 辰（one of the Terrestrial Branches)，long 龍 "dragon"，tong 童 "young, inferior"，yin 音 "sound" and zhang 章 "stanza".

5. 八

【人】天地之性最貴者也。此籀文象臂脛之形。凡人之屬皆從人。（如鄰切。）

人［Man］the worthiest of all beings between Heaven and Earth. This is the Large Seal style character depicting of a man with arms and legs. All things related to "man" are written with the radical 人. (Pronounced/nz-iěn/.)

6. 肖

【老】考也。七十曰老。從人、毛、匕，言鬚髮變白也。凡老之屬皆從老。（盧皓切。）

老［Old］means "aged". Seventy years is old. The character is composed of the characters "man" 人，"hair" 毛 and "change" 匕，saying that beard and hair have become white. All things related to "old age" are written with the radical 老［e. g. 耆 "auld"，壽 "long life"，孝 "obedient towards the elder"］. (Pronounced/l-au/.)

7. 土

【土】地之吐生物者也。二象地之下，地之中物出形也。凡土之屬皆從土。（它魯切。）

土［Soil］is what the earth produces of living creatures. The two horizontal strokes depict the surface of the soil and what is below，［and the vertical stroke] depicts what comes out of the earth. All things related to "earth" are written with the radical 土. (Pronounced/t^h-uo/.)

8.　　　　　　　　　　坤 or 隆

【地】元氣初分輕清陽為天，重濁陰為地。萬物所陳列也。從土、也聲。（徒內切。）【隓】籀文地，從隊。

地 [Earth] (/d^{h}i/) means, the primordial spirit in the beginning divided light, clear and bright things in the shape of Heaven from heavy, muddy and dark things symbolizing Earth. [Earth] is how the ten thousand beings are arranged. The character is composed of "soil" and the phonetic 也 (/jia/). 隓 is a Large Seal style character for 地, derived from 隊.

9.　　　　　　　　　　甲 or 甶

【甲】東方之孟陽氣萌動，從木戴孚甲之象。一曰：人頭空為甲。甲象人頭。凡甲之屬皆從甲。（古狎切。）【甶】古文甲，始於十，見於千，成於木之象。

甲 [Shield, or the first of the Celestial Stems] means, when the young sunrays from the east imbue the sprouts, they begin to move. The character depicts a wooden handle headed with a hard shield. One author says, that hollow skulls of humans were the used as shields, the character depicting a man's head. All things related to "shield" are written with the radical 甲 (Pronounced/k-ap/.) 甶 is an old-style character for 甲, symbolizing the beginning with ten, appearance with thousand, and completed in a tree.

10.　　　　　　　　　　子 or 子 or 𡿩

【子】十一月陽氣動萬物，滋人以為偁。象形。凡子之屬皆從子。李陽冰曰：子在中足併也。（即里切。）【𡿩】古文子，從川象髮也。【𡿩】籀文子，囟有髮臂脛在几上也。

子 [Son, or the first of the Terrestrial Branches] means, in the eleventh month, the yang spirit moves the ten thousand beings, nourishing man to full accordance with nature. The character is a picture (of a child). All things related to "child" are written with the radical 子. Li Yangbing says: It depicts a baby in its diapers, the feet side by side. (Pronounced/tsi/.) 孚 is an old-style character for 子, three strokes depicting the hair. 㜽 is the Large Seal Script character, the fontanel having hair, arms and legs and lying on a small table.

> ### ➤ 注释

　　summit　n. 顶峰,顶点

　　denomination　n. 命名,名称

　　obedient　adj. 顺从的,服从的

　　primordial　adj. 原初的,根本的

　　celestial　adj. 天上的,天空的

　　imbue　v. 渗透,浸染

　　terrestrial　adj. 陆生的,地球的,人间的

　　fontanel　n. 囟门

> ### ➤ 练习

　　1. How was *Shuowen Jiezi* organized by sections?

　　2. Please look up the following entries in *Shuowen Jiezi* and translate into English:

　　a. 法

　　b. 礼

　　c. 刑

　　d. 律

四、拓展阅读

➢ 背景知识

所谓"同音文 Homonym text",就是整个文章中的汉字只允许采用同一个音,四声不限,标点不限,大多是文言文 Classical Chinese,这样的文章叫做"同音文"。汉语中,声母和韵母相拼有四百多种音节组合,但是汉字的数量成千上万,所以汉语中必然存在着大量的同音字 Homophones。同音文的首创者为中国现代语言学先驱赵元任。赵元任是拼音方案的倡导者,他设计的这些极端的例子是为了告诉人们,现实口语中根本不会出现这种情况,从而从反面证明汉字拉丁化之可能性不大。

1.【原文】

季姬寂,集鸡,鸡即棘鸡。棘鸡饥叽,季姬及箕稷济鸡。鸡既济,跻姬笈,季姬忌,急咭鸡,鸡急,继圾几,季姬急,即籍箕击鸡,箕疾击几 伎,伎即齑,鸡叽集几基,季姬急极屐击鸡,鸡既殛,季姬激,即记《季姬击鸡记》。

【拼音】

Jì jī jì,jí jī,jī jí jí jī. Jí jī jī jī,jì jī jíjī jí jì jì jī. Jī jì jì,jī jī jī jí,jì jī jì,jí jī jī,jī jí,jì jī jī,jì jī jì,jí jī jī jī,jī jí jī jī jī,jì jī jī,jī jī jí jī jī,jì jī jí jī jí jī jī,jī jì Jī jí jī jī jī jī,jì jī jí,jì jī jī,jí jì"jì jī jī jī jì".

【释义】

季姬感到寂寞,罗集了一些鸡来养,是那种出自荆棘丛中的野鸡。野鸡饿了叫叽叽,季姬就拿竹箕中的小米喂它们。鸡吃饱了,跳到季姬的书箱上,季姬怕脏,忙叱赶鸡,鸡吓急了,就接着跳到几桌上,季姬更着急了,就借竹箕为赶鸡的工具,投击野鸡,竹箕的投速很快,却打中了几桌上的陶伎俑,那陶伎俑掉到地下,竟粉碎 了。季姬争眼一瞧,鸡躲在几桌下乱叫,季姬一怒之下,脱下木屐鞋来打鸡,把鸡打死了。想着养鸡的经过,季姬激动起来,就写了这篇《季姬击鸡记》。

【Google Translator's mistranslation】

Season Kyi silence, set the chicken, the chicken that chicken spine. Spine chicken hunger grumble, and Kei Ji Ji Ji quarter chicken. Chicken only economic, Ji Ji Ji, Ji Ji Ji, anxious cards chicken, chicken anxious, following a few rubbish, Ji Ji anxious that membership Kei hit chicken, Kei disease hit a few trick, trick that powdered chicken grumble set several groups, season Ji clog hit extremely anxious chicken, chicken both lightning, quarter Kyi excited that in mind, "season chicken Kyi hit record."

【Suggested translation】

Lady Ji is a lonely concubine. One day she sets to collect some chickens as her pets. These chickens are raised in the wild bushes of thorns. When they are hungry, they clucked loud. Lady Ji took out the bamboo quarter of millet to feed them. After the chickens were fed, they followed Lady Ji and jumped onto her book boxes, Lady Ji became anxious that the chickens would soil her books so she scared them off the boxes. Again, though, these chickens jump onto adjoining tea table and further irritated Lady Ji. As she threw her bamboo tool at the chickens, trying to drive them off, it speedily hit the pottery figurine. The pottery figurines fell to the ground and shattered into pieces. The chickens huddled under the table in terror and clucked even louder. Lady Ji exploded with great rage. She took off her wooden clog shoes to beat the chickens. Seeing they were dead, Lady Ji became emotional and recorded a memoir titled Lady Ji's chicken attack.

2.【原文】

石室诗士施氏,嗜狮,誓食十狮。施氏时时适市视狮。十时,适十狮适市。是时,适施氏适市。氏视是十狮,恃矢势,使是十狮逝世。氏拾是十狮尸,适石室。石室湿,氏使侍拭石室。石室拭,氏始试食是十狮。食时,始识是十狮,实十石狮尸。试释是事。

【拼音】

Shíshì shī shì shī shì, shì shī, shì shí shí shī. Shī shì shíshí shì shì shì shī. Shí shí, shì shí shī shì shì. Shì shí, shì shī shì shì shì. Shìshì shì shí shī, shì shí shì, shì shì shí shī shì shì. Shì shi shì shí shī shī, shì shíshì. Shíshì shī, shì shí shì shì shíshì. Shíshì shì, shì shí shì shì shì shí shī. Shí shí, shǐ shi shì shíshī, shí shí shí shī shī. Shì shì shì shì.

【释义】

石室里住着一位诗人姓施,爱吃狮子,决心要吃十只狮子。他常常去市场看狮子。十点钟,刚好有十只狮子到了市场。那时候,刚好施氏也到了市场。他看见那十只狮子,便放箭,把那十只狮子杀死了。他拾起那十只狮子的尸体,带到石室。石室湿了水,施氏叫侍从把石室擦干。石室擦干了,他才试着吃那十只狮子。吃的时候,才发现那十只狮子,原来是十只石头的狮子尸体。试试解释这件事吧。

【Google Translator's mistranslation】

Poet Shi Shi, addicted to lions, swore to eat ten lions. Shi Shi always sees the lion in the market. At ten o'clock, the ten lions are suitable for the market. At that time, Shishi is the right market. Shi sees ten lions as ten lions. Shi Shi is ten lion corpses, suitable for stone room. The stone chamber is wet, so the Shishi will wipe the stone chamber. Shishi tried ten lions. When eclipsing, I first knew the ten lions and realized the ten stone lion corpses. Trial explanation is a matter.

【Suggested translation】

The poet Shi that lived in a stone cell was fond of eating lions. Once he swore to eat ten lions. Shi frequently went to look for lions on the market. At ten o'clock, ten lions happened to come to the market. At that time, Shi also went to the market. Looking at the ten lions, Shi took out his bow and arrows, and killed the ten lions. Shi picked up the ten lions and went back to the stone cell. The stone cell was damp, Shi ordered a servant to wipe the stone cell dry. When the stone cell was wiped, Shi started to try to taste the ten lions. At the time of consuming the lions, Shi began realizing the ten lions were, in fact, ten dead bodies of stone lions. Now can you try to explain what the matter is?

➤ 注释

homonym　n. 同音异义词,同拼异义词

homophone　n. 同音异义词

Classical Chinese　n. 文言

➤ 练习

Explore more fun of homonym texts as exampled below:

1)《忐贪》

贪贪忐探探,坦探探贪贪。

探探摊贪祖,忐贪坍叹瘫。

2)《仁人忍刃》

人人仁人人忍人,认仁人忍人刃人。

仁人仁忍人人刃,人忍人人人人仁。

忍人仁人任人刃,任人刃人任仁人。

五、现代回声

➤ 背景知识

　　汉字的书写效率一直为西方诟病,有志改革者不断发出"废除汉字"的呼声。上世纪 60 年代后期,计算机处理文字成为可能,但汉字使西方计算机专家感到棘手,一时间,汉字将"死于计算机时代"的论调颇为流行。然而美国斯坦福大学历史学家学者汤姆·马拉尼(Tom Mullaney)认为,汉字在电报和打字机领域曾经遭遇尴尬的历史促使中国人充分利用电脑软件优

势,以至于现在用中文输入比用英语要快得多。

Chinese Characters Are Futuristic and the Alphabet Is Old News

——The QWERTY keyboard was once the envy of the world ,but not anymore.

By *Sarah Zhang*

the Atlantic

November 1,2016

On a bright fall morning at Stanford, Tom Mullaney is telling me what's wrong with QWERTY keyboards. Mullaney is not a technologist, nor is he one of those Dvorak keyboard enthusiasts. He's a historian of modern China and we're perusing his exhibit of Chinese typewriters and keyboards,the curation of which has led Mullaney to the conclusion that China is rising ahead technologically while the West falls behind,clinging to its QWERTY keyboard.

Now this was and still is an unusual view because Chinese—with its 75,000 individual characters rather than an alphabet—had historically been the language considered incompatible with modern technology. How do you send a telegram or use a typewriter with all those characters? How do you even communicate with the modern world? If you're a Cambridge-educated classicist enamored with the Greeks,you might just conclude Chinese script is" archaic. "Long live the alphabet.

But, Mullaney argues, the invention of the computer could turn China's enormous catalog of characters into an advantage.

Mullaney is the author of two forthcoming books on the Chinese typewriter and computer,and we discussed what he's learned while researching them. His argument is pretty fascinating to unpack because,at its heart, it is about more than China. It is about our relationship to computers, not just as physical objects but as conduits to intangible software. Typing English on a QWERTY computer keyboard, he says, "is about the most basic rudimentary way you can use a keyboard." You press the "a" key and "a" appears on your screen. "It doesn't make use of a computer's processing power and memory and the cheapening thereof." Type "a" on a QWERTY keyboard hooked up to a Chinese computer, on the other hand, and the computer is off anticipating the next characters. Typing in Chinese requires mediation from a layer of software that is obvious to the user.

In other words, to type a Chinese character is essentially to punch in a set of instructions—a code if you will, to retrieve a specific character. Mullaney calls Chinese typists "code conscious." Dozens of ways to input Chinese now exist, but the Western world mostly remains stuck typing letter-by-letter on a computer keyboard, without taking full advantage of software-augmented shortcuts. Because, he asks, "How do you convince a person who's been told for a century and a half that their alphabet is the greatest thing since sliced bread?"

It's China's awkward history with the telegraph and the typewriter, argues Mullaney, that primed Chinese speakers to take full advantage of software when it came along—to the point where it's now faster to input Chinese than English.

> **注释**

futuristic　adj. 前瞻的，未来的

QWERTY keyboard　n. 标准英文输入键盘

Dvorak keyboard　n. 德沃夏克键盘

incompatible　adj. 不相容的，不合时宜的

enamor   v. 迷恋,倾心

archaic   adj. 古老的,陈旧的,过时的

conduit   n. 管道,导管

intangible   adj. 无形的,抽象大的

rudimentary   adj. 基本的,未发展的

mediation   n. 中介

instruction   n. 指令

shortcut   n. 捷径

prime   v. 使准备好

➢ **练习**

1. What does Tom Mullaney mean by"code conscious"?

2. What, according to Tom Mullaney, makes Chinese typing a more developed input technology?

3. What is Tom Mullaney's main argument about technology and users? Share your opinions.

第三章　哲　　学

一、词源梳理

　　"philosophy"在西方历史悠久。多种西方语言中的"哲学"都来自希腊语 Philosophia，"philo"意为"爱"，"Sophia"意为"智慧"。亚里士多德在其《形而上学》中说："我们也想不出哪门学问比哲学更可贵。因为最神圣的学问也是最可贵的，而从两个方面看，只有哲学才最神圣"。在古希腊，智慧是生活的艺术，来自神谕，因此人们热爱并且追求它。这一术语后来在欧洲成为了关于世界观的学问，有其贯穿始终的学脉和研究范畴。

　　从文字学方面看，中国的"哲"与 philosophy 有异曲同工之处。《说文》将"哲"解释为"知也。从口折声。悊，哲或从心。"可见"哲"也是"智慧"之意。然而"哲学"这一术语在中国用以指称关于世界观的学问却经历了颇为复杂曲折的过程。

　　关于世界观的学问在中国古代有多种术语来指称，如"玄学"、"理学"、"道学"及"形上之道"等。明末欧洲耶稣会士入华，传播天主教的同时也向中国输入了西方的其它学科，哲学便是其中之一。他们在译介"哲学"时用的译名也并不统一，有音译"斐禄所费亚"，也有意译"爱知学"、"理学"、"理科""性学"等。但这些译名在中国都影响有限，未能流传下来。明治维新时期，日本在向西方学习的过程中也同样面临厘定西方学科术语的问题。学者西周潜心学习西方的物质和精神文明成果，研究了中国和日本已有的多种译名，最终摈弃"理学"等原有译名不用，于 19 世纪 70 年代新创"哲学"译名,这一新译名经过近二十年的时间在日本得到了广泛认可。十九二十世纪之交,这一日本译名又由向日本学习的中国知识分子引入中国,经当时诸多学者如黄遵宪、梁启超、严复及蔡元培等的讨论争鸣之后,最终作为学科之名得到了国人的认可。

二、引导阅读

➢ 背景知识

迈克尔·普埃特(Michael Puett),哈佛大学东亚语言与文明系教授,哈佛大学宗教研究会会长,哈佛大学亚洲研究中心代理主任。自 2006 年起,普埃特教授就开始向学生讲授中国哲学概论,他告诉学生,课程中涉及的哲学家们生活在近 2500 年前的中国,但他们的思想却与今日的美国息息相关。他向学生承诺,"这门课会改变他们的人生",很多学生也表示这并非虚言。在哈佛大学最受欢迎课程中,这门课位列第三位,仅次于最热门的《计算机科学导论》和《经济学原理》。普埃特教授以及他的课程也被诸多西方主流媒体报道,本文便是《纽约时报》2016 年 6 月的报道。

值得注意的是,普埃特教授及其课程的成功并不能说明中国哲学在西方或者是美国的普及。2015 年 9 月 11 日的《洛杉矶时报》就刊登了一篇名为《大学哲学课堂上缺失了什么? 中国哲学》的文章,该文作者指出,中国哲学家们的名字可能很多西方人都听说过,但真正读过其著作的却寥寥无几。这种状况不仅仅存在于美国的普罗大众之间,在美国知识界亦如此。美国所有大学中,有 100 多个哲学博士点,但是,其中仅 7 个聘任了专攻中国哲学的教职员,可见中国哲学在美国的影响之低微。普埃特教授的成功及其对中国哲学及其教学的思考可以为我们弘扬和传播中国哲学提供很有价值的镜鉴。

A Harvard Scholar on the Enduring Lessons of Chinese Philosophy

Since 2006,Michael Puett has taught an undergraduate survey course at Harvard University on Chinese philosophy,examining how classic Chinese texts are relevant today. The course is now one of Harvard's most popular, third only to"Introduction to Computer Science"and"Principles of Economics."Mr. Puett and the writer Christine Gross-Loh have distilled the essence of his course into"The Path: What Chinese Philosophers Can Teach Us About the Good Life."The book has been bought by publishers in 25 countries,including China,where the book will be published this year.

In an interview,Mr. Puett discussed the value of rituals,reading Du Fu as well as Shakespeare,and why embracing your true self is not the answer.

Some Chinese philosophical texts are already very popular in the West. There are innumerable translations, for example, of Laotzu's Tao Te Ching.

Some of the texts are indeed very popular,but one of my concerns is that they're often read according to our stereotypes. They are often thought of as"traditional"ideas,focused on teaching us to accord with the world as it is,as opposed to what we like to call"modern"ideas that are focused on liberating us as individuals to decide for ourselves how to live. So-called Confucianism,for example,is read as simply being about forcing people to accept their social roles,while so-called Taoism is about harmonizing with the larger natural world. So Confucianism is often presented as bad and Taoism as good. But in neither case are we really learning from them.

They come across as exotic and foreign.

Precisely. They've become simply foreign and exotic, made into things that we have nothing to learn from.

Is there another risk? That these ideas could be reduced to self-help tips?

A key idea of the book is precisely to oppose that. If we want to take these ideas seriously, we shouldn't domesticate them to our own way of thinking. When we read them as self-help, we are assuming our own definition of the self and then simply picking up pieces of these ideas that fit into such a vision. So, for example, people sometimes take Taoism as a way to "help me find myself and live well in the world." But these ideas are not about looking within and finding oneself. They are about overcoming the self. They are, in a sense, anti-self-help.

What is a key idea in China's philosophical tradition that challenges contemporary assumptions?

Today, we are often told that our goal should be to look within and find ourselves, and, once we do, to strive to be sincere and authentic to that true self, always loving ourselves and embracing ourselves for who we are. All of this sounds great and is a key part of what we think of as a properly "modern" way to live. But what if we're, on the contrary, messy selves that tend to fall into ruts and patterns of behavior? If so, the last thing we would want to be doing is embracing ourselves for who we are — embracing, in other words, a set of patterns we've fallen into. The goal should rather be to break these patterns and ruts, to train ourselves to interact better with those around us.

If we guide people too much, isn't it paternalism?

Certainly some strains of Chinese political theory will take this vision of the self — that we tend to fall into patterns of behavior — to argue for a more paternalistic state that will, to use a more recent term, "nudge" us into better patterns. But many of the texts we discuss in the book go the other way, and argue that the goal should be to break us from being such passive creatures — calling on us to do things that break us out of these patterns and allow us to train ourselves to start altering our behavior for the better.

——by Lan Johnson

> **注释**

distill　v. 提取,蒸馏,作为精华产生

stereotype　v. & n. 陈词滥调,成见;对……形成模式化看法

rut　n. 惯例

> **练习**

1. Who is your favorite Chinese philosopher? Please make a brief description of this philosopher and his thoughts.

2. According to you, how is classic Chinese philosophy relevant today?

三、阅读与比较:《道德经》的三种译本

> **背景知识**

《道德经》原名《老子》,又称《五千言》、《老子五千文》等,春秋时期老子所作。汉景帝时此书被尊为《道德经》,与《易经》和《论语》一起被认为是对中国影响最大的三部思想巨著。《道德经》不仅在中国影响深远,据联合国教科文组织统计,被译成外国文字发行量最多的文化名著,除了《圣经》就是《道德经》。早在唐朝,玄奘法师就将道德经译成梵文,传到印度等国。唐朝开元年间《道德经》又传入了日本。16 世纪末,早期罗马入华传教士将《道德经》翻译成了拉丁文,该译本的目的主要是传教,以中国古代典籍附会天主教,价值不大,但它开启了这本著作传入欧洲的旅程。迄今为止,《道德经》被翻译成了拉丁语、法语、德语和英语等近 30 种语言,外语译介本多达1000 多种,而且几乎每年都有新译本问世。

19 世纪早期,法国人开始翻译《道德经》。1823 年,雷慕莎选译了其中的四个章节,1842 年儒莲的法语全译本问世。英国人翻译《道德经》的历程要比法国人晚了近半个世纪。1868 年,湛约翰牧师的英文译本在伦敦出版,但译者本人承认他参考了儒莲的法文译本。此后其它英文译本如雨后春笋一般不断问世,

但其中最有影响力的应该还是牛津大学首任汉学教授理雅各 1891 年出版的译本。理雅各以传教士的视角阐释和译介中国古典哲学思想,在翻译中以归化为主,异化为辅,用典雅流畅的英文诠释了这本中国古典著作,对于原文中押韵的部分,也费尽心血使用诗体韵文翻译,其影响力至今不衰。

相比于西方人对《道德经》的译介,华人的翻译要晚了将近二百年。1936 年华英书局出版的英译本首开先河。此后华人译介的《道德经》译本渐渐增多,但迟至 21 世纪初,华人翻译的《道德经》也只有 50 种左右。与西方人的"拿来"相比,华人传播自身文化时的"送出"力度显然要小很多。在这些华人译者之中,林语堂、辜正坤和许渊冲的译本影响力比较大。本章选取了《道德经》原文以及理雅各译本和许渊冲译本的前四章,以资读者比较研习。

➢ 素材 1. 老子《道德经》原著节选

一章

道可道,非常道;名可名,非常名。

无,名天地之始;有,名万物之母。

故常无,欲以观其妙;常有,欲以观其徼。

此两者,同出而异名,同谓之玄。玄之又玄,众妙之门。

二章

天下皆知美之为美,斯恶矣;皆知善之

为善,斯不善矣。

有无相生,难易相成,长短相形,高下相

盈,音声相和,前后相随,恒也。

是以圣人处无为之事,行不言之教,万物作而弗始,生而弗有,为而不恃,功成而弗居。夫唯弗居,是以不去。

三章

不尚贤,使民不争。

不贵难得之货,使民不为盗。

不见可欲,使民心不乱。

是以圣人之治,虚其心,实其腹,弱其志,强其骨。

常使民无知无欲;使夫智者不敢为也。

为无为,则无不治。

四章

道冲,而用之或不盈。

渊兮,似万物之宗;

挫其锐,解其纷;

和其光,同其尘;

湛兮,似或存。

吾不知谁之子,象帝之先争。

➢ **素材 2. An extract from *Laws Divine and Human* by Xu Yuanchong**

Chapter I

The divine law may be spoken of,

but it is not the common law.

(Truth can be known,

but it may not be the well-known truth

or

Truth can be known,

but it may not be the truth you known)

Things may be named,

but names are not the things.

In the beginning heaven and earth are nameless;

when named, all things become known

So we should be free from desires

in order to understand the internal mystery of the divine law;

and we should have desires

in order to observe its external manifestations.

Internal mystery and external manifestations

come from the same origin,

but have different names.

ley may be called essence.

The essential of the essence

is the key to the understanding of all mysteries

Chapter II

If all men in the world know what is fair,

then they know what is unfair.

If all men know what is good,

then they know what is not good.

For"to be"and" not to be"co‐exist,

There cannot be one without the other:

without "difficult",there cannot be"easy";

without "long",there cannot be"short";

without"high",there cannot be"low";

without sound,there can be no voice;

without "before",there cannot be "after"

The contrary complement each other.

Therefore the sage does everything without interference,

teaches everyone without persuasion,

and lets everything begin uninitiated and grow unpossessed.

Everything is done without being his deed,

and succeeds without being his success.

Only when success belongs to nobody

does it belong to everyone.

Chapter III

Honor on man

so that none would contend for honor.

Value no rare goods

so that none would steal or rob.

Display nothing desirable

lest people be tempted and disturbed.

Therefore the sage rules

by purifying people's soul,

filling their bellies,

weakening their wills

and strengthening their bones.

He always keeps them knowledgeless and desireless

so that the clever dare not interfere.

Where there is no interference,

there is order.

Chapter IV

The divine law is formless,

its use is inexhaustible.

It is endless,

whence come all things;

where the sharp is blunted,

the knots are untied,

the glare is softened,

all look like dust.

Apparent,

it seems to exist.

i do not know whence it came,

it seems to exist before God.

> 素材 3. **An extract from *Tao Te Ching* by James Legge**

1

One

The Tao that can be trodden is not the enduring and unchanging Tao. The name that can be named is not the enduring and unchanging name.

Two

(Conceived of as) having no name, it is the Originator of heaven and earth; (conceived of as) having a name, it is the Mother of all things.

Three

Always without desire we must be found,

If its deep mystery we would sound;

But if desire always within us be,

Its outer fringe is all that we shall see.

Four

Under these two aspects, it is really the same; but as development takes place, it receives the different names.

Together we call them the Mystery. Where the Mystery is the deepest is the gate of all that is subtle and wonderful.

2

One

All in the world know the beauty of the beautiful, and in doing this they have(the idea of)what ugliness is; they all know the skill of the skillful, and in doing this they have(the idea of)what the want of skill is.

Two

So it is that existence and non-existence give birth the one to(the idea of) the other; that difficulty and ease produce the one(the idea of) the other; that length and shortness fashion out the one the figure of the other; that(the ideas of)height and lowness arise from the contrast of the one with the other; that the musical notes and tones become harmonious through the relation of one with another; and that being before and behind give the idea of one following another.

Three

Therefore the sage manages affairs without doing anything, and conveys his instructions without the use of speech.

Four

All things spring up, and there is not one which declines to show itself; they grow, and there is no claim made for their ownership; they go through their processes, and there is no expectation(of a reward for the results). The work is accomplished, and there is no resting in it(as an achievement).

The work is done, but how no one can see; 'Tis this that makes the power not cease to be.

3

One

Not to value and employ men of superior ability is the way to keep the people from rivalry among themselves; not to prize articles which are difficult to procure is the way to keep them from becoming thieves; not to show them what is likely to excite their desires is the way to keep their minds from disorder.

Two

Therefore the sage, in the exercise of his government, empties their minds, fills their bellies, weakens their wills, and strengthens their bones.

Three

He constantly(tries to)keep them without knowledge and without desire, and where there are those who have knowledge, to keep them from presuming to act(on it).

When there is this abstinence from action, good order is universal.

4

One

The Tao is(like)the emptiness of a vessel; and in our employment of it we must be on our guard against all fulness. How deep and unfathomable it is, as if it were the Honoured Ancestor of all things!

Two

We should blunt our sharp points, and unravel the complications of things; we should attempt our brightness, and bring ourselves into agreement with the obscurity of others. How pure and still the Tao is, as if it would ever so continue!

Three

I do not know whose son it is. It might appear to have been before God.

➢ **注释**

manifestation　n. 表现,显示

complement　v. & n. 补足;补足物

persuasion　n. 劝导,说服(力)

➢ **练习**

1. Read the above passages, pay special attention to those words with

cultural connotation, and then complete the form.

Chinese Version	Xu's Translation	Legge's Translation
道		
名		
无		
有		
无为		
帝		

2. Please refer to the above passages, choose one of your favorite sentence from the original version and comment on its different translations.

四、拓展阅读：对中国哲学的研究

➤ 背景知识

如本章第一部分所说，"哲学"这一术语在中国的确立与翻译和近代亚洲引入西方的"philosophy"密切相关，但中西方哲学的传统和学脉无疑存在着很大差别。西方虽有悠久的哲学传统，这一传统内部也并非整齐划一的大合唱。很多西方哲学家甚至在"什么是哲学"这一问题上也未能达成一致。即便如此，中国哲学家在表达和论证模式上与西方的差异仍然是显而易见的。因此也有学者提出，中国没有西方意义上的哲学，只有思想。这也在一定程度上造成了外国人翻译和接受中国哲学的困难。黑格尔就曾嘲笑中国没有哲学。因为在他看来，只有源自古希腊的对真理的抽象思辨才可以称之为哲学。而中国那些思想家的短小不连贯的"处世格言"根本不能算哲学。如果要为"哲学"这一专业术语寻求一个普世公认的定义和范畴，恐怕是极其困难的。但是中国哲学虽然产生于特定的时空环境，虽然有其独特的表达方式，在人们面对人生、宇宙、生死等大问题时却能够给全世界不同时代的人以启示，这便是它永久的价值所在。

本部分为读者提供了冯友兰所著《中国哲学简史》中《中国哲学家的表达方式》一节，以及德国著名汉学家顾彬2017年发表的《方法和阅读——对孔子和中国哲学的反思》一文，以供读者比较鉴赏。

➤ 素材 1. An extract from *A Brief History of Chinese Philosophy* by Feng Youlan

A Western student beginning the study of Chinese philosophy is instantly confronted with two obstacles. One, of course, is the language barrier; the other is the peculiar way in which the Chinese philosophers have expressed themselves. I will speak about the latter first.

When one begins to read Chinese philosophical works, the first impression one gets is perhaps the briefness and disconnectedness of the sayings and writings of their authors. Open the *Confucian Analects* and you will see that each paragraph consists of only a few words, and there is hardly any connection between one paragraph and the next. Open a book containing the philosophy of Lao Tzu, and you will find that the whole book consists of about five thousand words—no longer than a magazine article; yet in it one will find the whole of his philosophy. A student accustomed to elaborate reasoning and detailed argument would be at a loss to understand what these Chinese philosophers were saying. He would be inclined to think that there was disconnectedness in the thought itself. If this were so, there would be no Chinese philosophy. For disconnected thought is hardly worthy of the name of philosophy.

It may be said that the apparent disconnectedness of the sayings and writings of the Chinese philosophers is due to the fact that these sayings and writings are not formal philosophical works. According to Chinese tradition, the study of philosophy is not a profession. Everyone should study philosophy just as in the West every one should go to church. The purpose of the study of philosophy is to enable a man, as a man, to be a man, not some particular kind of man. Other studies—not the study of philosophy—enable a man to be some special kind of man. So there were no professional philosophers; and non-professional philosophers did not have to produce formal philosophical writings. In China, there were far more philosophers who produced no formal philosophical writings than those who did. If one wishes to study the philosophy of these men, one has to go to the records of their sayings or the letters they wrote to disciples and friends. These letters did not belong to just one period in the life of the person who wrote them, nor were the records written only by a single person. Disconnectedness or even inconsistency between them is, therefore, to be expected.

The foregoing may explain why the writings and saying of some philosophers are disconnected; but it does not explain why they are brief. In some philosophic writings, such as those of Mencius and Hstin Tzu, one does find systematic reasoning and arguments. But in comparison with the philosophic writings of the West, they are still not articulate enough. The fact is that Chinese philosophers were accustomed to express themselves in the form of aphorisms, apothegms, or allusions, and illustrations. The whole book of Lao-tzu consists of aphorisms, and most of the chapters of the Chuang-tzu are full of allusions and illustrations. This is very obvious. But even in writings such as those of Mencius and Hstin Tzu, mentioned above, when compared with the philosophical writings of the West, there are still too many aphorisms, allusions, and illustrations. Aphorisms must be very brief; allusions and illustrations must be disconnected.

Aphorisms, allusions, and illustrations are thus not articulate enough. Their insufficiency in articulateness is compensated for, however, by their suggestiveness. Articulateness and suggestiveness are, of course, incompatible. The more an expression is articulate, the less it is suggestive—just as ihe more an expression is prosaic, the less it is poetic. The sayings and writings of the Chinese philosophers are so inarticulate that their suggestiveness is almost boundless.

Suggestiveness, not articulateness, is the ideal of all Chinese art, whether it be poetry, painting, or anything else. In poetry, what the poet intends to communicate is often not what is directly said in the poetry, but what is not said in it. According to Chinese literary tradition, in good poetry the number of words is limited, but the ideas it suggests are limitless. So an intelligent reader of poetry reads what is outside the poem; and a good reader of books reads what is between the lines. Such is the ideal of Chinese art, and this ideal is reflected in the way in which Chinese philosophers have expressed themselves.

The ideal of Chinese art is not without its philosophical background. In the twenty-sixth chapter of the Chuang-tzu it is said: "A basket-trap is for catching fish, but when one has got the fish, one need think no more about the basket. A foot—trap is for catching hares; but when one has got the hare, one need think no more about the trap. Words are for holding ideas, but when one has got the idea, one need no longer think about the words. If only I could find someone who had stopped thinking about words and could have him with me to talk to!" To talk with someone who has stopped thinking about words is not to talk with words. In the Chuang-tzu the statement is made that two sages met without speaking a single word, because "when their eyes met, the Too was there. According to Taoism, the Too(the Way)cannot be told, but only suggested. So when words are used, it is the suggestiveness of the words, and not their fixed denotations or connotations, that reveals the Too. Words are something that should be forgotten when they have achieved their purpose. Why should we trouble ourselves with them any more than is necessary? This is true of the words and rhymes in poetry, and the lines and colors in painting.

During the third and fourth centuries A. D. , the most influential philosophy was the Neo—Taoist School, which was known in Chinese history as the hsiian hstteh(the dark or mystic learning). At that time there was a book entitled Shih-shuo Hsin-yil, which is a record of the clever sayings and romantic activities of the famous men of the age. Most of the sayings are very brief, some consisting of only a few words. It is stated in that book that a very high official once asked a philosopher(the high official was himself a philosopher), what was the difference and similarity between Lao-Chuang (i. e. , Lao Tzu and Chuang Tzu) and Confucius. The philosopher answered: "Are they not the same?" The high official was very much pleased with this answer, and instantly appointed the philosopher as his secretary. Since the answer consists of only three words in the Chinese language, this philosopher has been known as the three-word secretary. He could not say that Lao-Chuang and Confucius had nothing in common, nor could he say that they had everything in common. So he put his answer in the form of a question, which was really a good answer.

The brief sayings in the Confucian Analects and in the philosophy of the Lao-tzu are not simply conclusions from certain premises which have been lost. They are aphorisms full of suggestiveness. It is the suggestiveness that is attractive. One may gather together all the ideas one finds in the Lao-tzu and write them out in a new book consisting of fifty thousand or even five hundred thousand words. No matter how well this is done, however, it is just a new book. It may be read side by side with the original Lao-tzu, and may help people a great deal to understand the original, but it can never be a substitute for the original.

> **素材 2.** *Method and Reading——Reflections on Confucius and Chinese Philosophy* **by Wolfgang Kubin**

THERE are some scholars who claim Chinese philosophy isn't a genuine philosophy, and if it is, they say, it is either too simple or too hard to understand. You will hear similar opinions not only in Europe, but also in China.

In this article, I don't want to examine whethercases like these are only matters of opinion or fact. Instead, I want to highlight the problematic nature of the art of reading difficult Chinese texts. How dowe read a Chinese text which doesn't really speakto us innately?

As is well known in modern hermeneutics, awork that doesn't speak to us is a dead work. Nonetheless, we also know that something we are notyet ready to comprehend or appreciate today mightgain our fullest sympathy and attention tomorrow. How is this possible? And what exactly was it thathappened to us in such cases between these two incidents in our life?

Let me use myself as an example and therebyreiterate. Due to my early readings of *Hegel in Vienna* (1968), the words of my first Chinese teacherin Muenster (1969), and my university years duringthe "cultural revolution" in Beijing (1974—75), I wasnot at all interested in Confucius (551—479 BC). Heappeared to me as boring, trivial and, in comparison to Greek philosophy, which I favored at thattime, anything but philosophic.

Why is it then that I like to read *Confucian Analects* (*Lunyu*) today and often recite the words of themaster, and even defend them, as a response to certain negative developments in Western modernity?

It all has to do with a certain primal experience. In May 1999, I was doing research on Chineseaesthetics. I bought a German translation of the French book *In Praise of Blandness* , *Proceeding from Chinese Thought* , and *Aesthetics* by FrançoisJullien. It opens more or less with the close revisionof an inconspicuous passage from *Lunyu*.

In order to spare the readers the impression thathe looks at Confucius with a lack of philosophicalexpertise, Jullien right from the beginning pointsout the true character of the essence of Chinese culture as he sees it: Something that lies in the middleand appears unimportant at first glance, but whichis in fact truly essential.

Whoever takes Hegel's statement of the *Lunyu* as being trivial seriously should first properly studythe Chinese spirit before further debate, as the Chinese spirit defines itself quite differently from ours, namely through its withdrawal from the visible andthe structured.

Philosophy and Death

Chinese people are quite right to be afraid of everything designed and modeled, because all that isdesigned and well-formed confines us to somethingspecific. As the formed and defined version of myself, I am only what I reveal as my shaped self. This self is reduced to certain specific characteristics, butno longer implies the countless number of all possible options as a whole. That is, for instance, whyfashion plays such an important role in the Western world, as it allows people to design and define themselves in a very individual way.

On the other side, something unshaped and shapeless is limited only to itself and its potential, but without being perceptible as something special. Thus, from outer appearances it could be many things; however, it prefers to be everything possible in its inner self.

According to Georg Wilhelm Friedrich Hegel(1770—1831) a human being should in general(objectively)be what he is also for himself(subjectively), which means, a person should define himself by what he feels deep inside as well as by his outer appearance, thus resolving the dichotomy of being.

As a consequence of this thought, the concept of self realization appears as a new terminus in Hegel's works from 1816 onwards, and becomes a whole new scheme.

This scheme, however, differs signifcantly from the Chinese concept of "*xiushen.*" This binominal, which can be translated as "cultivating of one's moral character,"is central to Confucianism. Originally,"*xiushen*" meant the cleansing of all evil in river waters. Confucius regards this concept as a basis for personality development.

According to the classical work *The Great Learning*, one becomes a person by placing the act of physical cleansing in the context of the empire under heaven, the(vassal)state and the family.

How much a cosmological concept like this takes away from a single person what is a part of his individuality, in the view of the Occidental culture, becomes visible through a later key phrase from the Song Dynasty (960—1279):"Erase human desires and apply the heavenly principles." This phrase goes further than the former requirement of Confucius, by stating that a human being has to"overcome itself, to reinstate the social norms, the rite."

In all the cases named, what one gains is not one's very own unique form, but the form of being itself, the form of everybody and everything. In this way I am indistinguishable from other humans by my outer appearance. Instead I carry the reason for everything within my inner self. This is also why heaven, earth, and humans can be understood as an internal-worldly trinity.

This idea also explains why the former Chinese philosophy remained unspoken. Words form a text, and in this way narrow it down to a few possibilities. Plenty of words might seem to clarify a statement, but in fact,they muddy it.

In the case of Confucius we have to mentally fill in further thoughts between the Chinese characters and by doing so upgrade the unspoken statements to something philosophical and eloquent.

For instance,let us take a closer look at the following example from *Lunyu* (IV. 8): The Master said,"If a man in the morning hears the right way,he may die in the evening without regret. "

What does Confucius mean by this statement? From the mouth of Socrates(470—399 BC)we are familiar with the idea that philosophizing means to learn to die. So why not take a detour via Socrates to understand his Chinese peer?

From the European perspective,we might as well ask: Why can a man,who hears about the right way in the morning,not die by noon? Whoever raises questions like this and thereby complements a minimalist saying,will truly start to philosophize. As a consequence,death will become an object of his very own thoughts,just like it became one in the mind of Socrates.

The French philosopher François Jullien has complemented another short and well known passage of the *Confucian Analects* in this style, which also deals with the subject of death:

The Duke of She asked Zilu about Confucius,but Zilu did not answer him. The Master said:"Why didn't you say to him,'he is simply a man, who in his eager pursuit of knowledge forgets his food,who in the joy of its attainment forgets all his sorrows,and who does not perceive that old age is coming on?'"

Zilu's silence is characteristic,because a statement about the Master would have inevitably defined him as a certain something and singled him out as something in particular. However,Confucius himself does not seem to know difficulties like these. He talks about himself in dual images, which make clear what is important to him and what not. The images of eager pursuit and food, joy and sorrow, perception and age contrast each other.

However, we do not know what exactly it is that the Master is eagerly pursuing or feels joy about. Here, like in many other passages in the *Analects*, there is no clear object following the sentence's verb. Only the last verb "perceive" reveals an object: the coming on of age. As this verb is negated, the content of self-characterization seems to reveal a kind of calmness in the Master Confucius. The search will only end after death, which, however, the Master doesn't seem to fear at all.

What we deal with here is a phenomenon, an exercise, which plays an important role equally in Chinese and Western philosophy. However, this parallelism hasn't been paid much attention to up to now.

➢ 注释

disciple   n. 门徒,信徒,弟子

articulate   v. 清晰发音,明确表达

aphorism   n. 格言,警句

inconspicuous   a. 不显眼,不引人注目的

negate   v. 否定,无效

➢ 练习

1. Read the above passages, list some reasons that lead to the difference between Chinese and Western philosophies.

2. What kind of role did Chinese classic philosophy play in Chinese culture?

3. How do you understand *Xiushen* and self-realization?

五、现代回声

➢ 背景知识

　　了解和学习中国哲学,不仅应该了解中国以往哲学家的思想,更应该关注其在当下的意义,关注中国哲学有什么可以提供给当今世界,有什么有助于解决当下世界性难题的解决方案。在这一方面,很多中外学者都进行了有益的探索和思考,中国学者赵汀阳便是其中颇具影响力的一位。

　　赵汀阳,中国社会科学院哲学研究所研究员;中国人民大学哲学学院教授,博士生导师;欧洲跨文化研究院学术常委;哈佛燕京学社及哈佛大学东亚系蒲塞杰出访问学者。赵汀阳教授初期主要研究西方哲学,二十世纪末开始转而关注中国各种人文学科,潜心研究中国哲学,主要研究领域为政治哲学、伦理学及知识论等。自二十世纪末开始,赵汀阳教授在国内外发表和出版了上百种论文和专著,其中主要有《论可能生活》、《天下体系》、《哲学的支点》、《坏世界研究》、《天下的当代性》、《惠此中国》等。本部分选取了 2018 年 2 月《华盛顿邮报》刊载的赵汀阳教授关于"天下"的一篇文章,以供读者思考。

Can This Ancient Chinese Philosophy Save Us From Global Chaos?

Zhao Tingyang is one of China's most influential contemporary philosophers. He is the author of "The *Tianxia* System: An Introduction to the Philosophy of a World Institution" *and is a member of the Chinese Academy of Social Sciences.*

BEIJING — Today's world is full of conflict, hostility and continuing clashes among civilizations. All indications suggest we are headed beyond failed states to a failed world order. In this Hobbesian context of growing chaos and anarchy, U. S. President Donald Trump has emerged as an old-fashioned hero from early modern times, with his misperception of the world as a battlefield instead of a shared community. However, as globalization has connected economies and shared information around the world, such a course will surely end in failure.

Thus, I suggest another path, one rooted in the ancient Chinese concept of tianxia, which roughly translates to "all under heaven" coexisting harmoniously. This concept of world order was embraced for hundreds of years from around 1046 to 256 B. C. during the Zhou dynasty, China's longest-lasting.

The Rationality of *tianxia*

To explain the concept of *tianxia*, let me introduce an imitation test, a game that reveals the concept's philosophical roots. In this game, each player seeks to maximize his or her own self-interest within a Hobbesian state of nature, and each player learns and imitates the successful strategies deployed by the other players.

As a result, none of the successful strategies dominate for long, since all of them are copied by others and soon become common knowledge. The stable equilibrium among strategies finally comes about when all players have learned all available successful strategies and thus have become equally smart or equally stupid.

An imitated strategy could be one of hospitality or hostility. A strategy is irrational if it leads to self-defeating consequences when universally imitated. A rational strategy — where the first consideration is coexistence — continues to produce positive rewards when copied by other players. It is the only strategy not to incur any retaliation and thus successfully to withstand the challenge of others imitating it.

Tianxia is thus a rational worldview. In game theory, it is the best conception of an undefeatable strategy or a stable evolutionary strategy. And it is precisely what the world needs today at this historical juncture.

What Does *tianxia* Look Like?

The concept of *tianxia* defines an all-inclusive world with harmony for all. It often refers to the physical world in early literature, but it is essentially a political concept consisting of a trinity of realms.

First, *tianxia* means the Earth under the sky, "all under heaven. "Second, it refers to the general will of all peoples in the world, entailing a universal agreement. It involves the heart more than the mind, because the heart has feelings. And third, *tianxia* is a universal system that is responsible for world order. The world cannot achieve *tianxia* unless the physical, psychological and political realms all coincide.

About 3,000 years ago, the Zhou dynasty brought the *tianxia* system — the only one ever practiced — to prominence. The dynasty sought to bring the whole world together under one tent as a way to eliminate any negative external influence, and thereby conflict, within what was then considered the civilized world. *Tianxia* thus defines the concept of "the political" as the art of co-existing through transforming hostility into hospitality — a clear alternative to the more modern concepts of German legal theorist Carl Schmitt's recognition of politics as "us vs. them," Hans Morgenthau's "realist" struggle for power and Samuel Huntington's "clash of civilizations. "

How Can *tianxia* Be Made Accessible Now?

The idea of "perpetual peace," famously associated with philosopher Immanuel Kant, proved possible during the Zhou dynasty in a region that was mostly culturally homogenous, but it was ineffective in settling the kind of civilization clashes noted by Huntington. A "*tianxia* peace" for our hyper-connected, interdependent world would have to go a big step further. It would have to be built on the broader foundation of a compatible universalism that includes all civilizations — not an exclusive unilateral claim of one civilization to universality.

To put it in philosophical terms, and to go back to my imitation test, the methodology for possible tianxia must be what's called relational rationality. Or, to put it another way: existence presupposes coexistence. Everyone can live if — and only if — they let live; otherwise everyone will suffer from unbearable retaliation. This truth is captured in the Confucian concept of ren, which literally means that being is only defined in relation to others, not by individual existence.

Aversion to risk is much stronger when guided by relational rationality than when guided by individual rationality. As I define it, relational rationality emphasizes the minimization of mutual hostility over the maximization of self-interest. *Tianxia* suggests that relational rationality should have priority over individual rationality in political and economic practices.

Relational rationality and universal consent are essential for a sound world order that includes all peoples. Confucius was the first to have understood this and proffered his principle that one becomes established if and only if one lets others be established, and one is improved if and only if one lets others improve. Hence, *tianxia* could be named the "Confucian optimum" as a more acceptable alternative to the so-called self-interest-driven "Pareto optimal."

I can think of no better overarching concept for governing our present world, which is, more than ever, an interdependence of plural identities. Seeking to maximize self-interest in such a world is only a recipe for endless conflict to the detriment of all.

——by *Zhao Tingyang*

➢ **注释**

hobbesian   adj. 霍布斯哲学的

anarchy   n. 无政府状态

deploy   v. 配置,部署

incur　v. 招致,遭受

retaliation　n. 报复,反击

homogenous　adj. 同质的,同类的

pareto optimal　帕累托最优

➤ **练习**

1. Read the above passage and give a brief account of Professor Zhao's view of *tianxia*.

2. According to your view, can Chinese classic philosophy contribute to the world today something else?

第四章　文学(上)

一、词源梳理

　　"文学"在西方经历了一个漫长复杂的演变过程。拉丁文早期的"文学"(literatura)译自希腊语,这一术语有时指阅读和书写的知识,有时甚至指"刻写"或者"文字"本身。在法国,"文学"这个词在相当长的时期都用来指文学研究。"literature"早期在英语中的意思是"对于文学的研究或知识",即"学识"或"学养",尤其是对于拉丁文的知识。这一含义后来慢慢被"全部的文学作品"或者"某一地区或国家在一定时期的文字材料"所取代。在十八世纪,"literature"作为"文学作品"的意义被迅速民族化和本土化,然而这个词的含义仍然与文献、学识及作品等等交织在一起,但是也更多的时候开始指向想象性的文学作品。即使到今天,英语中的文学也包含两方面意思,一是指文学作品或者想象性的文学,二是指对文学的知识和研究。

　　从文字学方面看,中国的"文"也同样含义丰富。《说文·序》中说:"仓颉之初作书,该依类象形,故谓之文"。《说文》将文解释为"刻画之文饰"也。《易经》中"物相杂,故曰文",可见"文"最初就具有刻画、装饰和纹理等多种意思。后来,它又转指自然界或人类社会某些有规律性的现象,"天文"、"人文"即是。

　　关于"文学",国学大师章太炎说:"何以谓之文学? 以有文字,著于竹帛,故谓之文。论其法式,谓之文学。凡文理、文字、文辞,皆谓之文。而言其采色之焕发,则谓之彣。《说文》云:文,错画也,象交文。彣,彣也,彣有彣彰也。或谓文章当做彣彰,此说未是。要之,命其形质,则谓之文;状其华美,则谓之彣。凡彣者,必皆成文;而成文者,不必皆彣。是故言论文学,当以文字为主,不当以彣彰为主"。因此他将古代的图书、表谱等等都归入了"文"。根据这一说法,"文学"的外延丰富至极。民国知名学者刘咸炘的观点可能更符合中国古代文史哲不分家的传统,他说:"凡文字之所载,不外事、理、情三者,记事之文谓之史,说理之文谓之子,言情之文谓之诗"。到了现代,受西方学科分类精细化的影响,中文的"文学"基本仅仅指向狭义的文学作品,正如朱光潜先生说:"文学是以语言文字为媒介的艺术"。

二 引导阅读

➤ 背景知识

作为中国古典文学的巅峰之作,《红楼梦》自问世之日起就在中国广泛流传,有所谓"开讲不谈红楼梦,读尽诗书也枉然"之说,作为一门学问的"红学"也在曹雪芹去世后不久便形成了。鲁迅先生所说:"《红楼梦》是中国许多人所知道,至少,是知道这名目的书. 谁是作者和续者姑且勿论,单是命意,就因读者的眼光而有种种:经学家看见《易》,道学家看见淫,才子看见缠绵,革命家看见排满,流言家看见宫闱秘事……"可见《红楼梦》在中国文化中的影响之大,以及其解读和研究的角度之多。

然而,相比于中国其它叙事文学作品,《红楼梦》在英语世界的传播却颇显滞后。直至二十世纪七十年代,企鹅出版社出版了大卫. 霍克斯的译本之后,完整的《红楼梦》才在西方广泛流传开来。下面选择的英国著名电视节目主持人、历史学家迈克尔·伍德的文章用通俗流畅的语言介绍了《红楼梦》及其译者霍克斯,也为《红楼梦》在英语世界很晚才流行开来这一现象提供了一种解读。

Why Is China's Greatest Novel Virtually Unknown in the West?

Dream of the Red Chamber is a masterpiece that has been called
the 'book of the millennium' and it is high time it receives
the attention it deserves.

When I was a graduate student in Oxford many years ago I shared a house with a brilliant German sinologist who used to push translations my way, stroking his beard with a teasing smile: "Try this-you'll really enjoy it. "Many visitors popped into our terraced house on Abingdon Road, and one night around the kitchen table I met a fascinating character, rangy with white hair and beard, and a twinkly eye. His name was David Hawkes.

A gifted linguist, he had directed Japanese codebreakers in his early 20s, during the Second World War. As a student at Peking University, he had been in Tiananmen Square in 1949 when Mao proclaimed the People's Republic of China. Later, as a teacher, he had done a wonderful translation of *the Songs of the South*, part of a poetic tradition earlier than anything that has survived in the west. Then he became professor of Chinese in Oxford, but, as he put it, "I resigned in order to devote my time to translating a Chinese novel ⋯ well, the Chinese novel".

The book was *Dream of the Red Chamber*, also known as *The Story of the Stone*, written by Cao Xueqin. The critic Anthony West called it "one of the great novels of world literature⋯ to the Chinese as Proust is to the French or Karamazov to the Russians".

Hawkes eventually completed his great endeavour with the help of his son-in-law John Minford, who finished the last two volumes of the five, which were published by Penguin between 1973 and 1986. Hawkes's translation was greeted as an introduction to "a masterpiece", a "work of genius", a "candidate for the Book of the Millennium". When Chinese premier Wen Jiabao was given a copy of Shakespeare during his state visit to the UK, the new Chinese ambassador Fu Ying gave the queen the Hawkes translation.

The novel is an 18th-century saga, the tale of a noble family that falls from grace. It is full of incredible detail of the social, cultural and spiritual life of the time. Chairman Mao claimed to have read it five times-and thought everyone else should too. Today, everyone in China knows it, partly due to the much-loved 1987 TV version, which had the impact of the Colin Firth/Jennifer Ehle *Pride and Prejudice* in the UK.

Dream of the Red Chamber was written in the 1750s "by a great artist with his very lifeblood", said Hawkes. Cao's story mirrors the tale of his own family. His grandfather, Cao Yin, was an imperial bondservant, an important functionary in the south, who enjoyed high favour with the emperor Kangxi. But after Kangxi died, his son began a purge of corruption and incompetence, and the family were ruined. They lost their mansion in Nanjing and moved to a modest house among the alleys of Beijing, southeast of the Forbidden City.

So Yin's grandson grew up in straitened circumstances, a brilliant but watchful boy, wary of all power, and never forgetting his grandad's saying about the fickleness of fortune: "When the tree falls, the monkeys will be scattered. "He was good with the brush, both with paint and with words: but he had no aptitude for university, so he found himself down and out in his 30s, selling his paintings and working as a private teacher (he was eventually sacked for getting a maidservant pregnant.) By the end he was sleeping in barns and working in wine shops; he clearly drank too much.

The book was written in dribs and drabs: each new chapter circulated among family and friends, often in exchange for a meal and a pitcher of wine. He died in 1763, heartbroken it is said, by the death of his only son. *Dream of the Red Chamber* was finally published in print in 1791, but the text is still surrounded by controversy. There is a story that it had been censored because eminent people it satirised had been too thinly disguised. It is also debated whether the text we have is all his. Different endings survive, with a writer called Gao E claiming to have published the complete version according to the author's wishes. Today, "redology" (Red Chamber obsessives are known as "redologists") is a massive and still expanding field in China, with conferences, annual journals and a torrent of publications. Manuscripts still turn up. Mysteries remain unsolved.

Hawkes's version gives us the first 80 chapters by Cao and the last 40 redacted by Gao E, who it seems fair to assume was using an unfinished draft and clearly knew what the author had planned. It is a different kind of novel from earlier Chinese classics such as *Romance of the Three Kingdoms*, *The Water Margin and Monkey*, the latter a vast sprawling narrative, surreal and poignant, full of songs and poems. The female characters are especially strong. As Cao himself said: "Having made an utter failure of my life, one day I found myself in the midst of my poverty and wretchedness, thinking about the female companions of my youth. As I went over them in my mind's eye one by one it suddenly came over me that those slips of girls-which is all they were then-were in every way, both morally and intellectually, superior to the 'grave and moustached signor' I am now supposed to have become. The realisation brought with it an overpowering sense of shame…And I resolved then, however unsightly my shortcomings might be, I must not, for the sake of keeping them hid, allow those wonderful girls to pass into oblivion without a memorial. "

The book as it stands in the Penguin version runs to 2,500 pages-twice as long as *War and Peace*. Hard going at first because of the myriad characters (there are 40 main ones) and their (to a non-Chinese eye) difficult names. But once you are into it, it is a book into which the reader can completely immerse herself; it is like nothing else in all of literature. Having just watched his thrilling adaptation of *War and Peace*, all I can say is: "Over to you, Andrew Davies. "

——by Michael Wood

> **注释**

　　rangy　adj. 瘦高的,落魄的

　　imperial bondservant　包衣

　　functionary　n. 官员

　　fickleness　n. 变化无常,浮躁

　　dribs and drabs　点点滴滴,片断

　　poignant　adj. 尖锐的,心酸的

> **练习**

　　1. Read the above passage and give a brief introduction of *Dream of the Red Chamber*. Borrow from the passage as much as you like.

　　2. Have you read the novel *Dream of the Red Chamber*? In what way has the book influenced your development?

　　3. Who is your favorite character of the book? Please make a brief description of the character and comment on his/her fate.

三、阅读与比较:《红楼梦》的三个英译本

> **背景知识**

　　明末清初,中西文化交流空前活跃,《红楼梦》就是从 1830 年开始有了英译本,包括乔利(H. Bencraft Joly)译本在内总共四种。然而,由于中国国力衰微,英译《红楼梦》在英文文学体系中处于边缘状态。译者多为英国驻华外交官,主要目的是为了帮助在华外国人学习中文,翻译的故事情节非常不完整,其中最长的乔利译本也不及原著的一半。

　　五四运动之后,《红楼梦》重新成为中外学者瞩目的对象。很多西方学者对《红楼梦》有了全面深入的了解,认识到它的巨大艺术魅力足以与西方小说媲美。王良志和王际真就属于这类学者。他们的译本均于 20 年代成书于如日方升、不捐细流的美国,英译中国古典文学作品却并非"经典"或

"高雅"作品。西方人对东方异域风情的猎奇心，使得这一时期的两个译本带有非常强烈的迎合倾向，比如仅仅关注宝黛爱情悲剧，意译而非音译人物姓名，等等。但王际真的译笔水平高超，所选情节故事性极强，还专门请人作序，同时自己写说明，介绍小说内容、作者生平、版本出处，因此其译本在英美读者中产生了相当持久和广泛的影响。1932 年德国翻译家库恩翻译出版的德译本，也是在与王际真译本比较研究的基础上完成的旷世之作。

二战之后，国际文化交流更为频繁和平等，20 世纪 70 至 80 年代，能充分展示红楼艺术魅力的两个英文全译本应运而生，一是霍克思（David Hawks）和闵福德（John Minford）翁婿译本《石头记》（*The Story of Stone*），二是杨宪益和戴乃迭夫妇的译本《红楼梦》（*The Dream of Red Mansions*）。这两个英译本的译者皆学贯中西，更重要的是其翻译都旨在充分展现原著不朽的文化艺术价值，因此译者付出了长期艰苦的努力，在忠实原著、吸收红学研究的最新成果以及读者接受方面煞费苦心。霍译本甚至根据故事内容分卷，并根据各卷内容另行命名为"金色年华"、"海棠诗社"、"哀世之音"、"还泪情史"、"如梦方醒"。封内有作者简介，各卷有序言和附录，为西方普通读者和中国古典名著搭建桥梁。杨译促进文化交流的方式，则是大量使用脚注，解释小说人物和中国特殊文化现象。至此，《红楼梦》终于从世界文学的边缘向中心迈出了一大步。这两个译本也很大程度上影响了后来的其他译本。

除了英译本之外，《红楼梦》还有德译本六个（均为同一种译本）、匈译本三个（同一种译本）、法、俄、意、荷、希腊、罗、西译本各一个。

➤素材 1.《红楼梦》原著节选

士隐乃读书之人，不惯生理稼穑等事，勉强支持了一二年，越发穷了。封肃见面时，便说些现成话儿；且人前人后又怨他不会过，只一味好吃懒做。士隐知道了，心中未免悔恨，再兼上年惊唬，急忿怨痛，暮年之人，那禁得贫病交攻，竟渐渐的露出了那下世的光景来。

可巧这日拄了拐扎挣到街前散散心时，忽见那边来了一个跛足道人，疯狂落拓，麻鞋鹑衣，口内念着几句言词道：

世人都晓神仙好，惟有功名忘不了。

古今将相在何方？荒冢一堆草没了。

世人都晓神仙好，只有金银忘不了。

终朝只恨聚无多，及到多时眼闭了。

世人都晓神仙好，只有娇妻忘不了。

君生日日说恩情，君死又随人去了。

世人都晓神仙好，只有儿孙忘不了。

痴心父母古来多，孝顺子孙谁见了？

士隐听了，便迎上来道：“你满口说些什么？只听见些‘好’‘了’‘好’‘了’。”那道人笑道：“你若果听见‘好’‘了’二字，还算你明白：可知世上万般，好便是了，了便是好。若不了，便不好；若要好，须是了。我这歌儿便叫《好了歌》。”士隐本是有夙慧的，一闻此言，心中早已悟彻，因笑道：“且住，待我将你这《好了歌》注解出来何如？”道人笑道：“你就请解。”士隐乃说道：

陋室空堂，当年笏满床。衰草枯杨，曾为歌舞场。蛛丝儿结满雕梁，绿纱今又在蓬窗上。说甚么脂正浓、粉正香，如何两鬓又成霜？昨日黄土陇头埋白骨，今宵红绡帐底卧鸳鸯。

金满箱，银满箱，转眼乞丐人皆谤。正叹他人命不长，那知自己归来丧？训有方，保不定日后作强梁。择膏粱，谁承望流落在烟花巷！因嫌纱帽小，致使锁枷扛。昨怜破袄寒，今嫌紫蟒长：乱烘烘你方唱罢我登场，反认他乡是故乡。甚荒唐，到头来都是“为他人作嫁衣裳”。

那疯跛道人听了，拍掌大笑道：“解得切！解得切！”士隐便说一声“走罢”，将道人肩上的搭裢抢过来背上，竟不回家，同着疯道人飘飘而去。当下哄动街坊，众人当作一件新闻传说。封氏闻知此信，哭个死去活来。只得与父亲商议，遣人各处访寻，那讨音信？无奈何，只得依靠着他父母度日。幸而身边还有两个旧日的丫鬟伏侍，主仆三人，日夜作些针线，帮着父亲用度。那封肃虽然每日抱怨，也无可奈何了。

这日那甄家的大丫鬟在门前买线，忽听得街上喝道之声。众人都说：

"新太爷到任了！"丫鬟隐在门内看时，只见军牢快手一对一对过去，俄而大轿内抬着一个乌帽猩袍的官府来了。那丫鬟倒发了个怔，自思："这官儿好面善？倒像在那里见过的。"于是进入房中，也就丢过不在心上。至晚间正待歇息之时，忽听一片声打的门响，许多人乱嚷，说："本县太爷的差人来传人问话！"封肃听了，唬得目瞪口呆。

不知有何祸事，且听下回分解。

> ➤ **素材 2. An extract from _A Dream of the Red mansions_ by Yang Xianyi**

As a scholar, Shiyin had no knowledge of business or farming. He struggled along for a year or two, losing money all the time, while Feng Su kept admonishing him to his face and complaining to all and sundry behind his back of his incompetence, idleness and extravagance.

To the shock Shiyin had suffered the previous year and the toll taken by his subsequent misfortunes was now added the bitter realization that he had misplaced his trust. Ageing and a prey to poverty and ill health, he began to look like a man with one foot in the grave.

He made the effort one day to find some distraction by taking a walk in the street, leaning on his cane. Suddenly a Taoist limped towards him, a seeming maniac in hemp sandals and tattered clothes, who as he came chanted:

> "All men long to be immortals
> Yet to riches and rank each aspires;
> The great ones of old, where are they now?
> Their graves are a mass of briars.
> All men long to be immortals,
> Yet silver and gold they prize
> And grub for money all their lives
> Till death seals up their eyes.

All men long to be immortals

Yet dote on the wives they've wed,

Who swear to love their husband evermore

But remarry as soon as he's dead.

All men long to be immortals

Yet with getting sons won't have done.

Although fond parents are legion,

Who ever saw a really filial son?"

At the close of this song Shiyin stepped forward.

"What was that you just chanted?" he asked. "I had the impression that it was about the vanity of all things. "

"If you gathered that, you have some understanding," the Taoist remarked. "You should know that all good things in this world must end, and to make an end is good, for there is nothing good which does not end. My song is called *All Good Things Must End*. "

Shiyin with his innate intelligence at once grasped the other's meanmg. Putting on a smile he said, "Wait a minute, will you let me expound this song of yours?"

"By all means do," said the Taoist. Shiyin then declaimed:

"Mean huts and empty halls

Where emblems of nobility once hung;

Dead weeds and withered trees,

Where men have once danced and sung.

Carved beams are swathed in cobwebs

But briar-choked casements screened again with gauze;

While yet the rouge is fresh,the powder fragrant,

The hair at the temples turns hoary for what cause?

Yesterday,**yellow** clay received white bones;

Today, **red** lanterns light the love-birds' nest;

While men with gold and silver by the chest

Turn beggars,scorned by all the dispossessed.

A life cut short one moment makes one sight,

Who would have known it's her turn next to die?

No matter with what pains he schools his sons.

Who knows if they will turn to brigandry?

A pampered girl brought up in luxury

May slip into a quarter of ill fame;

Resentment at a low official rank

May lead to fetters and a felon's shame.

In ragged coat one shivered yesterday,

Today a **purple** robe he frowns upon;

All's strife and tumult on the stage,

As one man ends his song the next comes on.

To take strange parts as home

Is folly past compare;

And all our labour in the end

Is making clothes for someone else to wear. "

The lame, eccentric Taoist clapped his hands. "You have hit the nail on the head," he cried.

"Let's go," was Shiyin's brief reply.

He transferred the sack from the Taoist's shoulder to his own, and then, without even calling in at his home, he strode off with the priest.

This caused a sensation in the neighbourhood and words of it soon reached Shiyin's wife, who gave way to a storm of weeping. After consultation with her father she had a thorough search made, but there was no news of her husband. She had perforce to go back and live with her parents. Luckily she still had her two maids, and the three of them by sewing day and night helped to defray Feng Su's expenses. For his part, grumble as he might, he had to lump it.

One day the elder of the two maids was buying some thread at the gate when she heard men shouting to clear the street, and people said the new prefect had arrived to take up office. She hid in the doorway to watch. First soldiers and runners marched past two by two. Then came a large sedan-chair in which was seated an official in a black gauze cap and **red** robe. The maid stared in surprise and thought: His face looks familiar. Have I seen him somewhere before? But once back in the house she thought no more of the matter.

That evening, just as they were going to bed, there came a loud knocking on the gate and a clamour of voices. Messengers from the yamen ordered Feng Su to appear for questioning by the prefect. His jaw dropped and he gaped in consternation. Did this mean fresh calamity?

To find out, read the next chapter.

➤ 素材 3. An extract from *The Story of Stone* by David Hawkes

A scholar, with no experience of business or agricultural matters, Shiyin now found himself poorer after a year or two of struggle than when he had started. Feng Su would treat him to a few pearls of rustic wisdom whenever they met, but behind his back would grumble to all and sundry about "incompetents" and "people who liked their food but were too lazy to work for it", which caused Shi-yin great bitterness when it came to his ears. The anxieties and injustices which now beset him, coming on top of the shocks he had suffered a year or two previously, left a man of his years with little resistance to the joint onslaught of poverty and ill-health, and gradually he began to betray the unmistakable symptoms of a decline.

One day, wishing to take his mind off his troubles for a bit, he had dragged himself, stick in hand, to the main road, when it chanced that he suddenly caught sight of a Taoist with a limp—a crazy, erratic figure in hempen sandals and tattered clothes, who chanted the following words to himself as he advanced towards him:

"Men all know that salvation should be won,
But with ambition won't have done, have done.
Where are the famous ones of days gone by?
In grassygraves they lie now, every one.

Men all know that salvation should be won,
But with their riches won't have done, have done.
　　Each day they grumble they've not made enough.
　　When they've enough, it's goodnight everyone

Men all know that salvation should be won,
But with their loving wives they won't have done.
　　The darlings every day protest their love:

But once you're dead, they're off with another one.

> Men all know that salvation should be won,
>
> But with their children won't have done, have done.
>
> Yet though of patents fond there is no lack,

Of grateful children saw I ne'er a one. "

Shi-yin approached the Taoist and questioned him, "what is all this you are saying? All I can make out is alot of 'won' and 'done'. "

"If you can make out 'won' and 'done'," replied the Taoist with a smile, "you may be said to have understood; for in all the affairs of this world what is won is done, and what is done is won; for whoever has not yet done has not yet won, and in order to have won, one must first have done. I shall call my song the 'Won-Done Song'"

Shi-yin had always been quick-witted, and on hearing these words a flash of understanding had illuminated his mind. He therefore smiled back at the Taoist, "Wait a minute! How would you like me to provide your 'Won-Done Song' with a commentary?"

"Please do!" said the Taoist; and Shi-yin proceeded as follows:

> "Mean hovels and abandoned halls
>
> Where courtiers once paid daily calls:
>
> Bleak haunts where weeds and willows scarcely thrive
>
> Were once with mirth and revelry alive.
>
> Whilst cobwebs shroud the mansion's gilded beams,
>
> The cottage casement with choice muslin gleams.
>
> Would you of perfumed elegance recite?
>
> Even as you speak, the raven locks turn white.
>
> Who yesterday her lord's bones laid in clay,

On silken bridal-bed shall lie today.

Coffers with gold and silver filled:

Now, in a trice, a tramp by all reviled.

One at some other's short life gives a sigh,

Not knowing that he, too, goes home—to die!

The sheltered and well-educated lad,

In spite of all your care, may turn out bad;

And the delicate, fastidious maid

End in a foul stews, plying a shameful trade.

The judge whose hat is too small for his head

Wears, in the end, a convict's cangue instead.

Who shivering once in rags bemoaned his fate,

Today finds fault with **scarlet** robes of state.

In such commotion does the world's theatre rage:

As each one leaves, another takes the stage.

In vain we roam:

Each in the end must call a strange land home.

Each of us with that poor girl may compare

Who sews a wedding-gown for another bride to wear. "

"A very accurate commentary!" cried the mad, lame Taoist, clapping his hands delightedly.

But Shi-yin merely snatched the satchel that hung from the other's shoulder and slung it from his own, and with a shout of "Let's go!" and without even waiting to call back home, he strode off into the wide world in the company of the madman.

This event made a great uproar in the little town, and news of it was relayed from gossip to gossip until it reached the ears of Mrs Zhen, who cried herself into fits when she heard it. After consulting her father, she sent men out to inquire everywhere after her husband; but no news of him was to be.

It was now imperative that she should move in with her parents and look to them for support. Fortunately she still had the two maids who had stayed on with her from the Soochow days, and by sewing and embroidering morning, noon and night, she and her women were able to make some contribution to her father's income. The latter still found daily occasion to complain, but there was very little he could do about it.

One day the elder of the two maids was purchasing some silks at the door when she heard the criers clearing the street and all the people began to tell each other that the new mandarin had arrived. She hid in the doorway and watched the guards and runners marching past two by two. But when the mandarin in his black hat and **scarlet** robe of office was borne past in his great chair, she stared for some time as though puzzled. "where have I seen that mandarin before?" she wondered. "His face looks extraordinarily familiar. " But presently she went into the house again and gave the matter no further thought.

That night, just as they were getting ready for bed, there was suddenly a great commotion at the door and a confused hubbub of voices shouting that someone was wanted at the *yamen* for questioning, which so terrified Feng Su that he was momentarily struck dumb and could only stare.

If you wish to know what further calamity this portended, you will have to read the following chapter.

➤ 注释

admonish   vt. 告诫,劝告

sundry   adj. &n. 杂项(的)

maniac adj. &n. 疯狂的；疯子

hemp adj. &n. 麻类植物（的）

tatter v. 撕碎，使破烂

briar n. 荆棘

expound v. 详述，阐释

pamper v. 纵容，使过量

strife and tumult 动荡冲突

defray v. 支付

onslaught n. 猛攻，突击

erratic adj. & n. 古怪的（人）

hovel n. 小屋，茅舍

cangue n. 枷

satchel n. 包，背包

commotion n. 骚动，暴乱

hubbub n. 喧哗，骚动

➢ 练习

1. Read the above passages, pay special attention to those words with cultural connotation, and then complete the form.

Chinese Version	Yang's Translation	Hawkes's Translation
神仙		
功名		
好		
了		
夙慧		
悟彻		

2. Please refer to the above passages to explain the favored technique of foreshadowing in Chinese classical novels, where the story and the char-

acters' ultimate ending is implied at the very beginning?

四、《好了歌》的其他英译版本

➤ 背景知识

《好了歌》位于《红楼梦》第一章结尾,具有很强的预示情节、点明主题的作用。然而,由于中西之间语言和文化的巨大差异,翻译起来却障碍重重。本部分为读者提供了另外两个《好了歌》的译文,以供鉴赏比较。

乔利(H. Bencraft Joly,中文名周骊),原为英国驻澳门领事馆副领事,后为驻中国领事。他完整翻译了《红楼梦》第 1 回到第 56 回。上册二十四回,1892 年由香港别发洋行(Kelly and Walsh, Hong Kong)出版,下册三十二回,1893 年由澳门港务局出版。标题名字为《红楼梦》,但没有作者曹雪芹的字样,因为译者那时还不知道作者姓名。乔利本打算翻译整个 120 回,可惜因去世而未能如愿。在上册译本前的序言中,有译者小序一篇,说"翻译本书的动机,并非意欲跻身于汉学家之林,而是因为我本人在北京学习时,读完《自迩集》后陷入《红楼梦》的迷宫而困惑犯愁。……能对现在与将来学习汉语的学生,拙译哪怕能稍有帮助,我将感到十分满足。"人们对他的评价是:西译红楼梦第一人,但译笔不佳。然而在红楼梦的英译史上,乔利的英译本不但大大超越了此前零散的摘译片段,而且对后来的英文全译本译者霍克思和闵福德翁婿、杨宪益和戴乃迭夫妇有所启示,为他们指明了努力的方向和应该注意的问题,起了承上启下的重要作用,其历史贡献不容忽视。

王际真(Chi-Chen Wang,1899—2001),出生在山东省桓台县的一个富裕家庭,早年毕业于留美预备学堂——北京清华学校前身。1922 年获学校全额资助赴美留学,先后在威斯康辛及哥伦比亚大学获得学位。曾任纽约艺术博物馆(Metropolitan Museum of Art)东方部职员、哥伦比亚大学汉文教员。王际真一生因大部分时间在美国生活,国内很少有人提及他。他主持哥大中文系二十余年,为其教学科研打下了坚实基础。在西方,他因英译《红楼梦》和鲁迅小说而广为人知。

　　王际真翻译《红楼梦》这项工作始于哥大毕业之后。他将全书节译为 1 个楔子和 39 回，译名为 *Dream of the Red Chamber*。每回之中，根据故事情节分成若干小节，基本上是转述的意译，删节较多，1929 年同时在纽约和伦敦出版。但该译本有著名汉学家阿瑟·韦利（Arthur Welay）5000 字的序言，强调其重要性，译者本人也有一篇 7000 字的说明。天津《大公报》"文学副刊"署名评价王译本："译者删节颇得其要，译笔明显简洁，足以达意传情……喜其富于常识，深明西方读者之心理。"1958 年，王际真将节译本《红楼梦》增补后，由吐温出版社再次出版纽约版。王译本虽然只有原书一半回数，但在杨宪益和戴乃迭 1978 年合译英文全译本出版之前，一直是英美最为流行的《红楼梦》版本，在西方颇受推重。

➤ 素材 1. Haoliao Ge by. H. Bencraft Joly

All men spiritual life know to be good,

But fame to disregard they ne'er succeed!

From old till now the statemen where are they?

Waste lie their graves, a heap of grass extinct.

All men spiritual life know to be good,

But to forget gold, silver, ill succeed!

Through life they grudge their hoardings to be scant,

And when plenty has come, their eyelids close.

All men spiritual life hold to be good,

Yet to forget wives, maids, they ne'er succeed!

Who speak of grateful love while lives their lords,

And dead their lord, another they pursue.

All men spiritual life know to be good,

But sons and grandsons to forget never succeed!

From old till now of parents soft many，

But filial sons and grandsons who have seen?

➢ 素材 2. **Haoliao Ge by Chi-chen Wang**

They all know the freedom of the immortals

But Reward and Fame they cannot forget.

Where are the ministers and generals past and present? ——

Under the neglected graves overgrown with grass.

They all know the freedom of the immortals

But Gold and Silver they cannot forget.

All life long they save and hoard and wish for more——

Then suddenly their eyes are forever closed.

They all know the freedom of the immortals

But their wives they cannot forget.

They speak of love and constancy while you live——

They will marry again before your graves are dry.

They all know the freedom of the immortals

But their sons and grandsons they cannot forget.

Doting parents there have been many since ancient times——

But whoever saw filial and obedient offspring?

➢ 注释

grudge   n. &v. 怨恨，不满

hoardings   n. 储藏物

scant　adj. 不足的，缺乏的

doting　adj. 溺爱的，偏爱的

filial　adj. 孝敬的

➢ 练习

1. *Haoliao Ge* reflected a variety of conflicts in Chinese Culture, could you list some of them?

2. Read the above passages, comment on the four English versions of Haoliao Ge provided in Part 1 and Part 2.

3. After reading the passages, do you have a new understanding of real and unreal?

五、现代回声

➢ 背景知识

2016 年 9 月，在旧金山，中国古典小说《红楼梦》首次被搬上西方歌剧舞台。歌剧主创团队几乎都是华裔艺术家，盛宗亮和黄哲伦编剧，盛宗亮作曲，赖声川导演，叶锦添舞美及服装设计，旅欧中国男高音石倚洁扮演宝玉，旅美韩国女高音曹青扮演黛玉。这一演职员阵容被旧金山歌剧院院长马修·希尔瓦克称为"梦之队"。然而，将一部一百多回的皇皇巨著浓缩成不到三个小时的歌剧对于这一阵容仍然是巨大的挑战。最终，擅长在西方舞台上讲故事的黄哲伦和自称已成为半个红学家的盛宗亮大刀阔斧将纷繁复杂的原著人物精简为七个,并以宝、黛、钗三人爱情为主线,交织着贾、薛两大家庭因失皇宠而衰败的故事,最后的结局是黛玉投河、宝玉出家。

在旧金山演出六场,获得很大成功之后,这一英文版《红楼梦》歌剧登陆香港和中国大陆的舞台,然而,熟悉《红楼梦》的中国观众在对其予以肯定的同时,也对其情节、歌词等提出了批评意见。

Rebuilding Classics in Modern Era: *Dream of the Red Chamber*

Transforming *Dream of the Red Chamber* into an opera seems at once impossible and necessary. The eighteenth-century novel is a true classic of Chinese literature, one of the most treasured stories ever written, and it is full of plot devices that have long beguiled composers and audiences alike. There's a love triangle equal to the one in Aida; a trick marriage as devious as anything in Falstaff. But the original book is also quite lengthy—2,400 pages when translated into English. Author Cao Xueqin indulged himself in a meaningful and exhaustive tale that starts when a stone and a flower are changed into human form and goes on, in great detail, to include forty major characters and four hundred minor ones. The novel itself acknowledges that the "narration may border on the limits of incoherency and triviality," though, it adds, that it "possesses considerable zest."

The novel's principal narrative concerns young Bao Yu, who falls for his cousin, Dai Yu, but is pressured to marry his other cousin, Bao Chai, in order to secure his family's fortune. The novel unfolds with an excess of words and complexity that resists translation into dialogue, but its literary power comes from the runs of beautiful, flowery poetry it uses to make connections. A libretto doesn't come easy when the subtext of the main characters' relationship is that they were once a stone and a flower, but composer Bright Sheng and librettist David Henry Hwang told the story in less than three hours, including one intermission, at the world premiere at San Francisco Opera(seen Sept. 10). Sheng and Hwang, who collaborated on the libretto, dispatched the mythical backstory as economically as possible and moved right to the zest of the drama, focusing on the greed, ambition, fear, deceit, vanity, violence, and above all, lust that drives the action. For the sake of brevity, they hand over the story's set-up to a narrator in monk's garb, whose spoken word prologue is stilted and over exaggerated, not a good start. But there are numerous heart-wrenching moments that follow, including a stunning aria for Dai Yu in Act II, which has the soprano comparing her own fate as an excluded lover to that of fallen petals— "When their beauty and fragrance fade/Who cares for the fallen petals? / Treasured in the flush of your bloom/Yet soon discarded to decay. "

There are, of course, actual petals are falling upon the set at that point, just one of many scenic delights from designer Tim Yip. He's an Academy Award winner for the super-sized film Crouching Tiger, Hidden Dragon and he doesn't hold back. Some of it is what you'd expect—elaborate mansions appear on stage with pagoda roofs and carved wooded columns, and large watercolor landscapes serve as props. But there are also eye-catching projections that set scenes on fire and an amazing system of backdrops that rise and fall on cue, weaving together bits of rolling Chinese landscape in ways that are both literal and abstract. It was a lot to keep in order but director Stan Lai organized smooth transitions.

Sheng's score for the *Dream of the Red Chamber* drips with musical immoderation and deploys about double the high notes of most contemporary operas. The composer fully employs every instrument in the orchestra, understanding the dramatic punch each possesses. For a work so steeped in Chinese custom, he has chosen a broad array, stretching from violin and bassoon to gong and guqin(the stringed instrument related to the zither). Red Chamber is rooted firmly in classical European romance, though enhanced with well-considered ventures into Asian musical motifs. Under George Manahan's leadership, the orchestra was especially vigorous and loud, if not always in balance with the vocalists. The singing of all three leads—tenor Yijie Shi as Bao Yu, soprano Pureum Jo as Dai Yu and mezzo Irene Roberts as Bao Chai—had an exuberant, appealing freshness appropriate to characters whose moral sums are still in the process of adding up.

➢ **注释**

   beguile   v. 欺骗,使着迷

   libretto   n. 剧本,歌词集

   intermission   n. 幕间休息

   garb   n. 服装

   aria   n. 咏叹调

   vocalist   n. 歌手

   tenor   n. 男高音

   soprano   n. 女高音

   mezzo   n. 女中音

   exuberant   adj. 热情洋溢的

➢ 练习

1. In our time when pace of living is accelerating and digital technology is revolutionizing virtually all walks of life, how do we rebuild the classics remains a daunting mission. Do you have creative ideas to adapt the *Dream of the Red Chambers* for the general public, especially the young generation? (Consider various modern medias, gamification, festivals, etc.)

2. One of the challenge of inheriting classics is to keep its authentic value? What is the value of the book to your generation?

3. Conduct a research on the translations or adaptations of *Hong Lou Meng* both in China and the western world，choose one of them and write a review.

第五章 文学(下)

一 词源梳理

根据《说文解字》,"戏"字从"戈",它是三军之中附设的一个特殊兵种,也可能是一种兵器。《广韵》则把"戏"解释为"戏弄"之意。《汉书·西域传赞》中有"作巴俞都卢、海中砀极、漫衍鱼龙、角抵之**戏**以观视之"这样的记载,可见"戏"当时已经有了表演之意。诸多其它中国古代文献中也有关于"优"、"伶"或者"倡"人表演的记载。然而王国维《宋元戏曲史》云:"古之俳优,但以歌舞及戏谑为事。自汉以后则间演故事,而合歌舞以演一事者,实始于北齐"。徐慕云在其所著《中国戏剧史》中说:"北朝多异族而选主中原,与西域诸国,以交通及朝贡之频繁。各国之乐,间或流传华夏。故戏曲之发展,乃视南朝为盛。……正式之戏曲,实始基于此"。可见,中国戏曲真正出现,始于南北朝,是异域音乐影响的结果。但当时出现的只是"戏曲"。

"后代之戏剧,必合言语、动作、歌唱以演一故事,而后戏剧之意义始全。故真戏剧必与戏曲相表里。"戏剧之出现,始于宋,至元代才臻于完美。因为元代不仅戏剧进展神速,曲词之精妙亦冠绝古今。有人认为其中原因是元人以曲取士,但王国维反对此说,认为元代戏剧之盛是因为元代在相当长时期内废科举,士人之才无所用,转而用于撰写词曲。至元末明初,杂剧衰落,传奇取而代之成为了支撑明清两代戏剧繁荣的重要因素,汤显祖、孔尚任及洪昇等作家创作的戏剧也就成为了中国文学的经典之作。

西方戏剧的历史自古希腊开始就绵延不绝,源远流长。英语中的"drama"，"play"，"opera"以及"theatre"都有与中国戏剧相近的含义，但这些术语又各有侧重。"drama"有其希腊语词源，意思是"行动，事迹，场面"等，17世纪60年代才有了"作为艺术的戏剧文学"之意。"play"来自古英语，指"快速的动作或活动，消遣，练习"，到14世纪初期才衍生出"戏剧表演"的含义。"theatre"的古希腊词源为"theatron"，后半部分的"tron"是个表示地点的词缀，前半部分则表示"观看或者观看的座位"，因此它侧重的是戏剧表演的场所。而"opera"侧重的是歌剧。由此可见，中国的"戏剧"兼具以上多个英文术语之意，翻译为其中任何一个都嫌勉强，难怪有些译者直接用中文拼音将其翻译为"*Xiqu*"。

二、引导阅读

➤ 背景知识

　　汤显祖(1550—1616)，江西临川人，21岁中举而天下闻名。但他刚直不屈，先后得罪张居正及申时行等权臣而失去锦绣前程，又直言不讳，指摘万历皇帝及朝中重臣之过失而一再被贬。这反而使得汤显祖有时间和精力进行文学创作，"临川四梦"是他最重要的传世作品。

　　由于汤显祖与莎士比亚同为剧作家，且恰巧都于1616年逝世。日本著名中国戏曲研究专家青木正儿在20世纪早期就将汤显祖与莎士比亚相比，后世学者也不乏对两者进行比较研究者。然而在这两位伟大戏剧家逝世400周年之际，《经济学人》却刊发了下面这篇文章，对这一比附提出了质疑。这篇文章的观点当然不乏写作者的政治偏见，但对于我们如何认识自己的文学文化遗产，建立自己的文化名片及树立文化自信也提供了别样的角度。

How China Uses Shakespear to Promote Its Own Bard

There is Flattery in Friendship.

Like many countries, China had a busy schedule of Shakespeare-themed celebrations in 2016, 400 years after his death. There were plays, lectures and even plans announced for the rebuilding of his hometown, Stratford-upon-Avon, at Sanweng-upon-Min in Jiangxi province. But as many organisers saw it, Shakespeare was just an excuse. Their main aim was to use the English bard to promote one of their own: Tang Xianzu. Whatever the West can do, their message was, China can do at least as well.

Tang is well known in China, though even in his home country he does not enjoy anything like the literary status of his English counterpart—he wrote far fewer works(four plays, compared with Shakespeare's 37), and is not as quotable. But no matter. The timing was perfect. Tang died in 1616, the same year as Shashibiya, as Shakespeare is called in Chinese. President Xi Jinping described Tang as the "Shakespeare of the East" during a state visit to Britain in 2015. The Ministry of Culture later organised a Tang-themed exhibition, comparing his life and works to those of Shakespeare. It has shown this in more than 20 countries, from Mexico to France.

The two playwrights would not have heard of each other: contacts between China and Europe were rare at the time. But that has not deterred China's cultural commissars from trying to weave a common narrative. A Chinese opera company created "Coriolanus and Du Liniang", in which Shakespeare's Roman general encounters an aristocratic lady from Tang's best-known play, "The Peony Pavilion". The musical debuted in London, then travelled to Paris and Frankfurt. Last month Xinhua, an official news agency, released an animated music-video, "When Shakespeare meets Tang Xianzu". Its lines, set bizarrely to a rap tune, include: "You tell love with English letters, I use Chinese ink to depict Eastern romance."

The anniversary of Shakespeare's death is now over, but officially inspired adulation of Tang carries on(a musical about him premiered in September in Fuzhou, his birthplace—see picture). Chinese media say that a recent hit song, "The New Peony Pavilion", is likely to be performed at the end of this month on state television's annual gala which is broadcast on the eve of the lunar new year. It is often described as the world's most-watched television programme. Officials want to cultivate pride in Chinese literature, and boost foreign awareness of it. It is part of what they like to call China's "soft power".

Shakespeare's works only began to take root in China after Britain defeated the Qing empire in the first Opium War of 1839 —42. They were slow to spread. After the dynasty's collapse in the early 20th century, Chinese reformers viewed the lack of a complete translation of his works as humiliating. Mao was less keen on him. During his rule, Shakespeare's works were banned as "capitalist poisonous weeds". Since then, however, his popularity has surged in tandem with the country's growing engagement with the West.

Cong Cong, co-director of a recently opened Shakespeare Centre at Nanjing University, worries that without a push by the government, Tang might slip back into relative obscurity. But Ms Cong says the "Shakespeare of the East" label does Tang a disservice by implying that Shakespeare is the gold standard for literature. Tang worked in a very different cultural environment. That makes it difficult to compare the two directly, she says. Officials, however, will surely keep trying.

> **注释**

bard   n. 诗人

deter   vt. 劝阻

commissar   n. 委员,代表,政委贫困的

Coriolanus　n. 科里奥兰纳斯

adulation　n. 过分的赞扬,谄媚

surge　v. 突然增长,激烈波动

tandem　adj. 有大鬈曲八字胡的

in tandem　协同,联合,一起

obscurity　n. 默默无闻

disservice　n. 损害,伤害,虐待

> **练习**

1. Have you ever read or heard about any works written by Tang Xianzu? Give a brief review of it.

2. Have you ever read or heard about any works by Shakespeare? Give a brief review of it.

3. Do you think it proper to compare these two playwrights?

三、阅读与比较:《牡丹亭》的三个版本
> **背景知识**

《牡丹亭》,全名《牡丹亭还魂记》,是汤显祖的"临川四梦"之一,其中女主角杜丽娘春日游园,梦中遇见一书生便以身相许,梦醒后竟相思成疾,且一病不起。临终前杜丽娘画一自画像,埋在园中梅树之下,其梦中所见书生柳梦梅后来恰巧得到此像,挂在房中细细观赏。杜丽娘之魂魄自画像中走出与其缱绻多日。后柳梦梅解杜父于危难之中,具陈其事,并开棺使杜丽娘还魂,二人终成眷属。

早在 17 世纪,《牡丹亭》便传至日本,20 世纪又陆续被译成德文、法文、俄文和英文等西方文字,很多西方学者也发表了研究汤显祖及其《牡丹亭》的论著。下面节选的是汤显祖原著中的较为经典的第 10 出《惊梦》片段,以及美国学者西塞尔·伯奇(Cycil Birch)和中国学者汪榕培的译文。

➤素材 1.《惊梦》片段

（旦）不到园林，怎知春色如许！

【皂罗袍】原来姹紫嫣红开遍，似这般都付与断井颓垣。良辰美景奈何天，赏心乐事谁家院！恁般景致，我老爷和奶奶再不提起。（合）朝飞暮卷，云霞翠轩；雨丝风片，烟波画船——锦屏人忒看的这韶光贱！（贴）是花都放了，那牡丹还早。

【好姐姐】（旦）遍青山啼红了杜鹃，荼蘼外烟丝醉软。春香啊，牡丹虽好，他春归怎占的先！（贴）成对儿莺燕啊。（合）闲凝眄，生生燕语明如翦，呖呖莺歌溜的圆。（旦）去罢。（贴）这园子委是观之不足也。（旦）提他怎的！（行介）

【隔尾】观之不足由他缱，便赏遍了十二亭台是枉然。到不如兴尽回家闲过遣。（作到介）（贴）"开我西阁门，展我东阁床。瓶插映山紫，炉添沉水香。"小姐，你歇息片时，俺瞧老夫人去也。（下）（旦叹介）"默地游春转，小试宜春面。"春啊，得和你两留连，春去如何遣？咳，恁般天气，好困人也。春香那里？（作左右瞧介）（又低首沉吟介）天呵，春色恼人，信有之乎！常观诗词乐府，古之女子，因春感情，遇秋成恨，诚不谬矣。吾今年已二八，未逢折桂之夫；忽慕春情，怎得蟾宫之客？昔日韩夫人得遇于郎，张生偶逢崔氏，曾有《题红记》、《崔徽传》二书。此佳人才子，前以密约偷期，后皆得成秦晋。（长叹介）吾生于宦族，长在名门。年已及笄，不得早成佳配，诚为虚度青春，光阴如过隙耳。（泪介）可惜妾身颜色如花，岂料命如一叶乎！

【山坡羊】没乱里春情难遣，蓦地里怀人幽怨。则为俺生小婵娟，拣名门一例、一例里神仙眷。甚良缘，把青春抛的远！俺的睡情谁见？则索因循腼腆。想幽梦谁边，和春光暗流传？迁延，这衷怀那处言！淹煎，泼残生，除问天！身子困乏了，且自隐几而眠。（睡介）（梦生介）（生持柳枝上）"莺逢日暖歌声滑，人遇风情笑口开。一径落花随水入，今朝阮肇到天台。"小生顺路儿跟着杜小姐回来，怎生不见？（回看介）呀，小姐，小姐！（旦作惊起介）（相见介）（生）小生那一处不寻访小姐来，却在这里！（旦作斜视不语介）（生）恰好花园内，折取垂柳半枝。姐姐，你既淹通书史，可作诗以赏此柳枝乎？（旦作惊喜，欲言又止介）（背想）这生素昧平生，何因到此？（生笑介）小姐，咱爱杀你哩！

【山桃红】则为你如花美眷，似水流年，是答儿闲寻遍。在幽闺自怜。小姐，和你那答儿讲话去。（旦作含笑不行）（生作牵衣介）（旦低问）那边去？（生）转过这芍药栏前，紧靠着湖山石边。（旦低问）秀才，去怎的？（生低答）和你把领扣松，衣带宽，袖梢儿搵着牙儿苫也，则待你忍耐温存一晌眠。（旦作羞）（生前抱）（旦推介）（合）是那处曾相见，相看俨然，早难道这好处相逢无一言？（生强抱旦下）（末扮花神束发冠，红衣插花上）"催花御史惜花天，检点春工又一年。蘸客伤心红雨下，勾人悬梦采云边。"吾乃掌管南安府后花园花神是也。因杜知府小姐丽娘，与柳梦梅秀才，后日有姻缘之分。杜小姐游春感伤，致使柳秀才入梦。咱花神专掌惜玉怜香，竟来保护他，要他云雨十分欢幸也。

【鲍老催】（末）单则是混阳蒸变，看他似虫儿般蠢动把风情扇。一般儿娇凝翠绽魂儿颠。这是景上缘，想内成，因中见。呀，淫邪展污了花台殿。咱待拈片落花儿惊醒他。（向鬼门丢花介）他梦酣春透了怎留连？拈花闪碎的红如片。秀才才到的半梦儿；梦毕之时，好送杜小姐仍归香阁。吾神去也。（下）

【山桃红】（生、旦携手上）（生）这一霎天留人便，草借花眠。小姐可好？（旦低头介）（生）则把云鬟点，红松翠偏。小姐休忘了啊，见了你紧相偎，慢厮连，恨不得肉儿般团成片也，逗的个日下胭脂雨上鲜。（旦）秀才，你可去啊？（合）是那处曾相见，相看俨然，早难道这好处相逢无一言？（生）姐姐，你身子乏了，将息，将息。（送旦依前作睡介）（轻拍旦介）姐姐，俺去了。（作回顾介）姐姐，你可十分将息，我再来瞧你那。"行来春色三分雨，睡去巫山一片云。"（下）（旦作惊醒，低叫介）秀才，秀才，你去了也？（又作痴睡介）

（老旦上）"夫婿坐黄堂，娇娃立绣窗。怪他裙衩上，花鸟绣双双。"孩儿，孩儿，你为甚瞌睡在此？（旦作醒，叫秀才介）咳也。（老旦）孩儿怎的来？（旦作惊起介）奶奶到此！（老旦）我儿，何不做些针指，或观玩书史，舒展情怀？因何昼寝于此？（旦）孩儿适在花园中闲玩，忽值春暄恼人，故此回房。

无可消遣,不觉困倦少息。有失迎接,望母亲恕儿之罪。(老旦)孩儿,这后花园中冷静,少去闲行。(旦)领母亲严命。(老旦)孩儿,学堂看书去。(旦)先生不在,且自消停。(老旦叹介)女孩儿长成,自有许多情态,且自由他。正是:"宛转随儿女,辛勤做老娘。"(下)

➤ 素材 2. An extract from The *Peony Pavilion* by Wang Rongpei

Du Liniang:

Without coming to the garden, how could I have tasted the beauty of spring!

(*To the tune of* **Zaoluopao**)

The flowers glitter brightly in the air,

Around the wells and walls deserted here and there. Where is the "pleasant day and pretty sight,'?

Who can enjoy "contentment and delight"?

Mom and dad have never mentioned such pretty sights.

Du Liniang and Chunxiang:

The clouds at dawn and rain at dusk,

The bowers in the evening rays,

The threads of rain in gales of wind,

The painted boat and in hazy sprays:

All are foreign to secluded maids.

Chunxiang:

All the seasonal flowers are in full blossom, but it's still too early for the peony.

Du Liniang:

(*To the tune of* **Haojiejie**)

Amid the red azaleas cuckoos sing;

Upon roseleaf raspberries spider-threads cling.

Oh，Chunxiang，

The peony is fair indeed，

But comes the latest in the mead.

Chunxiang：

Look at the orioles and swallows in pairs！

Du Liniang and Chunxiang：

When we cast a casual eye，

The swallows chatter and swiftly fly

The orioles sing their way across the sky.

Du Liniang：

It's time to leave.

Chunxiang：

There's more than enough to be seen in the garden.

Du Liniang：

No more about it.

（*Du Liniang and Chunxiang begin to leave*）

（*To the tune of* **Quasi-Coda**）

It's true that there's more than enough to be seen，

But what though we visit all the scenic spots？

We'd better find more fun behind the screen.

（*They arrive at the chamber*）

Chunxiang：

"I open doors of chambers east and west

And sit on my own bed to take a rest.

I put azalea in the earthen vase

And add incense unto the proper place.

Mistress，please take a rest now and I'll go and see themadam.

（*Exit Chunxiang*）

Du Liniang:

⟨*Sighs*⟩

"Back from a brief spring tour,

I know my beauty now for sure. "Oh spring, now that I love you so much, what shall I do when you are gone? How dizzy I feel in such weather! Where's Chunxiang?

(*Looks around and lowers her head again, murmuring*) Oh heavens, now I believe that spring is annoying. It is true indeed what is written in various kinds of poems about maidens in ancient times who felt passionate in spring and grieved in autumn. I've turned sixteen now, but no one has come to ask for my hand. Stirred by the spring passion, where can I come across one who will go after me? In the past Lady Han met a scholar named Yu and Scholar Zhang came across Miss Cui. Their love stories have been recorded in the books *The Story of the Maple Leaves* and *The Life of Cui Hui*. These lovely ladies and talented scholars started with furtive datings but ended in happy reunion.

⟨*Heaves a Long sigh*⟩

Born and brought up in a renowned family of high officialdom, I've come of age but haven't found a fiance yet. I'm wasting my youth which will soon pass.

⟨*Weeps*⟩

What a pity that my face is as pretty as a flower but my fate is as dreary as a leaf!

(*To the tune of* **Shanpoyang**)

Indulged in springtime passion of all sorts,

I'm all of a sudden roused to plaintive thoughts.

I have a pretty face

And so my spouse must be as good,

With a noble place.

What is there to meet my fate

That I must waste my youth to wait!

When I go to bed,who'll peep

My shyness in my sleep?

With whom shall I lie in my secret dream,

Drifting down the springtime stream?

Tormented day by day,

To whom can I say?

About my woe,

About my wretched fate,

Only the heavens know!

I feel dizzy. I'll lean on the table and take a short nap.

(Falls asleep and begins to dream)

{Enter Liu Mengmei with a willow twig in his hand)

Liu Mengmei:

"In warm days oriole's songs ring apace

While man in deep affection has a smiling face

I chase the fragrant petals in the stream,

To find the fair lady in my dream. "

I follow the footsteps of Miss Du along the path,but howis it that I lose sight of her now?

{Looks back)

Hi,Miss Du!

(Du Liniang riser in astonishment and greets Liu Mengmei)

I've been looking for you here and there. Here I find you at last.

(Du Liniang looks aside without a word)

I just snapped a willow twig in the garden. Miss Du, as you are well versed in classics, why don't you write a poem to honour the twig?

(*In happy astonishment, Du Liniang is about to speak but holds back her tongue*)

Du Liniang:

(*Aside*)

I've never seen this young man before. Why does he come here?

Liu Mengmei:

(*Smiling*)

I'm up to the neck in love with you, Miss Du!

(*To the tune of* **Shantaohong**)

For you, a maiden fair,

With beauty that will soon fade,

I've been searching here and there

But alone in chamber you have stayed.

Come with me and let's have a chat there, Miss Du.

(*Du Liniang smiles but does not move. Liu Mengmei pulls her by the sleeve*)

Du Liniang:

(*In a subdued voice*)

Where to?

Liu Mengmei:

Beyond the peony grove,

Beside the mount we'll rove.

Du Liniang:

(*In a subdued voice*)

What to do, sir?

Liu Mengmei:

(*Also in a subdued voice*)

I shall unbutton your gown

And strip it down.

You'll bite your sleeve-top with your teeth,

Then hug with me and lie beneath.

(*Du Liniang is shy,but Liu Mengmei comes forward to embrace her.
She feigns to push him away*)

Liu Mengmei and Du Liniang:

Is it absurd

We seem to meet somewhere before

But stand here face to face without a word?

(*Exit Liu Mengmei ,holding Du Liniang in his arms*)(*Enter Flower
God with bunded hair'dressed in red and strewn with flowers*)

Flower God:

"The flower god looks after flowers here

And keeps the springtime busy year by year.

When petals fall from flowers in a rain,

The flower gazer starts to dream in vain. "

I am the flower god in charge of the prefect's back garden in Nan'an.
As the prefect's daughter Du Liniang and the scholar Liu Mengmei are
predestined to get married,Miss Du was so affected by her spring tour that
she has enticed Liu Mengmei into her dream. I am a flower god to take
care of all the beauties in this area,and so I've come here to protect her in
order that she will enjoy herself to the full.

〔*To the tune of* **Baolaocui**〕

In the surge of earth and sky,

He swirls like a busy bee

And glare the flowery maiden's eye.

That is a meeting in the dream,

A wedding in the mind,

An outcome of the fate

That brings defilement of the foulest kind.

I'll pick a flower petal to wake them up.

(*Scatters some petals to the entrance of the stage*)

How can they tear themselves away from dream?

They'll wake up when the petals gleam.

The scholar is still indulged in his dream, but when he wakes up, he'll see Miss Du to her chamber. I've got to go now. (*Exit the flower god*)

(*Enter Liu Mengmei and Du Liniang hand in hand*)

Liu Mengmei:

(*To the tune of* **Shantaohong**)

With heaven and earth as our bridal room,

We sleep on the grass and bloom.

Are you all right, my dear?

(*Du Liniang lowers her head*)

Look at her pretty hair,

Loosened here and there.

Please never forget the day when we

Lie together side by side,

Make love for hours and hours,

And hug as man and bride,

With your face red as flowers,

Du Liniang:

Are you leaving now, my love?

Liu Mengmei and Du Liniang:

Is it absurd

We seem to meet somewhere before

But stand here face to face without a word?

Liu Mengmei:

You must be tired, my dear. Sleep a while, sleep awhile.

(*Sees Du Liniang to her sleeping position, and pats her on the back*)

I'm going, my dear.

{*Looks back*}

Please sleep awhile, my dear, and I'll come and see you again. "She comes like gentle rain in spring

And wets me like clouds on the wing, (*Exit Liu Mengmei*)

Du Liniang:

(*Wakes up with a start and murmurs*)

Are you leaving, my love?

(*Dozes off again*)

(*Enter Zhen*)

Zhen:

"My husband holds high office here;

My daughter stays without much cheer.

Her worry comes from skirts she wears,

With blooms and birds adorned in pairs. "

How can you doze off like this, my child?

Du Liniang:

(*Wakes and calls the scholar*)

Oh! Oh!

Zhen:

What's wrong with you, my child?

Du Liniang:

{*Stands up with a start*}

Oh,it's you,mother I...

Zhen：

Why don't you,my child,enjoy yourself by doing someneedlework or reading some books?

Why are you dozing off like this?

Du Liniang：

Just now I took a walk in the back garden,but I was annoyed by the noise of the birds and so I came back to my chamber. As I could not find a way to while away the time,I dozed off for a moment. Please forgive me for having not greeted you at the door.

Zhen：

As the back garden is a desolate place,my child,don't go there again.

Du Liniang．

I'll follow your advice,mother.

Zhen；

Go and study in the classroom,my child.

Du Liniang：

As the tutor is on leave,I have a few days off.

Zhen：

(*Sighs*)

A girl has her own emotions when she has come of age. I'd better leave her alone. As the saying goes,

"Busy for the children all her life,

A mother always has her strife. "

(*Exit Zhen*)

➤ 素材 3. **An extract from *The Peony Pavilion* by Cycil Birch**

LI-NIANG：Without visiting this garden,how could I ever have realized this splendour of spring!

See how deepest purple, brightest scarlet

open their beauty only to the dry well's crumbling parapet.

"Bright the morn, lovely the scene?" listless and lost the heart

where is the garden "gay with joyous cries"?

My mother and father have never spoken of any such exquisite spot as this.

LI-NIANG, SPRING FRAGRANCE:

Flying clouds of dawn, rolling storm at dusk

pavilion in emerald shade against the sun-set glow

fine threads of rain, petals borne on breeze gilded pleasure-boat in waves of mist:

sights little treasured by the cloistered maid

who sees them only on a painted screen.

SPRING FRAGRANCE: All the flowers have come into bloom now, but it's still too early for the peony.

LI-NIANG:

The green hillside

bleeds with the cuckoo's tears of red azalea

shreds of mist lazy as wine-fumes thread the sweet briar.

However fine the peony

how can she rank as queen

coming to bloom when spring has said farewell!

SPRING FRAGRANCE: See them pairing, orioles and swallows!

SPRING FRAGRANCE, LI-NIANG:

Idle gaze resting

there where the voice of swallow shears the air

and liquid flows the trill of oriole.

Li-NIANG: We must go now.

SPRING FRAGRANCE: Really one would never weary of enjoying this garden.

LI-NIANG: How true. [They begin to walk back.]

Unwearying joy — how should we break its spell

even by visits each in turn

to each of the Twelve Towers of Fairy-land?

But better now, as first elation passes to find back in our chamber

some pastime for idle hours.

[They reach the house- SPRING FRAGRANCE

Open the west chamber door

in the east room make the bed

fill the vase with azalea

light aloes in the incense-burner.

Take your rest now, young mistress, while I go to report to Madam.
[She exits.]

LI-NIANG, sighing:

Back from spring stroll

to silent room

what to do but try on

the spring's new adornments?

Ah spring, now that you and I have formed so strong an attachment, what shall I find to fill my days when you are past? Oh this weather, how sleepy it makes one feel. Where has Spring Fragrance got to? [She looks about her, then lowers her head again, pondering:] Ah heaven, now I begin to realize how disturbing the spring's splendour can truly be. They were all telling the truth, those poems and ballads I read which spoke of girls of ancient times 'in springtime moved to passion, in autumn to regret. "Here am I at the"double eight," my sixteenth year, yet no fine scholar to break the cassia bough has come my way. My young passions stir to the young spring season, but where shall I find an"entrant of the moon's toad-palace"? Long ago the Lady Han found a way to a meeting with Yu Yu, and the scholar Chang met with Miss Ts'ui by chance. Their loves are told in the Poem on the Red Leaf and the Western Chamber, how these" fair maids and gifted youths "after clandestine meeting made marital unions"as between Ch'in and Tsin"— [She gives a long sigh:] Though born and bred of a noted line of holders of office, I have reached the age to "pin up my hair" without plan made for my betrothal to a suitable partner. The green spring-time of my own life passes unfulfilled, and swift the time speeds by as dawn and dusk interchange. [She weeps:] O, pity one whose beauty is a bright flower, when life endures no longer than leaf on tree!

From turbulent heart these springtime

thoughts of love

will not be banished

— O from what spring, what hidden source

comes this sudden discontent?

I was a pretty child, and so

of equal eminence must the family be

truly immortals, no less

to receive me in marriage.

But for what grand alliance

is this springtime of my youth

so cast away?

Who may perceive

these passions that lie dormant in my heart?

My only course this coy delaying

but in secret dreams

by whose side do I lie?

——hidden longings roll with the spring swelling stream,

Lingering

where to reveal my true desires!

Suffering

this wasting

where but to Heaven shall my lament be 'made!

I feel rather tired, I shall rest against this low table and drowse for a while. 〔She falls asleep and begins to dream of LIU MENG -MEI, who enters bearing a branch of willow in his hand.

LIU MENG -MEI: As song of oriole purls in warmth of sun so smiling lips open to greet romance. Tracing my path by petals borne on stream I find the Peach Blossom Source of my desire.

I came along this way with Miss Tu — how is it that she is not with me now? 〔He looks behind him and sees her: 〕 Ah, Miss Tu! 〔She rises, startled from sleep, and greets him. He continues: So this is where you were — I was looking for you everywhere. 〔She glances shyly at him but does not speak. 〕 I just chanced to break off this branch from a weeping willow in the garden. You are so deeply versed in works of literature, I should like you to compose a poem to honour it. 〔She starts in surprised delight, and opens her lips to speak but checks herself. Aside, she says: 〕 I have never seen this young man in my life — wbat is he doing here?

LIU, smiling at her: 〕 Lady, I am dying of love for you! I am the

partner born of fairest line

for whom you wait as the river of years

rolls past.

Everywhere l have searched for you

in compassion for you, secluded in your chamber.

Lady, come with me just over there where we can talk. [She gives him a shy smile but refuses to move; he tries to draw her by the sleeve, and she asks in a low voice:] Where do you mean?

LIU:

There, just beyond this railing peony-lined

against the mound of weathered T'ai-hu rocks.

[LI-NIANG, in a low voice:] But sir, what do you mean to do?

LIU also in a low voice:]

Open the fastening at your neck

loosen the girdle at your waist

while you

screening your eyes with your sleeve

white teeth clenched on the fabric as if

against pain

bear with me patiently a while

then drift into gentle slumber.

LI-NIANG turns away, blushing. LIU advances to take her in his arms, but she resists him. LIU, LI-NIANG]

Somewhere at some past time you and I

met.

Now we behold each other in solemn awe

but do not say

in this lovely place we should meet and

speak no word.

LIU exits carrying off LI-NIANG by force. Enter FLOWER SPIRIT in red cloak strewn with petals and ornamental headdress on piled-up hair.]

Commissioner of the Flowers' Blooming

come with new season

from Heaven of Blossom-Guard

to fulfil the springtime's labours.

Drenched in red petal rain

the beholder, heartsore

anchors his yearnings

beyond the shining clouds.

In my charge as Flower Spirit is this garden in the rear of the prefectural residence at Na - an. Between Li-niang, daughter of Prefect Tu, and the young graduate Liu Meng-Mei there exists a marriage-affinity which must some day be fulfilled, and now Miss Tu's heart has been so deeply moved by her spring strolling that she has summoned the graduate Liu into her dream. To cherish in compassion the "jade-like incense ones" is the special concern of a Flower Spirit, and that is why I am here to watch over her and to ensure that the "play of clouds and rain" will be a joyous experience for her.

Ah, how the male force surges and leaps

as in the way of wanton bee he stirs

the gale of her desire

while her soul trembles

at the dewy brink of a sweet, shaded vale.

A mating of shadows, this,

consummation within the mind

no fruitful

Effect

but-an apparition within the Cause.

Ha, but now my flower-palace is sullied by lust.

I must use a falling petal to wake her. (Scatters petals in the entrance to the stage:]

> Loth she may be to loose herself
>
> from the sweet spellbound dream of
>
> spring's delight
>
> but petals flutter down
>
> like crimson snow.

So graduate Liu, the dream is but half complete. When it is over, be sure to see Miss Tu safely back to her chamber. I leave you now. (Exits)

Enter LIU MENG-EI, leading LI-NIANG by the hand:] For this brief moment

> nature was our comforter
>
> leaves for pillow, our bed a bed of flowers.

Are you all right, Miss Tu? [She lowers her head.

> Disarrayed the clouds of her hair
>
> combs set with ruby and emerald
>
> falling aslant.
>
> O lady, never forget
>
> how close I clasped you
>
> and with what tenderness
>
> longing only to make
>
> of our two bodies one single flesh
>
> but bringing forth
>
> a glistening of rouge raindrops in the sun,

LI-NIANG: Sir, you must go now.

LI-NIANG, LIU:

Somewhere at some past time you and I

met.

Now we behold each other in solemn awe

but do not say

in this lovely place we should meet and

speak no word.

LIU: Lady, you must be tired now. Please take a rest. [He sees her back to the table against which she had been drowsing, and gently taps her sleeve:] Lady, I am going now — Looking back at her:] Lady, have a good rest now, I shall come to see you again.

Rain threatened the spring garden as she

approached

and when she slept the "clouds and rain"

broke over Wu-shan, hill of fairy love.

[He exits. LI-NIANG wakes with a start, and calls in a low voice:] Young sir, young sir, oh you have left me.

[She falls asteep again. Enter MADAM CHEN:]

Husband on Prefect's dais

daughter in cloistered chamber

— yet when she broiders patterns on a dress above the flowers the birds fly all in pairs.

Child, child, what are you doing asleep in a place like this?

[LI-NIANG wakes and calls again after LIU MENG-MEI: OH, OH.

MADAM CHEN:] Why child, what is the matter?

Startled, LI-NIANG rises to her feet:] Mother, it's you!

MADAM CHEN: Child, why aren't you passing your time pleasantly with needlework or a little reading? Why were you lying here sleeping in the middle of the day?

LI-NIANG: Just now I took an idle stroll in the garden, but all at once the raucousness of the birds began to distress me and so I came back to my room. Lacking any means to while away the time I must have fallen asleep for a moment. Please excuse my failure to receive you in proper fashion.

MADAM CHEN：The rear garden is too lonely and deserted, child. You must not go strolling there again.

LI-NIANG：I shall take care to do as you bid, mother.

MADAM CHEN：Off to the schoolroom with you now for your lesson.

LI-NIANG：We are having a break just now, the tutor is not here.

MADAM CHEN, signing：There must always be troubles when a girl approaches womanhood, and she must be left to her own way. Truly, moiling and toiling in the children's wake many the pains a mother needs must take.

➤ 注释

bower　n. 凉亭,树荫

seclude　v. 使隔离,使隔绝

azalea　n. 杜鹃花

oriole　n. 黄鹂

plaintive　adj. 哀伤的

rove　v. 流浪

entice　v. 诱使,怂恿

defilement　n. 污秽

toad palace　蟾宫

coy　adj. 腼腆的,忸怩的

heartsore　adj. 悲痛的,沮丧的

moiling and toiling　辛苦劳累

➢ **练习**

1. Read the above passages, pay special attention to those words with cultural connotation, and then complete the form.

Chinese Version	Wang's Translation	Birth's Translation
奈何天		
妾身		
春情		
残生		
书史		
香阁		

2. Please refer to the above passages and find some examples to illustrate the policy of domestication and alienation in the translation of texts rich in cultural information.

四、拓展阅读：汤显祖和莎士比亚的读者及其接受

➢ **背景知识**

同为十六十七世纪的戏剧大师，且同年逝世，汤显祖和莎士比亚被国内外很多学者作为比较研究的对象。2016 年英国布鲁斯伯里出版公司的阿登莎士比亚出版社出版了一本名为《1616：莎士比亚和汤显祖的中国》的论文集，汇集了中西学者相关研究的优秀成果，其编排方式也用心良苦，将研究两位戏剧大师的焦点相似的论文结对并列，极富价值。本部分截取了其中研究汤显祖和莎士比亚在同时代的接受情况的两篇论文中研究读者接受的部分，以资读者比较。

➢ **素材 1. Revising *Peony Pavilion* , Audience's Reception in Presenting Tang Xianzu's Text by Shih-pe Wang**

Theoretically, Tang's musical flaws might have compromised the singing; in practice, however, they do not appear to have posed any major problems for the performers. When his contemporary literati attempted to make *Peony Pavilion* more performable on stage, the actors just found a creative way of performing it as close to Tang's original as possible, even though a literatus musician like Shen Zijin still struggled to preserve the increasingly weak voice of his community in the more 'elite' form of a book of notations. How then shall we judge the goodwill of the literati who criticized in vain?

In order to understand the discrepancy between literati's and actors' standpoints, as well as their causes and consequences, we might seek the opinions of certain critics, playwrights and composers. Around 1616, some literati critics read and watched Tang's play with great enthusiasm and apparently without too much bias; their notes recorded the readers' and audience's preferences, which implicitly expressed their supportive attitude towards Peony Pavilion and its reception.

One critic's record is taken from the playwright Zhang Dafu about the true story of a contemporary female reader Yu Niang 俞娘. Yu loved *Peony Pavilion* and wrote a dense commentary on the script, but soon after completing it, with a destiny similar to that of the protagonist Du Liniang, she died at the age of seventeen, and her commentary was lost forever. Yu Niang's commentary spoke of female readers' passion for *Peony Pavilion*, attracted by Tang's fascinating words.

Another anecdote comes from an early Qing man of letters, Shen Mingsun 沈名蓀, who describes a late Ming legendary female actor Shang Xiaoling 商小玲. Shang was famous for her beauty and excellent performances, especially her playing of Du Liniang. She would become so involved with the emotional intensity of the role that she eventually died heartbroken on stage while playing the zhezixi of 'Pursuing the Dream'. In this case, Shang embodied the female actor's infatuation with Tang's words, and probably, through her passionate performance, the audience would be infected with it as well.

As Anjna Chouhan says, in her companion piece in this chapter, 'plays themselves offer important insight into audience management from the stage-end'. Another valuable source in documenting the audience's reaction comes from late Ming playwright Wu Bing's 吴炳 (1595—1648) play Jealousy Curing Stew (Liaodu geng 疗妒羹), which tells the popular legend of a talented beauty Xiaoqing 小青. Xiaoqing is the concubine of a rich man, who was treated miserably by his jealous wife and then died young. One scene of the full-length play, also a famous zhezixi performed on stage, 'tiqu' 题曲 (Commentary on the Play), could be viewed as a eulogy to Peony Pavilion. During a sleepless night, Xiaoqing reads Peony Pavilion. Closely identifying with the sorrow it depicts, she makes detailed comments on the play text in this scene. 'tiqu' describes a female reader's fascination with Tang's words, while its play text by Wu Bing could be regarded as a male reader's comment on and mimesis of Peony Pavilion, since he simply followed Tang's original version in playwriting rather than any other literati's revisions. In this way, 'tiqu' could be interpreted as a metaphoric 'drama review' or a miniature 'abridged adaptation' of Peony Pavilion.

Another critic, Pan Zhiheng, a friend of Tang and an avid theatregoer, discussed lots of actors and their performances in his anecdotes. He made comments on a performance of Peony Pavilion by a family troupe:

Wu Yueshi, a fellow member of my club, owns a family troupe of young actors. Once Wu ordered his actors to perform the play [Peony Pavilion]. The actor's figure, swaying and flickering, stirred my vision in most tiny ambiguous motions, my sorrows drifted beyond the tones.

His singing and performing was so perfect, without one word lost, without any detail overlooked.

Clearly, as both a member of the audience and a critic, Pan and the actors on stage all enjoyed each word and each detail of Tang's text. Pan tried to convey the most astute observation; for him, Peony Pavilion could inspire the souls of the actors and their audience in part through the interplay between the sublime lyrics and the performance. Pan's essay was titled '*Qingchi*' (the man who was obsessed with passion) and the source of "*qing*" (passion) in this case comes from the performance of Tang's powerful words.

No wonder the literati's revisions were doomed to failure. Another critic, Mao Yuanyi 茅元仪 (1594—1640), expressed the following opinion on Zang Maoxun's revision: 'Reading Zang's revision, I was annoyed with its mediocre words put in the original extraordinary plots, its mediocre tunes put in the original extraordinary words, and its mediocre rhymes put in the original extraordinary tunes. The playwright's [Tang Xianzu's] delicate design was totally spoiled; to the extent that it cannot even compare to most ordinary works. ' Obviously, any person who dared to revise Tang's words would be challenged on the level of literariness, as well as on the level of elegance, passion and rhetoric skill. It is amazing that actors, critics and audiences all stand on the side of literary value, rather than Zang's preference for stage value.

The tension between words and music continued and was not resolved until decades after Tang's death. A musical connoisseur, Niu Shaoya 钮少雅 (1564-after 1651), composed a work titled *Corrected Musical Tunes of Peony Pavilion* (*Gezheng Huanhun ji cidiao*《格正还魂记词调》, posthumously prefaced in 1694). Here only arias (song texts) are printed and dialogues and stage directions are not included. 23 Niu focused on amending the errors by amending the tunes but not the words. After Niu, the most successful and influential composer was Ye Tang 叶堂(1724? —97?), a legendary musician in the history of Chinese drama who published all of the entire 'adjusted' music notations of Tang's Four Dreams in 1792 and solved the controversies among Tang's opponents through his professional skill of composing. His strategy was to emend the musical errors by following Tang's original words. Since Ye Tang did his work, there is no longer any problem in singing *Peony Pavilion*. His book of music notation is significant in affirming the priority of Tang's text over the other literati's endeavours at revision. As Ye Tang explains in his rules of notation, 'because of the excellence of Tang's text, I did not dare to change it casually, so I change the tunes in various ways to fit in his words'.

Ye Tang also embodies the opinions of singers and actors through the ultimate method of expression. In contrast to some of the literati's revisions, those who actually performed Tang Xianzu's work revealed more of its literary value. Selected pieces in miscellanies maintained Tang's original taste for the delicacy of each scene or aria, while Ye Tang's full-length notations re-established a way in which Tang Xianzu's words could be fulfilled musically. These different kinds of audience reception suggest that it was almost impossible to revise or imitate a work of genius satisfactorily. Any rules or laws that are applied to it seem inferior to the work itself. Hence, around 1616, we find the best playwright in the history of Chinese drama, and also the most talented actors, readers and critics as audience in the history of theatre. The interplay which took place between the playwright and his audience, both his opponents and his supporters, gives us a glimpse of the unlimited exploration on Tang Xianzu and the theatrical landscape of his times.

> ➤ 素材 2. "No Epilogue, I Prey You——Audience Reception in Shakespeare-
>   an Theatre" by Anjna Choulan

Theatre historians have observed that while playwrights wrote for different companies of players throughout their careers, from Lyly and Marlowe to Shakespeare and Fletcher, they did become associated with specific theatres and, by extension, the audiences who frequented those layhouses. This forms the most striking parallel between Chinese and English audience-playwright relationships in the period, because traditional Chinese plays were written by and performed for the learned. Scholars were producing work for other scholars: stories of students falling in love with beautiful courtesans, and musical composition, were calculated to be recognizable by repeat audiences in spaces that were not, by definition, theatres. Plays in England were suited to the playhouse and plays in China were for one unique audience.

Audiences in England came in different shapes and sizes. And we do know that audiences had reputations at specific playhouses. Marston's epilogue to Jack Drum's Entertainment in 1600 mentions the types of people frequenting the Paul's company, calling them 'a good gentle audience'...

This explains why audience reputations gave playwrights flexibility to blame their less successful works on reception. Webster famously complained about his Red Bull audience in the epistle to *The White Devil*, published in 1612: 'most of the people that come to that playhouse, resemble those ignorant asses who visiting stationers' shops, their use is not to inquire for good books, but new books ...'. For Webster, the only thing wrong with the performance was the lack of 'a full and understanding auditory'. In this case he transitioned to print, thereby gaining a new kind of audience: a readership rather than auditors. Here, the play was in no way altered or edited to please the theatre audience. Fortunately for Webster, later Jacobean audiences of the finer indoor playhouses acquired a taste for *The White Devil*, thereby securing its place in the canon of great early modern tragedy.

The most tangible example of adaptation or revision comes from the few examples of post-performance complaints and lawsuits, which indicate that factual errors and offensive references could be edited out of plays. This is where the editing and rewriting, or in the case of Shakespeare, renaming came into play. Most famously, in the mid-1590s, Shakespeare was forced to rename his historical character, Sir John Oldcastle, creating the ever-popular Sir John Falstaff in his place. The less documented kind of revision comes from the nature of playing companies as repertory players. Gurr notes that with growing playing companies, playwrights were increasingly prolific, meaning that audiences came to expect new offerings on a weekly, sometimes daily basis. In turn, new plays were mingled with older plays to create a repertory unique to each company. Oslyn Knutson's study of repertory systems in the early 1600s indicates that, in Shakespeare's case, the acquisition of Blackfriars informed both the writing and choice of plays undertaken by the King's Men. But *the Revels Account* for court performances in spring 1604 includes *Measure for Measure*, *Othello*, *The Comedy of Errors*, *Love's Labour's Lost*, *The Merchant of Venice*, *The Merry Wives of Windsor* and *Henry V*. Most of these were old plays, revived and possibly adapted for court. Any number of revisions could have been made to these plays, in some cases ten years after their first performances. But, as Gary Taylor notes, the cost of hiring the playwright to produce additional scenes or make alterations, or even a stand-in playwright to adapt an older work, coupled with the expense of replacing worn-out costumes and props, would suggest that only the popular plays were worth reviving. In short, not new, specially ommissioned works, but the familiar plays were what audiences wanted.

So while this does not alter current thinking about audience reception in the early 1600s, it does place emphasis on the agency that audiences-in whatever shape and size-had in the writing and performing of a play, in a way that highlights the more scholarly concerns of Chinese theatre at the time. Whereas in China adaptation and revision were matters for learned argument, they were, in England, an ongoing dialogue between playwright and audience. Stern concludes her chapter on prologues and epilogues by arguing that "in performance(at least after c. 1600)stage-orations broad-casted a play's virginity and its author's fear, and were therefore a site of tension between author and play". Fear and tension are terms that concep-tualize one aspect of a playwright's relationship with his audience. But I would argue that with this fear came a degree of admiration for an audience's ability to reserve such objective judgement for any perform-ance. Playwrights like Shakespeare needed audiences and were dependent on them, but simultaneously were cautious *and even manipulative*. So when, in *A Midsummer Night's Dream*, Theseus claims that he wants nei-ther an excuse nor an epilogue for the short piece "Pyramus and Thisbe", and when Beaumont's grocer and his wife interpolate Rafe into their per-formance, it is the audience and not the players dictating the performance: its content, length and even the peripheral entertainments. The irony is that these playwrights have written those audiences and their responses, regaining their authorial and authoritative position, and manipulating true audience members into believing that every play is designed for and direct-ed towards them. For all the lamentations and trepidations of the play-wrights, it seems that playgoers in London by 1616, whether they were ig-norant asses or learned ears, were led to believe that they were the real test of a play's quality and endurance. Though this was most likely the case, it is amusing that in spite of Theseus's call to skip the epilogue to the play-within-the-play, Shakespeare proceeded to bolt one onto the end of his, along with something approaching an apology: "Gentles, do not reprehend. / If you pardon, we will mend".

➤ 注释

literatus   n. 学者;文学界(literati 的单数形式)

discrepancy   n. 矛盾,不符

infatuation   n. 迷恋,醉心

astute   adj. 机敏的,狡猾的

repertory   n. 全部剧目

omission   n. 冗长

interpolate   v. 篡改

➤ 练习

1. Read the above passages, give a brief account of the acceptance of Shakespeare and Tang Xianzu in their own times.

2. Do some research on the the two playwrights' posthumous fame.

五、现代回声

➤ 背景知识

1999 年 9 月,在林肯艺术中心,应邀参加"林肯中心艺术节"的中央芭蕾舞团携原创芭蕾舞剧《牡丹亭》在纽约林肯表演艺术中心大卫·寇克剧院进行首演,演出赢得现场观众热烈掌声,取得圆满成功。"林肯中心艺术节"艺术总监奈吉尔·雷登(Nigel Redden)先生说,邀请中央芭蕾舞团的代表芭蕾舞剧《牡丹亭》来参加林肯中心艺术节是非常正确的选择。他相信,文化的交流能增进彼此了解、成为中美人民相互友好交流的桥梁。英国《卫报》称赞该剧"原汁原味,引人入胜"。

　　自 2008 年北京天桥剧场首演以来，芭蕾舞剧《牡丹亭》曾受邀献演爱丁堡国际艺术节和香港艺术节。此次受邀参与的林肯艺术中心艺术节为世界顶尖的艺术盛会，也是《牡丹亭》首次被搬上西方歌剧舞台。这一芭蕾舞剧，将西方古典芭蕾和中国古典舞的美感艺术地结合在一起，获得了艺术界的好评。这对中国文化艺术界有着非同寻常的意义，也为中国传统文化走向世界提供了很有价值的启示。

➢ Great Leaps Forward—*The Peony Pavilion*

Jul. 10th, 2015

It is easy to see why the National Ballet of China(NBC)chose"The Peony Pavilion", a 16th-century Chinese opera, for adaptation into a ballet. The romance is familiar to a home audience that is not much acquainted with the dance form, while abroad having recognisable steps can help convey an exotic tale. Since its premiere in Beijing in 2008, the ballet has become a marquee production for the company. It has also found favour with critics when performed at the Edinburgh Festival and on stage in Australia. This week it made its American debut with three shows at the Lincoln Festival in New York City.

The ballet draws from a classical work that normally runs for 20 hours and covers everything from political duplicity to sexual awakening during the Song dynasty, its 12th-century Chinese setting. Re-envisioned for a new genre, though, it has been winnowed down to its the central plot and 120 minutes. Du Liniang, a young girl, dies pining for a scholar she meets in a dream, but is returned to her lover by fate. It has often been dubbed an oriental"Romeo and Juliet"—it was written just a few years after Shakespeare's 1594 play.

The ballet has a striking aesthetic. The curtain lifts to reveal a dark stage, empty except for the figure of the heroine dressed in white, seated in dreamy repose on the platform representing a pared-down pavilion. Behind her moves a sensual doppelgänger: a ballerina in red. A third image of Liniang is performed not by a ballerina, but a singer. She crosses the stage trilling passages from the classical kunqu-style opera, woven into an ambitious score that borrows themes from the likes of Ravel and Debussy.

"The Peony Pavilion" works best when there are fewer dancers on stage, as with the opening moments, and in the scenes that borrow from Chinese dance. In one memorable arrangement, the corps de ballet dance in a single line behind the scholar-hero Liu Mengmei. Each girl stretches out her arms at different angles—an image that is fresh to Western ballet, but nods to the Thousand-Armed Guanyin, a traditional dance about an Eastern goddess. Costumes by Emi Wada, an Oscar-winning Japanese designer, and sets by Michael Simon, are in a restricted palette. Fei Bo's choreography, though beautiful, is at times almost overwhelmed by the sum of the other parts.

Feng Ying, NBC's artistic director, has said that staging new works that establish a modern, uniquely Chinese style of ballet is a goal for the company. At the Lincoln Festival, NBC is also giving two performances of "The Red Detachment of Women", a ballet the company has danced for half a century, popularised early on by support from Jiang Qing, an actress and Mao Zedong's fourth wife. This work depicts a different dream—the communist one—but also the desire to reshape Chinese art through new forms. Back then, though, particular steps were discouraged for being "counter-revolutionary". Female dancers' hands were to be held open or in fists, not curled as to imply weakness. Partnering steps between men and women were limited for the same reason. The story of female liberation in "Detachment" is perhaps more progressive than the retrograde lovesickness in "Pavilion", but belied a rather illiberal art. Ms Feng is quite right that China needs a new balletic vision. It seems to be arriving.

➢ **注释**

marquee   n. 大天幕,华盖

duplicity   n. 口是心非,表里不一

doppelgänger   n. 幽灵,分身

palette   n. 调色板,颜料

choreography   n. 编舞

retrograde   adj. & v. 倒退

belie   v. 掩饰,证明……错误

➢ **练习**

1. According to the author, why is the modern Ballet adaptation of *The Peony Pavillion* successful both home and abroad?

2. Have you watched some modern adaptations of other ancient Chinese novels or dramas? choose one of them and write a review.

第六章 绘 画

一、词源梳理

中国古代画论典籍上并没有"美术"这个专用术语。发达的中国古代美术传统分散于一系列近似的词汇中,比如"刻削"、"丹青"、"图画"、"绘缋"及"刻镂"等等,大量的绘画、书法、雕刻及民间工艺等艺术创作形式共同汇成传统的"美术"范畴。

"绘画"也是现代文中的词汇,古代多分开使用。"绘"和"画"在《说文解字》中分别解释为"会合五彩的刺绣"和"用笔划定边界线。"先说"绘"字。其字形采用"糸"作边旁,采用"會"作声旁。《虞书》有记载:"山龙华虫作绘。"也就是说,绣出山、龙和各种色彩鲜艳的昆虫。而《论语》也说:"绘事后素"。即绘画是为了处理素色的背景。除此之外,还有其他一些记载,都证明了中国古代的绘绣关系。在看"画"字。畫,是古文写法的"畫"字,字形省略了横笔。劃,也是古文写法的"畫"字。"画"的繁体字字形像田畴四边的界线。"聿",表示用以画界的笔。所有与画相关的字,都采用"画"作边旁。在现代文中,"绘画"作为名词使用,表示造形艺术的一种,用色彩和线条在纸、布、墙壁或其他平面上绘写事物形象。

中西方截然不同的绘画传统,反映在语言文字上,就是英语中对应的词汇有 painting 和 drawing 两个。Painting,"油画",大约从公元 1200 年开始使用,表示"that which is painted, a picture depicted with paint," 从 14 世纪下半叶开始,有了艺术方面的含义,"art of depicting by means of paint"。

Drawing，由动词 draw 派生而来，作为"素描艺术"意义使用的时间比 painting 晚两百多年，始于 15 世纪末，作为"素描画"、"素描作品""picture or representation produced by drawing"使用则是 1660 年之后的事情了。从词源上可以看出，painting 才是西方美术史的正统，至今仍指软笔画，而 drawing 则指硬笔画，早期西方绘画中的硬笔专门用来快速绘制草图，类同于 sketch。

二、引导阅读
➢ 背景知识

中西方绘画艺术独立发展、各具特色，近代西学东渐以来，书画艺术可以算是为数不多的可以与西方抗衡的传统文化形式了。王国维曾说："自欧学东渐，吾国旧有之学遂以不振……而惟美术之学，则环球所推为独绝。言美术者必言东方，盖神州立国最古，其民族又具优秀之性"。

大都会博物馆是美国博物馆界收藏中国书画的后起之秀。它的亚洲部最初只有一件展品，后来却成为世界上最全面展示亚洲艺术的博物馆之一，其飞跃性的进展，很大程度上与 1971 年中国艺术史领军人方闻接任亚洲部艺术主任一职密不可分，尤其是他的整体收藏方案，一举让大都会成为欧美顶尖中国古代书画收藏博物馆。

何慕文（Maxwell K. Hearn）是方闻的学生，彼时刚刚耶鲁艺术史本科毕业，机缘巧合成为了方闻的助理，亲身经历了大都会博物馆亚洲部的华丽转变的 30 年，除了后来普林斯顿读博四年，他再也没离开过这里。2011 年何慕文成为亚洲艺术部主任，2015 年，为庆祝其亚洲艺术部建立 100 周年，大都会在他的主持之下举办了多场展览活动，展品囊括众多馆藏精华，如韩幹的《照夜白》和赵孟頫的《双松平远》。针对这一系列展览，何慕文编写了《如何读中国画——大都会艺术博物馆藏中国书画精品导览》一书，本文节选自该书引言。

How to Read a Chinese Painting

(Hearn, Maxwell K. , *How to Read A Chinese Painting*. Yale University Press, 2008.)

The Chinese way of appreciating a painting is often expressed by the words *du hua*, "to read a painting. "How does one do that?

The first work in this book, *Night Shining White* is an image of a horse. Originally little more than a foot square, it is now mounted as a handscroll that is twenty feet long as a result of thenumerous inscriptions and seals (marks of ownership) that have been added over the centuries, some directly on the painted surface, so that the horse is all but overwhelmed by this enthusiastic display of appreciation. Miraculously, the animal's energy shines through. It does so because the artist has managed to distill his observations of both living horses and earlier depictions to create an image that embodies the vitality and form of an iconic "dragon steed. "He has achieved this only with the most economical of means: brush and ink on paper.

This is the aim of the traditional Chinese painter: to capture not only the outer appearance of a subject but it's in its essence as well—its energy, life force, spirit. To accomplish his goal, the Chinese painter more often than not rejected the use of color. Like the photographer who prefers to work in black and white, the Chinese artist regarded color as a distraction. He also rejected the changeable qualities of light and shadow as a means of modeling, along with opaque colors to conceal mistakes. Indeed he relied on line—the intelligible mark of the ink brush.

The discipline that this kind of mastery requires derives from the practice of calligraphy. Traditionally, every literate person in China learned as a child to write by copying the standard forms of Chinese ideographs.

The student was gradually exposed to different stylistic interpretations of these characters. Overtime the practitioner evolved his own personal style, one that was a distillation and reinterpretation of early models.

The practice of calligraphy became high arts with the innovations of Wang Xizhi in the fourth century. By the eleventh century, a good hand was one criterion—together with a command of history and literary style—that determined who was recruited into government through civil service examination. Those who succeeded came to regard themselves as a new kind of elite, a meritocracy of "scholar-officials" responsible for maintaining moral and aesthetic standards established by the political and cultural paragons of the past. It was their command of history and its precedents that enabled them to influence current events. It was their interpretations of the past that established the structures by which an emperor might be constrained. And it was their poetry, diaries, commentaries that constituted the accounts by which a ruler would one day be judged.

These were the men who covered *Night Shining White* with inscriptions and seals. They recognized that the horse was meant as an emblem of China's military strength and, by extension, as a symbol of China itself. And they understood the poignancy of the image. *Night Shining White* was the favorite steed of an emperor who led his dynasty to the height of its glory but who, tethered by his unreasonable love with a concubine, neglected his charge and eventually lost his throne.

The emperor's failure to put his horse to good use may be understood as a metaphor for a ruler's failure to properly value his officials. This is undoubtedly how the retired scholar-official Zhao Mengfu intended his image of a horse, painted six hundred years later, to be interpreted. Expertise in judging fine horses had long been a metaphor for the ability to recognize men of talent.

Scholar officials were at times forced out of office, banished as a result of factionalism among those in power. In such cases, the alienated individual might turn to art to express his beliefs. But even when concealed in symbolic language, beliefs could incite reprisals: the eleventh-century official Su Shi, for example, was nearly put to death for writing poems that were deemed seditious. As a result, these men honed their skills in the art of indirection. Because of their highly personal nature, such works were almost always dedicated to a close friend and would have been viewed only by a select circle of like-minded individuals. But since these men acted both as policymakers and as the moral conscience of society, their art was highly influential.

Scholar-official painters most often worked in ink on paper and chose subjects—bamboo, old trees, rocks—that could be drawn using the same kind of disciplined brush skills required for calligraphy. This immediately distinguished their art from the colorful, illusionistic style of painting preferred by court artists and professionals. Proud of their status as amateurs, they created a new, distinctly personal form of paintings in which expressive calligraphic brush lines were the chief means employed to animate their subjects. Another distinguishing feature of what came to be known as scholar-amateur painting is its learned references to the past. The choice of a particular antique style immediately linked a work to the personality and ideals of an earlier painter or calligrapher. Style became a language by which to convey one's beliefs.

Since scholar-artists employed symbolism, style, and calligraphic brushwork to express their beliefs and feelings, they left the craft of formal portraiture to professional artisans. Such craftsmen might be skilled in capturing an individual's likeness, but they could never hope to convey the deeper aspects of a man's character.

Integrating calligraphy, poetry, and painting, scholar-artists for the first time combined the"three perfections"in a single work. In such paintings, poetic and pictorial imagery and energized calligraphic lines work in tandem to express the mind and emotions of the artist. Once poetic inscriptions had become an integral part of a composition, the recipient of the painting or a later appreciator would often add an inscription as his own"response. "Thus, a painting was not finalized when an artist set down his brush, but it would continue to evolve as later owners and admirers appended their own inscriptions or seals. Most such inscriptions take the form of colophons placed on the borders of a painting or on the end-papers of a handscroll or album; others might be added directly onto the painting. In this way, *Night Shining White* was embellished with a record of its transmission that spans more than a thousand years.

Both the court professional and the scholar-amateur made use of symbolism, but often to very different ends. While Zhao Mengfu's pines may reflect the artist's determination to preserve his political integrity, a landscape painting by a court painter might be read as the celebration of a well-ordered empire. A scholar-painting of narcissus reflects the artist's identification with the pure fragrance of the flower, a symbol of loyalty, while a court painter's lush depiction of orchids was probably intended to evoke the sensuous pleasures of the harem. Their key distinction is in the realization of the image: through calligraphically abbreviated black-and-white drawing on paper or through the highly illusionistic use of mineral colors on silk.

To"read"a Chinese painting is to enter into a dialogue with the past; the act of unrolling a scroll or leafing through an album provides a further, physical connection to the work. An intimate experience, it is one that has been shared and repeated over the centuries. And it is through such readings, enjoyed alone or in the company of friends, that meaning is gradually revealed.

> **注释**

scroll　n. (供书写的)长卷纸,卷轴

steed　n. 骏马,坐骑

opaque　adj. 不透明的

literate　adj. 有文化修养的,有读写能力的

ideograph　n. 象形文字

civil service examination　科举考试,公务员考试

meritocracy　n. 经营领导制度

aesthetic　adj. 美的,审美的

paragon　n. 典范,十全十美的人,完美无缺的人

poignancy　n. (不可数)辛酸,悲惨

tether　vt. 将(牲畜)…拴到

concubine　n. 妾,妃子

banish　v. 放逐,驱除,流放

incite　vt. (sb. to sth. /sth.)煽动;鼓动

reprisal　n. 报复;报复行动

seditious　adj. 煽动叛乱的;煽动反政府的;反动性的

hone　vt. 磨练,训练(尤指技艺)

sensuous　adj. 愉悦感官或精神的;让人舒服或给人以美感的

harem　n. (妻妾居住的)闺房,内室;后宫

> **练习**

1. To read a Chinese painting, one should be aware of the distinction between court professional artisans and scholar-amateur painters. Can you sum up their basic differences in painting?

2. What elements contributed to the scholar-amateur style of paintings?

3. How is symbolism used differently by court professionals and scholar officials?

三、阅读与比较

> **背景知识**

中国国画流派和技法各有不同,本部分将介绍两位中国艺术家眼中的国画之美。

第一篇文章选自 2008 年耶鲁大学和外文出版社联合出版发行的《中国绘画三千年(Three Thousand Years of Chinese Painting)》,主编及各位作者均为中美艺术史界的执牛耳者。本文作者杨新,艺术史论专业出身,曾任故宫博物院副院长达 13 年之久,现任故宫博物院研究员、国家文物鉴定委员会委员等职,活跃在在书画鉴定和艺术史学研究和实践的一线,积极致力于与国外学界沟通对话。

第二篇文章选自宗白华先生为数不多的著述之一《美学散步》。宗先生生于传统文化,在德国学习哲学和美学。他的这本代表作初次出版于 1981年,不重哲学分析而重趣谈和体验,不从逻辑定义和概念辨析出发,而是从美的感悟出发,将散步时所想所得用诗意而灵性的语言传递给读者。

> **素材 1. Approaches to Chinese Paintings**

(Barnhart, Richard, Xin, Yang, et. al. *Three Thousand Years of Chinese Painting*. Yale University Press. 1997.)

Chinese artists, philosophers, and critics have constantly discussed the role and qualities of painting throughout its long and complex history. What makes Chinese painting such an exquisite flower in the garden of Chinese civilization is the way the arts of the brush—painting, calligraphy, and poetry—together with the related art of seal engraving, interact, sometimes directly, sometimes indirectly, in producing so many of the master-pieces.

A complex yet important distinction for Chinese scholars as they have examined their painting tradition is between the detailed and technically proficient representation of a scene or object and the representation of its objectiveand subjective likeness. The former approach is associated largely with court painters, whose facility with the brush and whose naturalistic style culminated in many fine works, particularly during the Tang(618—907) and Song (960—1279) dynasties; the latter approach is associated largely with the Literati-artists whose works started to appear in significant numbers by the early Song. The contrast is not a total one. Still, the depiction of partly imagined likenesses, not strictly realistic ones, is at the heart of what most Chinese scholars see as distinctive about the Chinese painting tradition. "One should learn from nature and paint the image in one's mind," as the painter Zhang Zao wrote in the eighth century.

In the early periods in the development of Chinese painting, a prominent artistic goal was the realistic representation of the subject matter. Han Fei(280? —233 b. c.), a thinker of the Warring States period, argued that the easiest subjects to paint were ghosts and devils; the most difficult, dogs, horses, and other real things. Why? Because people are familiar with dogs and horses, but nobody has ever seen a ghost or a devil, so they will not know whether an exact likeness has been achieved. Murals in early tombs and in the Dunhuang caves, painted during the Tang dynasty, attest to their great accomplishments.

In line with this approach, Xie He, an art critic and painter of the Southern Qi(479—502), argued that there are "six principles of painting," one of which is "fidelity to the object in portraying forms." Zhang Yanyuan, an art historian of the Tang dynasty, agreed. "The subject matter," he said, "must be painted to its exact likeness. " But other critics, even early on, believed that paintings need not — should not — be judged solely by a standard of objective realism. Good paintings, they said, achieve the unity of the objective and the subjective, showing both the image as it exists in reality and the image in the painter's mind.

Here we see the emergence of *xieyi*, or "sketching the idea. " This, more than realistic depiction, is what many critics have considered to be truly important in painting. *Deyi* , "getting the idea" of the image in the artist's mind, becomes the chief point to grasp when looking at a painting. The viewer has to see beyond the image to the implied meaning. Only by "comprehending the ideas," or *huiyi* , can one appreciate the best paintings in the Chinese art tradition.

Artists taking this approach may highlight certain areas and leave large areas blank, except for certain details related to the theme. The spaces of various sizes and shapes form a pattern in themselves, drawing attention to the main subject matter while providing the viewer with room to imagine and wander in. Reality is implied, not necessarily rendered with scrupulous accuracy. A moonlit scene outdoors and a lamplit scene indoors may be painted like the same scene in daylight, with only a moon in the sky or a bright lamp to signal nighttime. In *The Night Revels of Han Xizai* , a scroll painting by Gu Hongzhong of the Five Dynasties period(907—960), burning candles show that the scene is set at night.

Another example of this widespread approach to reality relates to the depiction of buildings. Chinese painters tend to present buildings as seen straight on or from slightly above, seldom as seen from below. Li Cheng, another artist of the Five Dynasties period, once tried to paint pavilions, pagodas, and other structures atop hills exactly as they appeared to him from below; that is, he did not paint the tiles on the roofs, just the woodwork and frame below the eaves. His experiment was criticized by Shen Kuo, a famous Song-dynasty scholar, who said that Li did not understand how to "perceive smallness from largeness." In succeeding dynasties no artist ever again took Li's approach.

Neither Shen nor other Chinese critics have argued that such works distort reality, however. The opposite is the case. Realistic copying can never show the innate meaning or true nature of a subject, they would say. Only with imaginative representation can the depths of reality be depicted. By the end of the Tang dynasty in the tenth century, this approach to painting began to find its great forms of expression.

Works executed by court painters into the tenth century before the establishment of the Song dynasty prominently featured human figures, the use of lines to define forms, rich and varied coloring, and realistic representation of the subject matter. This approach fit well with the social and cultural functions that the paintings were designed to fulfill. During the Qin(221—206 B. C.) and Han(206 B. C. —A. D. 220) dynasties, for example, the government used portraits to publicize and praise loyal ministers and martyrs and to denounce traitors. Later Xie He even remarked, "All paintings stand for poetic justice; lessons about the rise and fall of ministers over the course of one thousand years can be drawn from paintings."

Scholars and officials of the Tang dynasty went a step further and attempted to bring painting into line with Confucian ideology. In *Lidai minghua ji* (Record of famous paintings of successive dynasties), Zhang Yanyuan argued that the "art of painting exists to enlighten ethics, improve human relationships, divine the changes of nature, and explore hidden truths. It functions like the Six [Confucian] Classics and works regardless of the changing seasons. The catalogue of the court collection of

paintings entitled *Xuanhe huapu*, compiled at the end of the Northern
Song(960—1127), attempted to define the social function of figure painting, even arguing that landscape painting, bird-and-flower painting, and
animal painting should fulfill a similar ethical function.

In the *Xuanhe huapu*, paintings were divided into ten categories according to subject: religious themes, figures, palace buildings, foreign people, dragons and fish, landscapes, animals, birds and flowers, bamboo, and
vegetables and fruit. These categories carefully reflected the official Confucian value system of the time. Landscape paintings, for example, were
prized for their portrayal of the Five Sacred Mountains and the Four Great
Rivers — places of imperial significance. The merit of birds and flowers
initially lay in their "metaphorical and allegorical meaning," while that of
vegetables and fruit lay in their use "as sacrifices to deities'" In short,
paintings were judged largely in terms of how well their subject matter
served the gods, the Buddha, sages, and emperors.

The compiler of the *Xuanhe huapu* certainly knew that birds and
bamboo were not directly connected to human affairs, but they had to be
made metaphorically relevant if they were to symbolize moral and ethical
values. Thus, pine trees, bamboo, plum blossoms, chrysanthemums,
gulls, egrets, geese, and ducks became symbols of hermits or men of noble
character; peonies and peacocks became symbols of wealth and rank; willow trees, symbols of amorous sentiments; and tall pine trees and ancient
cypresses, symbols of constancy and uprightness. In this way, bird-and-
flower paintings could serve an instructional purpose.

By the end of the Tang and during the Five Dynasties, before the *Xuanhe huapu* was written, landscape painting and bird-and-flower painting
on silk achieved maturity, in the process changing the traditional, simplis-
tic use of sketched lines to define forms. As landscapes came to convey

tranquility or poetic melancholy and refinement, the tendency to use less color or even just water and ink became prevalent. Painters also increasingly used scrolls as a medium.

In art circles in China it is believed that Wu Daozi(active ca. 710—760)marked the peak of court painting. Unfortunately,none of his works have survived,but some copies are said to be based on his original drawings.

A couple of centuries later, in the Northern Song period,came the rise of the literati-artist, whose influence on the development of Chinese painting was formidable. The literati-artists were well trained in poetry and calligraphy. Partly to distinguish themselves from professional painters, they often looked at painting in terms of those arts, adopting many of the aesthetic conceptions set forth in *Ershisi shipin* (The twenty-four aspects of poetry)by Sikong Tu of the Tang dynasty, a milestone in the history of poetry criticism. To fully explain such notions as vigor,thinness, primitive simplicity, elegance,naturalness, and implicitness, Sikong Tu described natural settings appropriate to each. Elegance, for instance, could be expressed by depicting scenes with "gentlemen listening to the falling rain in a thatched cottage while drinking from a jade pot; seated gentlemen flanked by tall bamboo groves; or floating white clouds and a few birds chasing each other in a sky clearing after rain. "

Another theory of poetry that proved highly influential among literati-painters and art critics was set forth by Mei Yaochen, a Song poet who sought to achieve "depth and primitive simplicity" in his works. Once he remarked that poems "must be able to portray hard-to-catch scenes as if they leap up before the eyes, and imply meaning between the lines. A masterpiece is superior even to this. " By "meaning between the lines" he referred to something the author had in mind and the reader could perceive only by intuition, that is, a meaning that could be apprehended but not expressed. The literati-artists saw the applicability of this idea to painting.

Another aspect of the shift from court painting to literati painting was the growing emphasis on painting as an enjoyable activity; intended to please oneself and one's friends. Su Shi, a poet, calligrapher, and painter of the Song dynasty, was one advocate of enjoyment. He once wrote a poem to a friend that read: I asked why you painted a portrait of me; you said you are a portraitist to amuse yourself. " Throughout the Yuan (1271—1368), Ming(1368—1644), and Qing(16^—1911) dynasties, particularly toward the close of each, when government power waned and corruption grew rife, the idea of using paintings to "enlighten ethics and improve human relationships" was seldom mentioned by literati-artists.

The practice of annotating a painting with a poem evidently originated among the literati of the Song period. A number of Song poets composed poems about paintings, and some of these are found written on the mountings of handscrolls. The earliest known pieces extant today are attributed to Emperor Huizong (r. 1101—1125), a celebrated painter in his own right; among these is the earliest existing example of a painting inscribed with a poem composed by the artist himself. Later painters followed suit; the practice became popular during the Yuan dynasty and common during the Ming and Qing dynasties, when paintings were likely to bear poetry or other inscriptions.

That Chinese characters developed from pictographs led to a belief that painting and calligraphy had a common origin. Over time, literati, who were well versed in calligraphy, employed in their paintings brushwork techniques affected by their calligraphic style, and came to see the form and content of the inscription as an integral part of the painting. Drawn to the art of calligraphy, they began to pay close attention in painting to the aesthetic appeal of lines and to the distinctive ways of doing brushwork, instead of just employing lines to compose forms. In the Yuan dynasty, Zhao Mengfu (1254—1322) inscribed a poem on a painting of rocks and bamboo that concluded with the statement that calligraphy and painting are identical. Later artists did not take this view but instead cultivated a distinctive personal calligraphic style that was naturally reflected in their paintings.

The inscription on a painting accentuates and complements the image. In the Song and Yuan periods, paintings were usually inscribed after completion to fill up any remaining space, but in the Ming and Qing periods, placement of the inscription was considered when an artist planned the initial composition. In some works the inscribed poem is essential to creating the perfect visual effect.

Seals, which typically imprint characters engraved in an ancient calligraphic style, likewise enhance a painting. The practice of affixing seals possibly originated with collectors who stamped their seals on collections to designate ownership. According to the *Xuanhe huapu*, paintings executed before the Tang dynasty were not stamped. The Tang emperor Taizong invented the practice by having his seals applied to paintings in the imperial household. During the Northern Song, painters began to stamp their own works, often to guard against forgery. Using seals, however practical, added aesthetic appeal to the paintings, as literati-painters realized. The red stamp could enliven a picture otherwise dull in color, and the choice of seal indicated certain interests and values of the painter, often with subtle cultural, personal, or political implications.

The incorporation of seals into pictures made Chinese painting into a comprehensive art that combines several others. A painting is often the joint product of a painter, a poet, a calligrapher, and a seal maker. In exceptional cases, as with Wu Changshuo and Qi Baishi(1864—1957), the painters are well versed in all these arts themselves. This bringing together of so many art forms ultimately became the most characteristic feature of Chinese painting and the reason why so many works resonate with the culture and civilization of China.

> **素材 2.《中国古代的绘画美学思想》节选**

（宗白华.《美学散步》,上海人民出版社,1981 年。）

（一）从线条中透露出形象姿态

我们以前讲过,埃及、希腊的建筑、雕刻是一种团块的造型。米开朗琪罗说过:一个好的雕刻作品,就是从山上滚下来滚不坏的。他们的画也是团块。中国就很不同。中国古代艺术家要打破这团块,使它有虚有实,使它疏通。中国的"形"字,字旁就是三根毛,以三根毛来代表形体上的线条。这也说明中国艺术的形象的组织是线纹。

由于把形体化成为飞动的线条,着重于线条的流动,因此使得中国的绘画带有舞蹈的意味。这从汉代石刻画和敦煌壁画（飞天）可以看得很清楚。有的线条不一定是客观实在所有的线条,而是画家的构思、画家的意境中要求一种有节奏的联系。例如东汉石画像上一幅画,有两根流动的线条就是画家凭空加上的。这使得整个形象显得更美,同时更深一层的表现内容的内部节奏。这好比是舞台上的伴奏音乐。伴奏音乐烘托和强化舞蹈动作,使之成为艺术。用自然主义的眼光是不可能理解的。

荷兰大画家伦勃朗是光的诗人。他用光和影组成他的画,画的形象就如同从光和影里凸出的一个雕刻。法国大雕刻家罗丹的韵律也是光的韵律,中国的画却是线的韵律,光不要了,影也不要了。"客有为周君画荚者"的故事中讲的那种漆画,要等待阳光从一定角度的照射,才能突出形象,在韩非子看来,价值就不高,甚至不能算作画了。

（二）气韵生动和迁想妙得

六朝齐的谢赫,在《古画品录》序中提出了绘画"六法"成为中国后来绘画思想、艺术思想的指导原理。"六法"就是:(1)气韵生动;(2)骨法用笔;(3)应物象形;(4)随类赋彩;(5)经营位置;(6)传移模写。

希腊人很早就提出"模仿自然"。谢赫"六法"中的:"应物象形"、随类赋彩"是模仿自然,它要求艺术家睁眼看世界:形象、颜色,并把它表现出来。但是艺术家不能停留在这里,否则就是自然主义。艺术家要进一步表达出形象内部的生命,这就是"气韵生动"的要求。气韵生动,这是绘画创作追求的最高目标,最高的境界,也是绘画批评的主要标准。

气韵,就是宇宙中鼓动万物的"气"的节奏与和谐。绘画有气韵,就能给欣赏者一种音乐感。六朝山水画家宗炳,对着山水画弹琴说:"欲令众山皆响",这说明山水画里有音乐的韵律。明代画家徐渭的《驴背吟诗图》,使人产生一种驴蹄行进的节奏感,似乎听见了驴蹄的的答答的声音,这是画家微妙的音乐感觉的传达。

再说"生动"。谢赫提出这个美学范畴,是有历史背景的。在汉代,无论绘画、雕塑、舞蹈、杂技,都是热烈飞动、虎虎有生气的。画家喜欢画龙、画虎、画飞鸟、画舞蹈中的人物。雕塑也大多表现动物。所以,谢赫的"气韵生动",不仅仅是提出了一个美学要求,而且首先是对于汉代以来的艺术实践的一个理论概括和总结。

谢赫以后,历代画论家对于"六法"继续有所发挥。为了达到"气韵生动",达到对象的核心的真实,艺术家要发挥自己的艺术想象。这就是顾恺之论画时说的"迁想妙得"。一幅画既然不仅仅描写外形,而且要表现出内在神情,就要靠内心的体会,把自己的想象迁入对象形象内部去,这就叫"迁想";经过一番曲折之后,把握了对象的真正神情,是为"妙得"。颊上三毛,可以说是"迁想妙得"了——也就是把客观对象真正特性,把客观对象的内在精神表现出来了。

总之,"迁想妙得"就是艺术想象,或如现在有些人用的术语:形象思维。它概括了艺术创造、艺术表现方法的特殊性。后来荆浩《笔法记》提出的图画六要中的"思"("思者,删拨大要,凝想形物"),也就是这个"迁想妙得"。

（三）骨力、骨法、风骨

前面说到，笔墨是中国画的一个重要特点。笔有笔力。卫夫人说："点如坠石"，即一个点要凝聚了过去的运动的力量。这种力量是艺术家内心的表现，但并非剑拔弩张，而是既有力，又秀气。这就叫做"骨"。

所谓"骨法"，在绘画中，粗浅来说，有如下两方面的含义。

第一，形象、色彩有其内部的核心，这是形象的"骨"。画一只老虎，要使人感到它有"骨"。"骨"，是生命和行动的支持点（引伸到精神方面，就是有气节，有骨头，站得住），是表现一种坚定的力量，表现形象内部的坚固的组织。因此"骨"也就反映了艺术家主观的感觉、感受，表现了艺术家主观的情感态度。

第二，"骨"的表现要依赖于"用笔"。张彦远说："夫象物必在于形似，而形似须全其骨气；骨气形似，皆本于立意而归于用笔"（《历代名画记》）。这里讲到了"骨气"和"用笔"的关系。为什么"用笔"这么要紧？这要考虑到中国画的"笔"的特点。中国画用毛笔。毛笔有笔锋，有弹性。一笔下去，墨在纸上可以呈现出轻重浓淡的种种变化。无论是点，是面，都不是几何学上的点与面（那是图案画），不是平的点与面，而是圆的，有立体感。中国画家最反对平扁，认为平扁不是艺术。就是写字，也不是平扁的。中国书法家用中锋的字，背阳光一照，正中间有道黑线，黑线周围是淡墨，叫作"绵裹铁"。圆滚滚的，产生了立体的感觉，也就是引起了"骨"的感觉。

"骨法用笔"，并不是同"墨"没有关系。在中国绘画中，笔和墨总是相互包皮含、相互为用的。所以不能离开"墨"来理解"骨法用笔"。对于这一点，吕风子有过很好的说明。他说：

"'赋彩画'和'水墨画'有时即用彩色水墨涂染成形，不用线作形廓，旧称'没骨画'。应该知道线是点的延长，块是点的扩大；又该知道点是有体积的，点是力之积，积力成线会使人有'生死刚正'之感，叫做骨。难道同样会使人有'生死刚正'之感的点和块，就不配叫做骨吗？画不用线构成，就须用色点或墨点、色块或墨块构成。中国画是以骨为质的，这是中国画的基本特征，怎么能叫不用线构的画做'没骨画'呢？叫它做没线画是对的，叫做'没骨画'便欠妥当了。"

现在我们再来谈谈"风骨"。对于"风骨"的理解,现在学术界很有争论"骨"是否只是一个词藻(铺辞)的问题?我认为"骨"和词是有关系的。但词是有概念内容的。词清楚了,它所表现的现实形象或对于形象的思想也清楚了。"结言端直",就是一句话要明白正确,不是歪曲,不是诡辩。这种正确的表达,就产生了文骨。但光有"骨"还不够,还必须从逻辑性走到艺术性,才能感动人。所以"骨"之外还要有"风"。"风"可以动人,"风"是从情感中来的。中国古典美学理论既重视思想——表现为"骨",又重视情感——表现为"风"。一篇有风有骨的文章就是好文章,这就同歌唱艺术中讲究"咬字行腔"一样。咬字是骨,即结言端直,行腔是风,即意气骏爽、动人情感。

(四)"山水之法,以大观小"

中国画不注重从固定角度刻画空间幻景和透视法。由于中国陆地广大深远,苍苍茫茫,中国人多喜欢登高望远(重阳登高的习惯),不是站在固定角度透视,而是从高处把握全面。这就形成中国山水画中"以大观小"的特点。宋代李成在画中"仰画飞檐",沈括嘲笑他是"掀屋角"。

画家的眼睛不是从固定角度集中于一个透视的焦点,而是流动着飘瞥上下四方,一目千里,把握大自然的内部节奏,把全部景色组织成一幅气韵生动的艺术画面。"诗云:鸢飞戾天,鱼跃于渊,言其上下察也。"(《中庸》),这就是沈括说的"折高折远"的"妙理"。而从固定角度用透视法构成的画,他却认为那不是画,不成画。中国和欧洲绘画在空间观点上有这样大的不同。值得我们的注意。谁是谁非?

> **注释**

　　mural　n.(大型的)壁画

　　attest　v.(to sth.)证实;是……的证据

　　scrupulous　adj.仔细的;细致的;一丝不苟的

　　metaphorical　adj.隐喻的,含比喻的,比喻性的

　　allegorical　adj.寓言的,寓意的

tranquility   n. 平静,安宁

melancholy   n. 忧郁,悲伤,闷闷不乐

refinement   n. 优雅,高贵,极致

thatched   adj. 茅草盖的

forgery   n. 伪造,伪造物

➢ 练习

1. What are the respective emphases of the two articles?

2. How do the two authors develop their own articles on the similar topic of "Chinese paintings"?

3. Which famous painters and connoisseurs have both authors mentioned?

四、拓展阅读

➢ 背景知识

书山浩瀚,学海无涯,如前人择要编撰出综合全面的资料性书籍,后来者的研究便有了可以倚仗的罗盘。《中国画论类编》和 *Early Chinese Texts on Painting* 都是免去了许多入门者和学者检索之苦的功德之书。编者用心良苦,又为进一步研究和跨文化研究留出了线索,为继续深入创造了条件。

《中国画论类编》原名《中国古代画论类编》,由著名美术史论学家俞剑华先生编著。始于 1936 年,历经抗战和新中国成立,大量搜集,陆续而成,且经傅抱石、潘天寿等权威审阅,几经修改,于 1956 年定稿。该书虽名画论,其实包罗很广。凡历代经传文集中有关画论之作都在收集之列。内容也颇为翔实,如画论、画理、画法、画诀、画诗、画品、画评、画谱、画说、画鉴、画跋等无不酌加收录,以求完备。为了便于读者寻根找据,编者不但注明出处,撰写了作者小传,还适量增加了按语。

Early Chinese Texts on Painting(《中国早期的绘画文本》)自 1985 年

出版以来，就成为海内外中国艺术研究者的宝贵资料，常常和《类编》配套使用。该译本选集时间跨度广，门类丰富，开篇有介绍性导读，书末附专有术语及人物生平，翻译语言精准，且通俗易读。

➤ **素材 1.《古画品录·序》**

（谢赫，选自《中国画论类编》俞剑华编著 人民美术出版社 1957 年 p355）

　　夫画品者，盖众画之优劣也。图绘者，莫不明劝戒，著升沉，千载寂寥，披图可鉴。虽画有六法，罕能尽该。而自古及今，各善一节。六法者何？一，气韵生动是也；二，骨法用笔是也；三，应物象形是也；四，随类赋彩是也；五，经营位置是也；六，传移模写是也。唯陆探微、卫协备该之矣。然迹有巧拙，艺无古今，谨依远近，随其品第，裁成序引。故此所述不广其源，但传出自神仙，莫之闻见也。

(Hsieh Ho(active ca. 500—535?). Translated by William R. B. Acker. Susan Bush and Hsio-yen Shih, *Early Chinese Texts on Painting*, Hong Kong University Press, 2012, p71.)

Now by classification of painters is meant the relative superiority and inferiority of all painters. As for painters, there is not one who does not illustrate some exhortation or warning, or show the rise and fall [in man's affairs]. The solitudes and silences of a thousand years may be seen as in a mirror by merely opening a scroll.

Even though painting has its Six Elements [or Laws], few are able to combine them thoroughly, and from ancient times until now each painter has excelled in one particular branch. What are these Six Elements? First, Spirit Resonance which means vitality; second, Bone Method which is [a way of] using the brush; third, Correspondence to the Object which means the depicting of forms; fourth, Suitability to Type which has to do with the laying on of colors; fifth, Division and Planning, that is, placing and arrangement; and sixth, Transmission by Copying, that is to say the copying of models.

Only Lu T'an-wei [5th century] and Wei Hsieh [active late 3rd-early 4th century] were thoroughly proficient in all of these.

But, while works of art may be skillful or clumsy, aesthetics knows no ancient and modern. Respectfully relying upon remote and recent [sources] and following their classifications, I have edited and completed the preface and citations. Hence what is presented is not too far-ranging. As for the origins [of painting], it is merely reported that it proceeded from gods and immortals, but none was witness to such.

➤ 素材 2.《画记》

（白居易，选自《中国画论类编》俞剑华编著 人民美术出版社 1957 年 p25）

张氏子得天之和，心之术，积为行，发为艺。艺尤者其画欤！画无常工，以似为工，学无常师，以真为师。故其措一意，状一物，往往运思中与神会……凡十馀轴。无动植，无大小，皆曲尽其能。莫不向背无遗势，洪纤无遁形。迫而视之，有似乎水中，了然分其影者。然后知学在骨髓者，自心术得；工侔造化者，由天和来。张但得于心，传于手，亦不自知其然而然也。至若笔精之英华，指趣之律度，予非画之流也，不可得而知之。今所得者，但觉其形真而圆，神和而全，炳然，俨然，如出于图之前而已耳。

Record on Painting

(Po Chü-i(772—846). Translated by Susan Bush. Susan Bush and Hsio-yen Shih, *Early Chinese Texts on Painting*, Hong Kong University Press, 2012, p71.)

Young Chang Tun-chien achieved the harmony of nature and the art of the mind, which accumulated to become action and emerged as art. His painting is the ultimate of art. There is no fixed [formula of] skillfulness in painting, resemblance is its skill, just as there is no constant model in learning, truth is the model. In sketching an idea or forming a thing, usually what has been turned over in the mind seems like spiritual insight (*shen-hui*) … [In Chang's paintings] he completely exhausted the potential of everything, moving or fixed, large or small, and there were absolutely no circumstances overlooked on any side, no forms concealed on any scale. When one stood back for viewing, it was as if they were [mirrored] in water that clearly defined their reflections. Afterwards one realized that learning that is in the bones and marrow is achieved by mental art, and skill matching creation comes from natural harmony. Chang merely received from his mind and transmitted to his hand, and it was so without his being conscious of its being so. When it comes to the beauty of the brushwork and the modulations of [a work's] tone, I am not a painter and am unable to tell about it. As for what I perceive, I merely see that the forms are true and complete and the spirit harmonious and whole, brilliantly and awesomely, they seem to emerge in front of the painting.

➤ 素材 3. 书画(节选)

(沈括,《中国画论类编》俞剑华编著 人民美术出版社 1957 年 p43)

　　藏书画者,多取空名。偶传为钟、王、顾、陆之笔,见者争售,此所谓"耳鉴"。又有观画而以手摸之,相传以谓色不隐指者为佳画,此又在耳鉴之下,谓之"揣骨听声"。……

　　书画之妙,当以神会,难可以形器求也。世之观画者,多能指摘其间形象、位置、彩色瑕疵而已;至于奥理冥造者,罕见其人。如彦远评画,言王维画物,多不问四时,如画花往往以桃、杏、芙蓉、莲花同画一景。余家所藏摩诘画《袁安卧雪图》,有雪中芭蕉,此乃得心应手,意到便成,故其理入神,迥得天意,此难可与俗人论也。……此真为识画也。

Casual Writings from the Garden of the Stream of Dreams, Book 17, "Calligraphy and Painting"

(Shen Kua(1031—1095).

Translated by Roderick Whitfield. Susan Bush and Hsio-yen Shih, *Early Chinese Texts on Painting*, Hong Kong University Press, 2012, p99—100.)

Of those who collect calligraphy and painting, the majority rely on names alone. If there is a work reputed to be from the brush of [such calligraphers as] Chung Yu [151—230] and Wang Hsi-chih [309-ca. 365], or [such painters as] Ku K'ai-chih [ca. 45-ca. 406] and Lu Tan-wei [5th century], those who see it compete to acquire it. This is known as "appreciating by ear. " Or again, there are those who, on looking at a painting, must rub it with their hand, believing the legend that those paintings are excellent whose coloring [in relief] is not concealed from the fingers. This is even lower than appreciation by ear, and is known as "trying a bone for sound" ...

The wonders of calligraphy and painting must be intuitively apprehended (*shen-hui*), they can hardly be sought through formal elements. Nowadays, those who look at paintings can usually just pick out faults of form or placement and blemishes in coloring, but one rarely meets anyone who has penetrated their subtle ordering and mysterious creation. Thus, in discussing painting, Chang Yen-yüan [?] said that Wang Wei usually painted things without regard for the four seasons: when painting flowers, he often depicted peach, apricot, hibiscus, and lotus flowers in a single scene. In my collection there is a painting by Wang Wei, *Yuan An Lying in Bed After the Snowfall* [at Lo-yang], that has a banana palm growing in the snow. Here then what was conceived in the mind was echoed by the hand, and as ideas arose they were immediately brought to completion. Hence the principles of his [mode of] creation partook of the divine，and in a special way he obtained the ideas of nature. This would be difficult to discuss with ordinary people … This is true knowledge of painting.

➤ 注释

exhortation　n. 敦促，极力劝诫

solitude　n. 孤独，幽静(的地方)

resonance　n. 共鸣，反响

marrow　n. 骨髓

hibiscus　n. 芙蓉，木槿

partook　vi.（of sth.）吃、喝、享用(尤其是给予的东西)

➤ 练习

1. Read the above passages and their corresponding translations. Pay special attention the key expressions about comments on paintings in English.

画　品	
气韵生动	
骨法用笔	
画无常工，以似为工	
神　会	
向背无遗势，洪纤无遁形	
耳　鉴	
得心应手，意到便成	

2. The three authors are well known，but not all of them are known as a connoisseur. Do you think their perspectives of commenting paintings and painters are influenced by their professions?

五、现代回声

➢ **背景知识**

  大量遍布世界各地的中国古画需要修复,但其技艺独特,相比作于宣纸或绢上的中国画,西方的版画和油画质地结实,相对而言容易修复。如今具有这门特殊技艺的人才短缺是一个世界现象,国内一些大学甚至开设了相关专业。邱锦仙,上海人,知青回城后进入上海博物馆学习,跟随师傅学习摸索如何修复古画,十多年慢慢练就过硬的手艺。和同期的其他 20 多人一样,无论是在中国,还是漂洋过海到纽约或伦敦,她一生与博物馆联系在一起。

The Guardian of Ancient Chinese Treasures at the British Museum

By Jian Sun/ in Times cultures/ on Saturday,07 Sep 2019 12:23 PM/ 60 Comments

  http://times-publications. com/index. php/2019/09/07/the-guardian-of-ancient-chinese-treasures-at-the-british-museum/

  The British Museum's rich collection of ancient Chinese paintings has attracted many visitors, especially Chinese tourists over the past 30 years. At the heart of this preservation and revival of Chinese art history is senior conservator Qiu Jinxian.

  Joanna Kosek, head of art preservation at the British Museum, told the Times Publications that Qiu is considered one of the museum's most priceless treasures. "We let the treasure treat the treasure," Kosek said, in tribute to Qiu's unparalleled expertise and restoration skills that have enabled her to perform countless miracles.

  Prior to joining the British Museum in 1987, Qiu had mastered the craft of repairing and mounting ancient art over a 15-year career at Shanghai Museum. Qiu and her colleagues studied diligently under the instruction of Xu Maokang and Hua Qiming, masters of renowned Chinese restoration technique Su and Yang. Qiu became experienced in repairing and mounting many forms of artwork and calligraphy including paper and silk hand scrolls, vertical and horizontal slope and lenses.

In 1987, Qiu was introduced by University of London's Professor Whitfield, a consultant in Chinese ancient art, to Mrs. Jessica Rawson, the director of British Museum oriental department. At the time there were no conservators specialised in ancient Chinese art at the British Museum. The large collection of Chinese ancient paintings and cultural relics in the museum were mainly repaired by Japanese and British methods and materials. As these methods were not suitable for Chinese paintings, the art collection was kept in storage for a long time instead of on public display.

Just before Christmas 1987, Qiu Jinxian had her first appointment at the British Museum. She was asked to repair an ancient scroll by Fu Baoshi, which had been badly damaged by fire. Qiu's methods, which included washing with warm water to separate the glue in order to repair the paper, shocked and stunned the curators. Some curators even got out the camera to record her methods as they'd never seen this way of restoring ancient art. "They didn't actually expect me to fix it."Qiu Jinxian stated simply when asked to recall that moment.

Mrs. Rawson the director of the oriental department was completely amazed by Qiu Jinxian's incredible skills. She immediately invited Qiu Jinxian to join the British Museum and helped her to apply for a working visa through the UK Ministry of Foreign Affairs. Due to the museum's focus on urgently rescuing and restoring its collection of Chinese art,

Mrs. Rawson gave Qiu an unprecedented position as senior conservator of Chinese painting. Qiu was subsequently given an exceptional talent visa by the British government.

Chinese ancient paintings are notoriously difficult to repair because of their large size, complex materials, diverse colours, and rich composition. The most important thing is to understand the long history, meaning and culture behind the painting. Repair is an extremely time and energy intensive process. Each painting normally takes several months from cleaning to restoration and drying. Since 1987, Qiu has repaired more than 400 artworks.

In 2014, Qiu and her team restored the 1,600-year-old Tang Dynasty copy of The Admonitions of the Instructress to the Court Ladies(*The Admonitions Scroll*)after 2 laborious months. It has become a major resource for studying the Eastern Jin Dynasty(317—420)painter Gu Kaizhi's original work as well as the evolution of early Chinese figure painting.

"So the British Museum and Ms. Qiu have played amazing roles in bring her extremely super skills and techniques over here in the first place in the 20 century. She established proper Chinese strong mounting in Europe. She is the one and only expert in Europe". Joanna Kosek told Times Publications that nobody can replace Qiu. She said she hopes there will be a successor but she hasn't seen one who can match Qiu's prowess yet. They have had trainees working as fellows with Qiu for years. However, it is a lengthy training process.

Joanna emphasized the craft of restoration is about deeply understanding language, culture and history. "You cannot teach quickly," Joanna said. "It may be difficult to see the results even after a decade, but the number of conservators of Chinese paintings will slowly grow in Europe."

The outstanding performance of Qiu Jinxian at the British Museum has made her position as senior conservator of Chinese paintings inde-structible. Due to annual funding cuts, the British Museum has had to lay off employees for years. 30 years ago, the museum employed more than 2, 000 people. But now the museum has only 800 employees. The layoffs are nearly 60%. Despite this, museum management have always prioritised the retainment of a senior conservator of Chinese painting.

Qiu told the media that she is very proud of her work. She feels that it is her mission to rescue and repair these ancient paintings so that they can be displayed in public exhibitions, where they can be studied by schol-ars and enjoyed by the general public from around the world. She wants more people to understand and appreciate Chinese history and culture through art. Although the artworks originated from China, they now be-long to the people of the world. Despite reaching retirement age, she still works at the British Museum 3—4 days a week. Her passion for storytell-ing through art still burns as strong as it did 32 years ago.

> **注释**

conservator　n. 文物修复员

expertise　n. 专门的知识或技艺

admonition   n. 告诫,劝诫,温和的责备

layoff   n. 暂时解雇,停工

retainment   n. 保留,保持

➢ 练习

1. Why is Ms. Qiu Jinxian considered one of the British Museum's most priceless treasures?

2. Why are Chinese ancient paintings difficult to repair?

3. What is Ms. Qiu's attitude towards her career as a conservator of Chinese paintings?

第七章　建　　筑

一、词源梳理

古汉语与建筑事物相关程度最高的十个汉字为"土、木、构、筑、营、修、缮、葺、建、造","建"与"筑"这两个字连用,在古汉语中很少,即便有通常也仅仅是两个动词的叠加,含义与现代中文"建筑"这个词不同。其中"建"在《说文解字》里的解释为"立朝律也",对应社会制度。建与立同义,泛指营造活动,如"皇帝有熊氏始建宫殿"和"宝月楼乾隆戊寅年建"。"筑"在《正字通》中解释为"凡土工曰筑",对应建造活动。其中"构"、"筑"二字集中反映了中国古代建筑在结构施工方面的不同特点,结合起来就有了"筑土构木"之说。"筑土"来源于古代的穴居,"构木"来源于古代的巢居。例如,《淮南子·氾论训》记载说:"古者民泽处复穴,冬日则不胜霜雪雾露,夏日则不胜暑蛰蚊虻;圣人乃作,为之筑土构木以为富室,上栋下宇以避风雨、以避寒暑,而百姓安之。"

中国古代的建筑则一直被视为一种匠作,而不是学科或艺术。以往也有所谓"匠作之学"一说,但不具有今日的学术地位。在古代知识体系中,相关内容主要在"考工"中,而"考工"属于"政书类",这一分类收集章典制度文献,而不是技术相关文献。而且,那时的建筑与土木工程混为一体,设计与施工不分家,现在的建筑学则是侧重于技术与艺术等方面的设计,土木工程学侧重于结构与施工。

英语中对应建筑的词是"architecture",表示关于建筑物的技术和艺术的系统知识,由"architect"派生而来。古英语中的"heahcræftiga"(highcrafter)就是从拉丁语"architectus"翻译而来。但这个单词可以追溯到希腊文"arkhitekton","*arkhi-*"意味"chief","*tekton-*"意为"builder,carpenter",整个单词意为"master builder,chief workman"。中世纪时,它通过从拉丁文进入法语,再进入英语。经由法语进入英语。建筑作为反映营造活动的动词,可以与英语中的"build"相对应使用,作为反映营造活动之成果,即建筑物的名词,可以与英语中的"building",而"architecture"对应的是"建筑"作为学问、风格的含义。

二、引导阅读
➢ 背景知识

　　原本面临拆迁的徽式老宅,竟然飞越重洋,在美国东北部的小镇整体重建,焕发生机,主管博物馆甚至为它设计了精美的网站,尊重与用心可见一斑。这是荫余堂的幸运,也是西方长久以来对中国古代建筑浓厚兴趣的延续。

　　西方对中国古代建筑的兴趣始于西欧。18世纪初,传教士对中国生活的描述掀起了欧洲"中国热",为了提供参考,英国学者开始零星介绍中国建筑。19世纪开始,日本人为了寻根溯源,也来到中国,进行了大规模实地考察,写成了大量极具价值的学术文献。美国的汉学研究起步较晚,但进展神速,比如促成"荫余堂"项目的白铃安(Nancy Berliner)便是上世纪80年代毕业于哈佛大学艺术及建筑史专业的博士。

　　"一生痴绝处,无梦到徽州",这是明代戏剧家汤显祖留下的千古绝唱,而撑起这一切美好的根源,是青砖黛瓦的徽派建筑,和淡淡炊烟笼罩的马头墙,荫余堂便是这样一座典型的徽派建筑。它奇迹般的命运转折,被中外媒体广泛报道,CBS的网络新闻简要生动地讲述了故事的来龙去脉。

Chinese House Finds Home In U. S.

(https://www.cbsnews.com/news/chinese-house-finds-home-in-us/)

Two hundred years ago,in a remote village in the Huizhou region of

China, a wealthy family built a beautiful house. They gave it a name, Yin Yu Tang.

It was about to meet the same fate as so many other historic wooden houses in China-torn down, the wood sold for scrap-when, completely by chance, the perfect person to save it simply walked up to the front door.

Nancy Berliner, curator of Chinese art and culture at the Peabody-Essex Museum in Salem, Massachusetts, happened upon Yin Yu Tang the very day that family members had gathered and decided to sell the house.

"An elderly man came up to me and he said, 'You like this house?'" Berliner recalls. "I said, 'It's beautiful,' and he said, 'Do you want to buy it?'"

Little did he know that day in 1996, that the Peabody-Essex Museum has an entire collection of old houses, and one of the world's great collections of Asian art and design. There was probably no better place, anywhere, for the house to end up.

The museum was just about to build a $125 million new building. There was just enough time to organize the elaborate cultural exchange necessary to acquire the house, and to redesign the new museum so Yin Yu Tang would be front and center.

Dan Monroe, director of the Peabody-Essex Museum, explains, "We did give it a place of honor and also a place of where it has its own standing and integrity. We considered things like feng shui. Even the placement...it's actually sited here in exactly the same manner it was sited in the village."

But first, the grand old house had to be moved.

Huang She Chi grew up in the house, which had been in his family for seven generations. Before Yin Yu Tang was dismantled, he consulted his ancestors to tell them what was about to happen. Then, each roof tile, each wall panel, each beam was catalogued, crated, and loaded into containers.

Yin Yu Tang embarked on a 13,000-mile journey. In January 1998, it arrived at a warehouse in Melrose, Mass. There, all of the pieces were unpacked and laid out like millions of giant Legos to be reassembled in Salem. The Chinese carpenters who took it apart were flown over to help put it back together.

Most people associate Salem with the colonial-era witch trials, but the legacy of Salem's 18th and early 19th century sea captains-merchants who went to sea to make their fortunes-is the bigger story. In 1799, just about the same time the Chinese house was built, some of these Salem adventurers opened what has evolved into the Peabody-Essex Museum.

Walk through the museum or any of the historic houses it owns and the link between Salem and the world of the Chinese house is obvious: especially in the Crowninshield Bentley House. Like the Chinese house, one family owned it for nearly 200 years.

The Crowninshield family of Salem and the Huang family of the Huizhou region in China actually lived remarkably similar lives.

"The men all lived outside the house," Berliner explains. "It was really only women and children who lived in the house. The men were merchants and had their businesses elsewhere. They would come back to get married, and then once every three years they might come back for about six months."

The name Yin Yu Tang can be interpreted to mean, hope that the house would shelter the family for many generations.

The house will not be restored to look as it might have 200 years ago. It will be left as a testament to members of one Chinese family living the history of their country. It's battered, but still beautiful.

"Everything is fit in with fine joinery to hold it down, and there are very, very few nails in the house," says Berliner. "Because the house was really a kit of parts, all the components could be built off-site and then they were brought to the site and just put right together and everybody knew what piece was what. Completely prefab."

But the secret of how it was done-and more importantly, how to do it again-involves restoration carpenter Zhou Zhiu Ming and his team. A house speaks its own language, and the Americans reassembling Yin Yu Tang needed interpreters.

So every few months, Zhou Zhiu Ming and his men leave their homes in China and move here to work alongside their American counterparts, sometimes for as long as six months at a stretch. In four years of working together, the two teams have devised their own way of communicating.

The process of joining the old house and the new museum began in earnest last summer. Passersby have noticed a strange fusion taking place-the weary beams of the Chinese home somehow bringing life to the hardhat zone of a 21st century construction site.

The building of one and the rebuilding of the other won't be complete until this coming June, but it already looks as though Yin Yu Tang and Salem are a good fit.

> **注释**

curator   n. (博物馆或美术馆等的)馆长,负责人

dismantle   vt. 拆开,拆卸

crate   vt. 把……装进木箱

trial   n. 审讯。文中的 trials 委婉代指 Salem Witch Trials。17 世纪末的北美殖民地,崇尚超自然还是日常生活的一部分,1692 年到 1693 年,当马萨诸塞州塞勒姆镇的居民陆续得了怪病,惨遭病痛折麽,人们相信是他

们是被巫术迫害,不少人被指控为巫师并接受审判乃至刑罚,尤其以女性居多。这是美国历史上有名的"塞勒姆审巫案"。

testament　n. 确实的证明

kit　n. 成套用品

prefab　n. 预制装备式建筑;adj.（建筑、结构）预制的,组装的

hardhat　n. 建筑工人;adj. 需要带安全帽的

> 练习

1. What would have been the fate of Yin Yu Tang, had Ms. Berliner not happened upon the old house that very day?

2. Please sum up the complete 13,000-mile journey of Yin Yu Tang from China to US.

3. Why does the author believe that there is an obvious link between Salem, especially in the Crowninshield Bentley House, and the world of the Chinese house?

三、阅读与比较:中国建筑的特别之处

> 背景知识

中国人自己的建筑学史起步于 20 世纪 30 年代,之前对中国传统建筑感兴趣的都是外国人,中国古代观念中,建筑被鄙薄为匠作之事。奠定中国建筑史学基础的是成立于 1930 年的中国营造学社,对中国传统建筑研究和保护作出了空前绝后的贡献。

学社最杰出的代表之一,莫过于梁思成。他深受父亲梁启超的家国情怀影响,又有深厚的古文修养,英文、西方自然科学和人文社会知识也都很扎实。他同终生伴侣林徽因携手赴美深造,全面了解了国内外对中国传统建筑的研究,熟读珍贵的《营造法式》和《工部工程作法则例》,最终把古文献上抽象隐约的文字印象,落实成为清晰明白的术语、准确详细的图纸、科学

系统的分析论述,写成了中国第一部有体系的简明传统建筑史《图像中国建筑史》。第一章第一节首次对中国古建筑的特点进行了全方位的精准概括,本文为该部分的汉译。

中国建筑史的建立和飞速发展,将海外的中国建筑史研究带到了一个崭新的高度。罗纳尔多·G. 纳普(Ronald G. Knapp)是美国知名的亚洲老建筑研究专家,对中国文化地理和历史地理有颇多著述,包括 *Tradition, Resilience, and Change*（2003）, *China's Old Dwellings*（2000）, *and China's Walled Cities*（2000）。在他的文章中,我们既能看到梁的吸收和借鉴,也能看到对梁的补充和发展。

➤ 素材 1. 中国建筑之特征

（梁思成,《中国建筑史》,百花文艺出版社,2005。）

建筑显著特征之所以形成,有两个因素:有属于实物结构技术上之取法及发展者,有缘于环境思想之趋向者。治建筑史者必事先把握,不惑于他时他族建筑与我之异同,不作偏激之毁誉。今略举中国建筑之主要特征。

一、属于结构取法及发展方面之特征,有以下可注意者四点:

（一）以木料为主要构材　凡一座建筑物皆因其材料而产生其结构法,更因此结构而产生其形式上之特征。世界他系建筑,多渐采用石料以替代其原始之木构,故仅于石面浮雕木质构材之形,以为装饰,其主要造法则依石料垒砌之法,产生其形制。中国始终保持木材为主要建筑材料,故其形式为木造结构之直接表现。其在结构方面之努力,则尽木材应用之能事,以臻实际之需要,而同时完成其本身完美之形体。匠师既重视传统经验,又忠于材料之应用,故中国木构因历代之演变,乃形成遵古之艺术。唐宋少数遗物在结构上造诣之精,实积千余年之工程经验,所产生之最高美术风格也。

（二）历用构架制之结构原则　既以木材为主,此结构原则乃为"梁柱式建筑"之"构架制"。以立柱四根,上施梁枋,牵制成为一"间"(前后横木为枋,左右为梁)。梁可数层重叠称"梁架"。通常一座建筑物均由若干"间"组成。此种构架制之特点,在使建筑物上部之一切荷载均由构架负担;承重者为其立柱与其梁枋,不借力于高墙厚壁之垒砌。建筑物中所有墙壁,无论其为砖石或为木板,均为"隔断墙",非负重之部分。是故门窗之分配毫不受墙壁之限制,而墙壁之设施,亦仅视分隔之需要。欧洲建筑中,惟现代之钢架及钢筋混凝土之构架在原则上与此木质之构架建筑相同。所异者材料及科学程度之不同耳。

（三）以斗栱为结构之关键,并为度量单位　在木构架之横梁及立柱间过渡处,施横材方木相互垒叠,前后伸出作"斗栱",与屋顶结构有密切关系。其功用在以伸出之栱承受上部结构之荷载,转纳于下部之立柱上,故为大建筑物所必用。后世斗栱之制日趋标准化,全部建筑物之权衡比例遂以横栱之"材"为度量单位,犹罗马建筑之柱式(Order),以柱径为度量单位,治建筑学者必习焉(第 2 图)。虽砖石之建筑物,如汉阙、佛塔等,率多叠砌雕凿,仿木架斗栱形制。斗栱之组织与比例大小,历代不同,每可借其结构演变之序,以鉴定建筑物之年代,故对于斗栱之认识,实为研究中国建筑者所必具之基础知识。

（四）外部轮廓之特异　外部特征明显,迥异于他系建筑,乃造成其自身风格之特素。中国建筑之外轮廓予人以优美之印象,且富于吸引力。今分别言之如下:

1. 翼展之屋顶部分　屋顶为实际必需之一部,其在中国建筑中,至迟自殷代始,已极受注意。历代匠师不惮烦难,集中构造之努力于此。屋顶坡面、脊端,及檐边、转角各种曲线,柔和壮丽,为中国建筑物之冠冕,而被视为神秘风格之特征,其功用且收"上尊而宇卑,则吐水疾而霤远"之实效。而其最可注意者,尤在屋顶结构之合理与自然。其所形成之曲线,乃其结构工程之当然结果,非勉强造作而成也。

2. 崇厚阶基之衬托　中国建筑特征之一为阶基之重要,与崇峻屋瓦互为呼应。周、秦、西汉时尤甚。高台之风与游猎骑射并盛,其后日渐衰弛,至近世台基、阶陛遂渐趋扁平,仅成文弱之衬托,非若当年之台榭,居高临下,作雄视山河之势。但宋、辽以后之"台随檐出"及"须弥座"等仍为建筑外形显著之轮廓。

3. 前面玲珑木质之屋身　屋顶与台基间乃立面主要之中部，无论中国建筑物之外表若何魁伟，此段正面之表现仍为并立之木质楹柱与玲珑之窗户相间而成，鲜用墙壁。左右两面如为山墙，则又少有开窗辟门者。厚墙开辟窗洞之法，除箭楼、仓廒等特殊建筑外，不常见于殿堂，与垒石之建筑状貌大异。

4. 院落之组织　凡主要殿堂必有其附属建筑物，联络周绕，如配厢、夹室、廊庑、周屋、山门、前殿、围墙、角楼之属，成为庭院之组织，始完成中国建筑物之全貌。除佛塔以外，单座之建筑物鲜有呈露其四周全部轮廓，使人得以远望其形状者。单座殿屋立面之印象，乃在短距离之庭院中呈现其一。此与欧洲建筑所予人印象，独立于空旷之周围中者大异。中国建筑物之完整印象，必须并与其院落合观之。国画中之宫殿楼阁，常为登高俯视鸟瞰之图。其故殆亦为此耶。

5. 彩色之施用　彩色之施用于内外构材之表面，为中国建筑传统之法。其装饰之原则有严格之规定，分划结构，保留素面，以冷色青绿与纯丹作反衬之用，其结果为异常成功之艺术，非滥用彩色，徒作无度之涂饰者可比也。故中国建筑物虽名为多色，其大体重在有节制之点缀，气象庄严，雍容华贵，故虽有较繁缛者，亦可免淆杂俚俗之弊焉。

6. 绝对均称与绝对自由之两种平面布局　以多座建筑合组而成之宫殿、官署、庙宇乃至于住宅，通常均取左右均齐之绝对整齐对称之布局。庭院四周，绕以建筑物。庭院数目无定。其所最注重者，乃主要中线之成立。一切组织均根据中线以发展，其部署秩序均为左右分立，适于礼仪（Formal）之庄严场合；公者如朝会大典，私者如婚丧喜庆之属。反之如优游闲处之庭园建筑，则常一反对称之隆重，出之以自由随意之变化。部署取高低曲折之趣，间以池沼、花木，接近自然，而入诗画之境。此两种传统之平面部署，在不觉中，含蕴中国精神生活之各面，至为深刻。

7. 用石方法之失败　中国建筑数千年来，始终以木为主要构材，砖、石常居辅材之位,故重要工程,以石营建者较少。究其原因有二:(1)匠人对于石质力学缺乏了解。(2)不知垫灰之主要功用,古希腊、罗马对于此方面均早已认识,罗马工师大刀阔斧,以大量富于粘性而坚固之垫灰垫托,且更进而用为混凝土,以供应其大量之建筑事业。

二、属于环境思想方面,与其他建筑之历史背景迥然不同者,至少有以下可注意者四:

(一)不求原物长存之观念　此建筑系统之寿命,虽已可追溯至四千年以上,而地面所遗实物,其最古者,虽待考之先秦土垣残基之类,已属凤毛麟角,次者如汉、唐石阙、砖塔,不止年代较近,且亦非可以居止之殿堂。整中国自始即未有如古埃及刻意求永久不灭之工程,欲以人工与自然物体竟久存之实,且既安于新陈代谢之理,以自然生灭为定律。

(二)建筑活动受道德观念之制裁　古代统治阶级崇尚俭德,而其建置,皆征发民役经营,故以建筑为劳民害农之事,坛社亲庙、城阙朝市,虽尊为宗法、仪礼、制度之依归,而宫馆、台榭、第宅、园林,则抑为君王骄奢、臣民侈僭之征兆。古史记载或不美其事,或不详其实,恒因其奢侈逾制始略举以警后世,示其"非礼",其记述非为叙述建筑形状方法而作也。

(三)着重部署之规制　古之政治尚典章制度,至儒教兴盛,尤重礼仪。故先秦、两汉传记所载建筑,率重其名称方位、部署规制,鲜涉殿堂之结构。嗣后建筑之见于史籍者,多见于五行志及礼仪志中。结构所产生立体形貌之感人处,则多见于文章诗赋之赞颂中。中国诗画之意境,与建筑艺术显有密切之关系,但此艺术之旨趣,固未尝如规制部署等第等之为史家所重也。

(四)建筑之术,师徒传授,不重书籍　数千年来古籍中,传世术书,惟宋、清两朝官刊各一部耳。然术书专偏,士人不解,匠人又困于文字之难,术语日久失用,造法亦渐不解,其书乃为后世之谜。如欧西、文艺复兴后之重视建筑工程及艺术,视为地方时代文化之表现而加以研究者,尚属近二三十年来之崭新观点,最初有赖于西方学者先开考察研究之风,继而社会对建筑之态度渐改,愈增其了解焉。

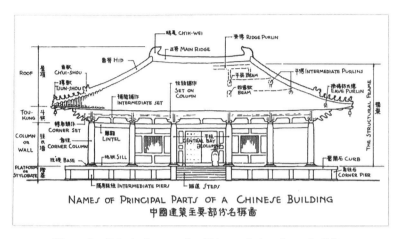

Figure 1　Principal parts of a Chinese timber-frame building

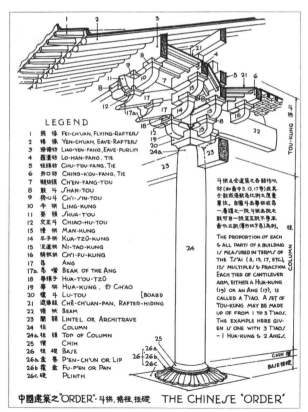

Figure 2　The Chinese order(the most frequently
reprinted of Liang's drawings)

➢ 素材 2. Chinese Houses: Similarities and Differences

(Knapp, Ronald G., Chinese Houses: the Architectural Heritage of a Nation. Tuttle, 2005)

With land area approximately the same as that of the United States and twice that of Europe, as well as widely varying climatic conditions, China includes fifty-six disparate nationalities and a remarkable diversity even among its dominant Han ethnic majority. It is thus not surprising that Chinese houses are at least as varied as those found in multinational Europe and are more diverse than those in the United States. These large structures include hierarchically organized quadrangular courtyard residences in the Beijing area, unique below-ground cave-like dwellings in the north and northwest, expensive manor complexes in the north, extraordinarily beautiful two- and three-story merchant dwellings in central China, massive multi-storied fortresses in the hilly south, portable tents and cantileveredpile-dwellings occupied by ethnic minority populations, as well as boats of many types along the coast and embayed rivers.

While there is no single style can be called "a Chinese house"across time and space, it is possible to point to a set of remarkably similar elements shared by many-if not most-houses, whether simple or grand. Chinese builders throughout the country historically favored a number of conventional building plans and structural principles. In addition, special attention was paid to the environmental conditions of specific building sites and to manipulating building parts in order to acquire some control of natural conditions, including access to sunlight and prevailing winds, in addition to blocking cold winds and collecting rainwater. Rooted deeply in Chinese building traditions, these fundamental building rudiments have influenced as well the building traditions found in Japan, Korea, and to some degree Vietnam.

Chinese builders not only create structures—space that is enclosed with walls and a roof—but also recognize the need to create exposed spaces for living, work, and leisure. Open spaces, often loosely referred to as "courtyards," are an important category in the special layout of any fully formed Chinese house. They are found in seemingly endless variations in relatively tiny houses as well as complicated expansive ones in which enclosed open spaces even include within them other buildings surrounding open spaces.

In "composing a house," to use Nelson Wu's apt phrase, open spaces are part of a "house-yard" complex. "The student of Chinese architecture," he continues, "will miss the point if he does not focus his attention on the space and impalpable relationships between members of this complex, but, rather, fixes his eyes on the solids of the building alone."

At least one open space is an important element of any Chinese house. Even when the space is merely the outdoors immediately in front of a rectangular structure and without surrounding structures. Full enclosure with buildings on three sides—an inverted U-shape—is quite common throughout China. Sometimes the fourth side is defined by a wall, which from the outside may make it appear as if the dwelling is wrapped by structures on four sides when that is not, in fact, the case.

The common English term "courtyards" itself, or even its many Chinese language equivalents, is insufficient in differentiating the many types of open spaces seen from place to place in China. Still, in general, the proportion of open space to enclose space is significantly less in southeast and southwest China compared to the north and northeast. In northeastern and northern China, courtyards are comparatively broad, while in southern China they are usually condensed in size, sometimes becoming a mere shaft open space. The Chinese term *tianjin* translated as"skywell,"catches well the meaning of constricted southern"courtyards".

Whether compact or spread out,many Chinese houses exhibit a clear spatial hierarchy that mirrors the relationships among the family living within it and their interaction with visitors. Adjacent open and closed spaces help define this spatial hierarchy,aided in fundamental ways by the purposeful use of gates,screen walls and steps. Casual visitors,for example,in the past were only invited into the front part of the house,perhaps only the entry vestibule near the main gate or into the first slender courtyard. The large courtyard and main hall were accessible only to family members. In addition,privileged spaces for women in the family were placed deeper in northern houses and in upper stories of southern houses, far from places where non-family visitors would see them. Separate passageways and doors sometimes helped enforce segregation. In some extensive residential complexes,moreover,a barely noticeable increase in elevation from the exterior to the interior,with each structure a few steps higher than the preceding courtyard,was employed to accentuate status differences from the outside deep into the interior.

Indeed,whenever possible,open space is—whatever the dimensions, and however enclosed by buildings— nearly obligatory elements of traditional Chinese houses. Open spaces offer abundant advantages in terms of providing enhanced ventilation and sunlight,a place to gather and work, and privacy and safety. Buildings are typically arranged symmetrically,facing each other around courtyards,with the principal building, usually where the main ceremonial hall is located,oriented towards the south or southeast. In many areas of northern China,this principal building is referred to as"northern building"or"upper building",both indicating a superior position. Side halls then can easily be designated"east hall"and"west hall"using descriptions that are both tied to the cardinal directions and hierarchy.

Weather found in a grand palace or a humble home,the common denominator of any Chinese structure is a modular building unit known as a *jian*. A *jian* is not only a fundamental measure of width,the span between two lateral columns that constitutes a bay,but it also represents the two-dimensional floor space bounded between four columns as well as the volumetric measure of the void defined by the floor and walls. Sometimes a *jian* forms"a room"although often a room is made up of several structural *jian*. In Chinese dwellings,it is rare for any effort to be made to hide structural columns that give shape to a *jian* that each stands not only as a mark of shape but as a natural aesthetic element as well.

Chinese houses and other buildings generally take shape from conventional set of elementary parts—foundation,wooden framework,and roof—using readily available building materials such as earth,timber and stone. Many old dwellings throughout the country lack a wooden framework. So that load bearing walls directly support the roof system,a condition that is almost universal with contemporary Chinese houses. Basement are rare in Chinese dwellings and most houses traditionally were built directly on compacted earth that had been leveled or slightly raised on a solid platform of time to earth or layered stone. Stone foundations can be seen supporting the walls of small and large dwellings of China in order to create a dry and secure base. Foundations of this sort are stable enough to support a damped earth,adobe,or fire brick wall above,which then either support the roof structure directly or merely serves as a curtain wall around a timber framework.

Load-bearing walls,that is,walls that directly support a roof structure, have a long history of use in common houses throughout China. With higher quality dwelling, however, walls do not support the weight of the roof above, but are merely curtain walls set between complicated structural wooden frameworks that lift the roof rather than using the walls themselves for this purpose. Independent of the walls, which are thus non-load-bearing, the timber framework is a kind of "osseous" structure similar to the human skeleton. Liang Sicheng, China's revered architectural historian, claimed that the use of a timber framework permits complete freedom in walling and penetration and, by the simple adjustment of the proportion between walls and openings, renders a house practical and comfortable in any climate from that of tropical Indochina to that of subarctic Manchuria. Due to this extreme flexibility and adaptability, this method of construction could be employed whether Chinese civilization spread and would effectively shelter occupants from the elements, however diverse they might be. Perhaps nothing similar is found in western architecture until the invention of reinforced concrete and the steel framing systems after the twentieth century".

Wood and structural frameworks lifting the roof were universally used in the construction of Chinese temples and palaces as well as the houses of those with the means to purchase expensive timber parts for the pillars and beams. The houses built by ordinary Chinese, on the other hand, almost always utilized limited amounts of timber because of costs and other factors, and thus generally were built with load-bearing walls. In no other feature of traditional Chinese housing was the prosperity of the owner so clearly expressed than that of the wooden frame since the cost of timber always far exceeded that of the earth required to compose the walls, even when fire bricks were used.

Although a roof is principally a functional canopy, sheltering a structure and its interior living place space from the elements, it may also be an expressive feature with sometimes powerful symbolism attached to it. The materials used to cover a roof, its degree of slope, as well as its profile are strongly influenced by both climatic and economic factors. In areas of substantial rainfall, the major concern is quickly moving falling water to the eaves in order to minimize the infiltration of moisture into the building. Pitched roofs—with surfaces that operate to disperse water like the scales of fish or the feathers of birds—are most common on Chinese dwellings. Roofs also contribute to insulating the inside of the dwelling, shielding the inhabitants from either heat or cold. Probably most Chinese roofs are merely utilitarian, providing crude water shedding and waterproofing. The profiles of many, however, exhibit a powerful elegance in terms of their curvature and covering, conditions that are more common in the residences of those with greater means than those who live in humble dwellings. Some scholars have claimed that Chinese pay as much attention to the appearance of the roof as westerners do to the facade.

Chinese craftsmen employ standard measurements, locally available building materials, experience and skill, and an acute awareness of environmental conditions in order to build Chinese houses. Structural and spatial variations throughout China reflect pragmatism and a strikingempiricism as builders act in response to local conditions, even as they are guided by building traditions from elsewhere. Whether built of earth, wood, stone, or some combination of these materials, Chinese houses are relatively easy and economical to repair or modify. Parts that are damaged by water or fire, because of the modularity of Chinese construction techniques, can be swapped out and replaced. The recycling of old materials and the adoptable reuse of old spaces are fundamental traditional practices. Evolving over thousands of years to meet changing environmental and social conditions, the courtyard in its extensive and condensed forms continues to unfold as an appropriate component in the spatial composition of Chinese residences throughout the country.

➢ **注释**

hierarchically adv. 分等级地. 分级体系地

cantilever n. 悬臂

embay vt. 使入湾,成港湾状

rudiments n. (the ～ of sth)基础,基本原理(或技能)

impalpable adj. 难掌握的,难琢磨的

shaft n. 通风井,天井

vestibule n. 门厅,前厅

accentuate vt. 强调,着重指出

ventilation n. 通风透气

bay n. 分隔间(户外或室内的,用以停放车辆、存放货物等)

osseous adj. 有骨的,多骨的

canopy n. (建筑的)顶棚,顶盖

pragmatism n. 实用主义,实用的观点或方法

empiricism n. 实证论,经验主义

➢ **练习**

1. Please make a mind map of Liang Sicheng's article "Features of Chinese Architecture" and translate all the relevant expressions into English.

2. The second article elaborates on similarities and differences of Chinese houses influenced by natural environment. What do you think is the author's scope of discussion, compared with that of the first article by Mr. Liang?

四、拓展阅读

➢ **背景知识**

中国的古典园林,集建筑、园艺、书画、文学、戏剧、雕刻等精华于一身,

是世界公认的艺术瑰宝。从魏晋开始,人们效仿自然山水修建园林,在现实生活中寄托隐逸情怀,到明清达到鼎盛,形成了一套完备的设计理念。白居易曾这样描绘他的宅园:"沧浪峡水子陵滩,路远江深欲去难。何如家池通小院,卧房阶下插鱼竿。"

以下两篇文章分别出自中国园林之父陈从周和苏格兰园林景观设计师麦琪·凯恩克(Maggie Keswick)之手。没有陈从周,就不会有上海豫园东部、苏州网师园和退思园的精心修复,也不会有纽约大都会博物馆内"明轩"的惊艳亮相,他的《说园》,以园林修复专家的一手经验,向读者介绍了中国造园技艺的精华;而麦琪·凯恩克的《中国园林》算得上最早的英文科普之一,本节选回顾了西方在18世纪接触中国园林之初的震惊和痴迷,同时也通过对比、书信摘录等方式展示了中国皇家园林无与伦比的美。

➤ 素材 1. 说园
(陈从周《说园(中英文本)》,同济大学出版社,2007)

我国造园具有悠久的历史,在世界园林中树立着独特风格,自来学者从各方面进行分析研究,各抒高见,如今就我在接触园林中所见闻掇拾到的,提出来谈谈,姑名"说园"。

园有静观、动观之分,这一点我们在造园之先,首要考虑。小园应以静观为主,动观为辅,庭院专主静现。大园则以动观为主,静观为辅。前者如苏州网师园,后者则苏州拙政园差可似之。人们进入网师园宜坐宜留之建筑多,绕池一周,有槛前细数游鱼,有亭中待月迎风,而轩外花影移墙,峰峦当窗,宛然如画,静中生趣。至于拙政园径缘池转,廊引人随,与"日午画船桥下过,衣香人影太匆匆"的瘦西湖相仿佛,妙在移步换影,这是动观。立意在先,文循意出。

中国园林是由建筑、山水、花木等组合而成的一个综合艺术品,富有诗情画意。叠山理水要造成"虽由人作,宛自天开"的境界。山与水的关系究竟如何呢? 简言之,模山范水,用局部之景而非缩小(网师园水池仿虎丘白莲池，极妙），处理原则悉符画本。如果我们能初步理解这个道理，就不至于离自然太远，多少能呈现水石交融的美妙境界。

中国园林的树木栽植，不仅为了绿化，要具有画意。宋人郭熙说得好："山水以山为血脉，以草为毛发，以烟云为神采"。草尚如此，何况树木呢？我总觉得一地方的园林应该有那个地方的植物特色，并且土生土长的树木存活率大，成长得快，几年可茂然成林。它与植物园有别，是以观赏为主，而非以种多斗奇。要能做到"园以景胜，景因园异"，那真是不容易。这当然也包括花卉在内。同中求不同，不同中求同，我国园林是各具风格的。古代园林在这方面下过功夫，虽亭台楼阁，山石水池，而能做到风花雪月，光景常新。

园林景物有仰观、俯观之别，在处理上亦应区别对待。楼阁掩映，山石森严，曲水湾环，都存乎此理。"小红桥外小红亭，小红亭畔、高柳万蝉声。""绿杨影里，海棠亭畔，红杏梢头。"这些词句不但写出园景层次，有空间感和声感，同时高柳、杏梢，又都把人们视线引向仰观。文学家最敏感，我们造园者应向他们学习。至于"一丘藏曲折，缓步百跻攀"，则又皆留心俯视所致。因此园林建筑物的顶，假山的脚，水口，树梢，都不能草率从事，要着意安排。山际安亭，水边留矶，是能引人仰观、俯观的方法。

中国园林妙在含蓄，一山一石，耐入寻味。立峰是一种抽象雕刻品，美人峰细看才象，九狮山亦然。奈何今天有许多好心肠的人，惟恐游者不了解，水池中装了人工大鱼，熊猫馆前站着泥塑熊猫，如做着大广告，与含蓄两字背道而驰，失去了中国园林的精神所在，真太煞风景。过去有些园名，如寒碧山庄、梅园、网师园，都可顾名思义，园内的特色是白皮松、梅、水。尽人皆知的西湖十景，更是佳例。亭榭之额真是赏景的说明书。拙政园的荷风四面亭，人临其境，即无荷风，亦觉风在其中，发人遐思。而对联文字之隽永，书法之美妙。更令人一唱三叹，徘徊不已。镇江焦山顶的别峰庵，为郑板桥读书处，小斋三间，一庭花树，门联写着"室雅无须大；花香不在多"。游者见到，顿觉心怀舒畅，亲切地感到景物宜人，博得人人称好，游罢个个传诵。

园林中曲与直是相对的,要曲中寓直,灵活应用。曲直自如。画家讲画树,要无一笔不曲,斯理至当。曲桥、曲径、曲廊,本来在交通意义上,是由一点到另一点而设置的。园林中两侧都有风景,随直曲折一下,使行者左右顾盼有景,信步其间使距程延长,趣味加深。由此可见,曲本直生,重在曲折有度。有些曲桥,定要九曲,既不临水面(园林桥一般要低于两岸,有凌波之意),生硬屈曲。行桥宛若受刑,其因在于不明此理(上海豫园前九曲桥即坏例)。

造园在选地后,就要因地制宜,突出重点,作为此园之特征,表达出预想的境界。北京圆明园,我说它是"因水成景,借景西山",园内景物皆因水而筑,招西山入园,终成"万园之园"。无锡寄畅园为山麓园,景物皆面山而构,纳园外山景于预园内。网师园以水为中心。殿春簃一院虽无水,西南角凿冷泉,贯通全园水脉,有此一眼,绝处逢生,终不脱题。新建东部,设计上既背固有设计原则,且复无水,遂成僵局,是事先对全园未作周密的分析,不加思索而造成的。

紧凑不觉其大,游无倦意,宽绰不觉局促,览之有物,故以静、动观园,有缩地扩基之妙。而大胆落墨,小心收拾(画家语),更为要谛,使宽处可容走马,密处难以藏针(书家语)。故颐和园有烟波浩渺之昆明湖,复有深居山间的谐趣园,于此可悟消息。造园有法而无式。在于人们的巧妙运用其规律。计成所说的"因借(因地制宜,借景)",就是法。《园冶》一书终未列式。苏州网师园是公认为小园极则,无旱船、大桥、大山、建筑物尺度略小,数量适可而止,亭亭当当,象一个小园格局。反之,狮子林增添了大船,与水面不称,不伦不类,就是不"得体"。

古代园林张灯夜游是一件大事,屡见诗文,但张灯是盛会,许多名贵之灯是临时悬挂的,张后即移藏,非永久固定于一地。灯也是园林一部分,其品类与悬挂亦如屏联一样,皆有定格,大小形式各具特征。现在有些园林为了适应夜游,都装上电灯,往往破坏园林风格,正如宜兴善卷洞一样,五色缤纷,宛或餐厅,几不知其为洞穴,要还我自然。苏州狮子林在亭的戗角头装灯,甚是触目。对古代建筑也好,园林也好,名胜也好,应该审慎一些,不协调的东西少强加于它。

➢ 素材 2. Western Reactions to the Chinese Gardens

(By Maggie Keswick. The Chinese Garden: History, Art and Architecture, Harvard University Press, Cambridge, Massachusetts, 2003)

When the first descriptions of Chinese gardens reached Europe in the eighteenth century, they started a revolution in taste. Until then, ever since the Egyptians first laid out pleasure gardens on the banks of the Nile, the gardens of the West had been based on straight lines and rectangles. Versailles, of course, was the most extreme example of this approach: at ground level the parterres might seem a little confusing, but from the high windows above all was revealed in perfect clarity with each pattern on the left balanced by its like on the right. Water, which in nature seeps and winds, was everywhere contained and either appeared fixed and static, like very rectangular mirrors laid out on the landscape, or sprouted from the mouths of mermaids and dolphins.

The first complete description of a Chinese garden was published in Paris in 1749, in a letter from Father Attiret, one of several Jesuits whom the Qianlong Emperor employed as painters to his court in Peking. For this emperor, landscaping was an obsessive passion. No sooner was one layout finished than he would start on another, and gradually several old Imperial gardens, as well as uncultivated and agricultural land, were absorbed into his domain. The result was a vast complex of lakes and palaces collectively known as "the Garden of Pure Brightness", or Yuan Ming Yuan. It was one of the most fantastic pleasure gardens ever built on earth.

For us today, the idea of an irregularly planned garden is familiar enough. To Father Attiret it was a revelation. His letter describes how

clear streams wound—seemingly as they willed—through gentle valleys
hidden from each other by charming hills. On the slopes, as if by chance,
plum and willow trees grew in profusion and through them paths mean-
dered with the line of the land ornamented all along with little pavilions
and grottoes. The streams themselves were edged with different pieces of
rock, some jutting out, some receding, but 'plac'd with so much art that
you would take it to be the work of nature. For what was so intriguing
was that the whole exquisite park was every bit as manmade as the landscapes of Le Nôtre: Only in this case the Art of the whole endeavor lay in
concealing, completely, any signs of the artificial. So Father Attiret continues,

> in some parts the water is wide, in others narrow; here it ser-
> pentizes, and there spreads away, as if it was really pushed off by the
> hills and rocks. The banks are sprinkled with flowers which rise up
> even thro' the hollows of the rockworks, as if they have been pro-
> duced there naturally.

Every valley had its own pleasure house—each one different, each filled
with its own collection of antiquities, books, and objects of virtu. And link-
ing these pavilions over the streams were the zigzag bridges which, if
stretched out straight, would have measured over two hundred meters in
length. On such bridges 'as afford the most engaging prospects' there were
little gazebos, in which people could rest themselves, while, below them, the
streams ran on until they met together to form wide lakes and waterways.
One of these were nearly five miles round, but what was the most charming
thing of all, is an island or rock in the middle of the sea, rais'd in a natural
and rustic matter; about six feet above the surface of the water. On this

rock there is a little palace, which, however, contains a hundred different apartments. It has four fronts and is built with inexpressible beauty and taste. The sight of it strikes one with admiration. From it you have a view of all the palaces, scattered at proper distances around the shores of the sea; all the hills, that terminate about it; all the small rivers, which tend thither, either to discharge their waters into it, or to receive them from it; all the bridges, either at the mouth or ends of these rivulets; all the pavilions, and triumphal arches, that decorate any of these bridges; and all the groves, that are planted to separate and screen the different palaces.

The irregularity of the Emperor's garden was not due to any lack of skill in the art of forming straight lines and right angles. In Peking, Father Attiret noticed that the street plan of the city itself, the great Palace, the Courts of Justice, and homes of 'the better sort of people' were all arranged with the strictest regard to geometric order. For many commentators, the orderly succession of rooms and courtyards in Chinese domestic architecture have often been seen as an expression of the Chinese ideal of harmonious social relationships: formal, decorous, regular and clearly defined.

This special respect for the landscape had a philosophical basis. Side by side with the Confucian emphasis on man in society, a totally different view of the world, and how to live in it, had grown up in China. The people who had formulated its doctrines were known as Terrorists, and they looked on man not as the measure of all things, but as an inseparable part of the great universe in which he existed. They sought to discover how this universe worked, and removed themselves from involvement in worldly concerns. Rejecting the Confucian's fine distinctions, they believed in the fundamental unity of all things. To them, book learning and intellectual thought were inferior too receptive and intuitive knowledge. And rather than actively working towards improving the world, they believed that all would be well so long as things were left to run their natural course.

When Father Attiret felt obliged to explain his enthusiasm for Chinese gardens, however, he did so only on aesthetic grounds, claiming that 'all is in good taste'. The gardens have conveyed their own message to him, as they were meant to do, through the senses rather than the mind. Although he may not have understood their philosophical background, his descriptions still manage to suggest the richness of meanings inherent in the Chinese garden as well as something of their extraordinary magic—the senses, which is not lost upon further acquaintance, of being transported to a fairy landscape quite unlike any other on earth. This is not just a fanciful conceit.

➢ 注释

Versailles　凡尔赛

seep　vi.（＋adv. / prep.）（尤指液体）渗；渗透

meander　vi.（＋adv. / prep.）（河流、道路等）蜿蜒而行；迂回曲折

grotto　n.（吸引人的）岩洞，洞穴

Le Nôtre　勒诺特尔，17 世纪法国巴黎的宫廷园林设计世家，其中，André Le Nôtre 法国国王路易十四的首席园林设计师，设计建造了凡尔赛宫，被誉为“皇家造园师与造园师之王”。

virtu　n. 艺术品爱好，古董；

gazebo　n. 瞭望台，露台

rustic　adj. 乡村的，质朴的

thither　adv. 到那边，到那方

stucco　n.（不可数）（涂墙壁或天花板用的）粉饰灰泥

➢ 练习

1. What principles should a Chinese garden designer follow according to Professor CHEN Congzhou? What examples did he use to support his

ideas?

2. Why did the first descriptions of Chinese gardens start a revolution in Europe? Explain the phenomenon on both aesthetic and philosophical grounds.

五、现代回声

> **背景知识**

　　普利兹建筑奖每年都表彰一位在世的建筑师,表彰他们在建筑设计中表现出的才智、想象力和责任感,以及通过建筑艺术对建筑环境和人性做出持久而杰出的贡献。该奖目光犀利,下手精准,从第一届得主菲利普·约翰逊(1979 年)开始,到凯文·罗奇(1982 年)、丹下健三(1987 年)、雷姆·库哈斯(2000 年),它勾勒出了一条影响深远的现代主义和后现代主义的建筑思潮脉络。因为获奖作品强大的说服力强,普利兹奖从创建至今不到半个世纪,已是建筑界公认的至高奖项。

　　第一位获得该奖的中国人是华裔设计师贝聿铭,1983 年。第一位获得该奖的中国本土建筑设计师是王澍,2012 年。王澍个性不羁,虽已获得好些颇有分量的国内外奖项,专业名声却毁誉参半。例如他将工作室命名为"业余工作室",意在"强调自由比准则有更高的价值"。他曾说,"我们传统的文化被彻底地摧毁了,……这个城市所有的和中国传统的一切都会彻底的铲平,剩下了几个像文物一样的保护点,剩下的东西放在博物馆里。"从评审团评议词可以看出,普利兹奖的评委显然是认同他保护传统文化和历史环境的尝试和努力的。

Jury Citations for WANG Shu, the 2012 Laureate

The architecture of the 2012 Pritzker Prize Laureate Wang Shu, opens new horizons while at the same time resonates with place and memory. His buildings have the unique ability to evoke the past, without making di-

rect references to history. Born in 1963 and educated in China, Wang Shu's architecture is exemplary in its strong sense of cultural continuity and re-invigorated tradition. In works undertaken by the office he founded with his partner and wife Lu Wenyu, Amateur Architecture Studio, the past is literally given new life as the relationship between past and present is explored. The question of the proper relation of present to past is particularly timely, for the recent process of urbanization in China invites debate as to whether architecture should be anchored in tradition or should look only toward the future. As with any great architecture, Wang Shu's work is able to transcend that debate, producing an architecture that is timeless, deeply rooted in its context and yet universal.

Wang Shu's buildings have a very rare attribute—a commanding and even, at times, monumental presence, while functioning superbly and creating a calm environment for life and daily activities. The History Museum at Ningbo is one of those unique buildings that while striking in photos, is even more moving when experienced. The museum is an urban icon, a well-tuned repository for history and a setting where the visitor comes first. The richness of the spatial experience, both in the exterior and interior is remarkable. This building embodies strength, pragmatism and emotion all in one.

Wang Shu knows how to embrace the challenges of construction and employ them to his advantage. His approach to building is both critical and experimental. Using recycled materials, he is able to send several messages on the careful use of resources and respect for tradition and context as well as give a frank appraisal of technology and the quality of construction today, particularly in China. Wang Shu's works that use recycled building materials, such as roof tiles and bricks from dismantled walls, create rich textural and tactile collages. Working in collaboration with construction workers, the outcome sometimes has an element of unpredictability, which in his case, gives the buildings a freshness and spontaneity.

In spite of his age, young for an architect, he has shown his ability to work successfully at various scales. The Xiangshan Campus of China Academy of Arts in Hangzhou is like a small town, providing a setting for learning and living for students, professors and staff. The exterior and interior connections between buildings and private and public spaces provide a rich environment where an emphasis on livability prevails. He is also capable of creating buildings on an intimate scale, such as the small exhibition hall or pavilions inserted into the fabric of the historic center of Hangzhou. As in all great architecture, he does this with a master's naturalness, making it look as if it were an effortless exercise.

He calls his office Amateur Architecture Studio, but the work is that of a virtuoso in full command of the instruments of architecture—form, scale, material, space and light. The 2012 Pritzker Architecture Prize is given to Wang Shu for the exceptional nature and quality of his executed work, and also for his ongoing commitment to pursuing an uncompromising, responsible architecture arising from a sense of specific culture and place.

➤ **注释**

resonate   vi. 共鸣,共振

exemplary　adj. 典型的,示范的

anchor　vt.（sth. /sb. in/to sth.）使扎根;使基于

repository　n. 学识渊博的人;智囊;知识宝典

appraisal　n. 评价;估价;估计;鉴定

collage　n. 拼贴艺术;拼贴画

virtuoso　n. 技艺超群的人;(尤指)演奏家

➤ **练习**

Please translate the following sentence into Chinese.

1. The architecture of Wang Shu opens new horizons while at the same time resonates with place and memory.

2. Wang Shu's work is able to transcend that debate, producing an architecture that is timeless, deeply rooted in its context and yet universal.

3. Wang Shu's works that use recycled building materials, such as roof tiles and bricks from dismantled walls, create rich textural and tactile collages.

4. He calls his office Amateur Architecture Studio, but the work is that of a virtuoso in full command of the instruments of architecture—form, scale, material, space and light.

第八章　中　医

一、词源梳理

中文的"医"是会意字,《说文》解释为:"盛弓弩矢器也。"从"殹"(yī),从酉(yǒu),"殹",治病时的扣击声。"酉",用以医疗的酒。医,作为动词有治疗、治愈之意,作为名词则是治病之人。

"药"则是形声字,从艸,乐声。其本义是治病的物品,即药物、药材。中国古代的药一般是植物,故从艸,但草木虫石谷皆可入药,即五药。"药"也可泛指能使人改过迁善,有益身心的东西,如"药石之言"就是劝人改过的话。

《国语》中说:"上医医国,其次疾人",后世将其发展为"上医医国,中医医人,下医医病"。可见中国古代有将医术与其它学识贯通的倾向,具体到治病,也是将人看作一个整体,头疼医头的治疗理念是中国古代医疗思想所不取的。

英语中的"doctor"词源来自拉丁语"doctus",其本意为教师。作为"行医者"的用法虽散见于中世纪英语中,却到十六世纪晚期才正式确立。"Medicine"的词源也可追溯至拉丁语,意为"治愈"。从词源上看起来,西方古代的"doctor"也涵义广泛,但西方医生的专业化却很早就露出了端倪了,在医生之中又细分出了着重于内科的"physician"、着重于外科的"surgeon",以及专门看牙齿的"dentist"。

二、引导阅读

➢ 背景知识

屠呦呦,1930 年 12 月出生,浙江宁波人,1955 年北京医学院药学系毕业后,分配到中国中医科学院中药研究所工作至今。中国中医科学院终身研究员、首席研究员,中国中医科学院青蒿素研究中心主任。

屠呦呦的科学贡献是发现青蒿素。她从中医古籍中得到启迪,改变青蒿传统提取工艺,创建了低温提取青蒿抗疟有效部位的方法,成为青蒿素发现的关键性突破,从此带动了全国对青蒿提取物的抗疟研究;她和她的团队最先从青蒿抗疟有效部位中分离得到抗疟有效单一成分"青蒿素";率先开展"醚中干"、青蒿素单体的临床试验,证实了其治疗疟疾的临床有效性;并与合作单位共同确定青蒿素的化学结构,为其衍生物开发提供了条件。青蒿素是与已知抗疟药化学结构、作用机制完全不同的新化合物,标志着人类抗疟药物发展的新方向。从上世纪 90 年代起,世界卫生组织(WHO)推荐以青蒿素类为主的复合疗法(ACT)作为治疗疟疾的首选方案,现已为全球疟疾流行地区所广泛使用。据 WHO《2015 年世界疟疾报告》,由于采取有效防治措施,包括 ACT 的治疗,2000 年全球疟疾发病 2.14 亿例、死亡 73.8 万人,到 2015 年发病率、死亡率分别下降 37% 和 60%,挽救了大约 590 万名儿童的生命。

屠呦呦及其团队因研制青蒿素获得多项国内重要奖励。2011 年屠呦呦因为"发现了青蒿素,一种治疗疟疾的药物,在全球,特别是发展中国家,挽救了数百万人的生命",获美国拉斯克临床医学奖;2015 年 10 月,屠呦呦又以"从中医药古典文献中获取灵感,先驱性地发现青蒿素,开创疟疾治疗新方法",获得诺贝尔生理学或医学奖。

下面是屠呦呦 2011 年 10 月发表于《自然》的论文《来自中医药的礼物——青蒿素的发现》的节选,读者从中可以看出这位诺奖得主对于科学以及中国传统医学的态度。

The discovery of artemisinin(qinghaosu) and gifts from Chinese medicine

—— By Youyou TU

Joseph Goldstein has written in this journal that creation(through invention)and revelation(through discovery)are two different routes to advancement in the biomedical sciences. In my work as a phytochemist,particularly during the period from the late 1960s to the 1980s, I have been fortunate enough to travel both routes.

I graduated from the Beijing Medical University School of Pharmacy in 1955. Since then,I have been involved in research on Chinese herbal medicine in the China Academy of Chinese Medical Sciences(previously known as the Academy of Traditional Chinese Medicine). From 1959 to 1962,I was released from work to participate in a training course in Chinese medicine that was especially designed for professionals with backgrounds in Western medicine. The 2. 5-year training guided me to the wonderful treasure to be found in Chinese medicine and toward understanding the beauty in the philosophical thinking that underlies a holistic view of human beings and the universe.

Discovery of antimalarial effect of qinghao

Malaria,caused by *Plasmodium falciparum* (恶性疟原虫),has been a life-threatening disease for thousands of years. After the failure of international attempts to eradicate malaria in the 1950s,the disease rebounded, largely due to the emergence of parasites resistant to the existing antimalarial drugs of the time,such as chloroquine(氯喹). This created an urgent need for new antimalarial medicines. In 1967,a national project against malaria was set up in China under the leadership of the Project 523 office. My institute quickly became involved in the project and appointed me to be the head of amalaria research group comprising bothphytochemical and pharmacological researchers. Our group of young investigators started working on the extraction and isolation of constituents with possible anti-malarial activities from Chinese herbal materials.

During the first stage of our work, we investigated more than 2,000 Chinese herb preparations and identified 640 hits that had possible antimalarial activities. More than 380 extracts obtained from 200 Chinese herbs were evaluated against a mouse model of malaria. However, progress was not smooth, and no significant results emerged easily.

The turning point came when an *Artemisia annua* L.(黄花蒿) extract showed a promising degree of inhibition against parasitegrowth. However, this observation was not reproducible in subse quent experiments and appeared to be contradictory to what was recorded in the literature. Seeking an explanation, we carried out an intensive review of the literature. The only reference relevant to use of qinghao(the Chinese name of Artemisia annua L.) for alleviating malaria symptoms appeared in Ge Hong's *A Handbook of Prescriptions for Emergencies*: "A handful of qinghao immersed with 2 liters of water, wring out the juice and drink it all". This sentence gave me the idea that the heating involved in the conventional extraction step we had used might have destroyed the active components, and that extraction at a lower temperature might be necessary to preserve anti-malarial activity. Indeed, we obtained much better activity after switching to a lower- temperature procedure.

We subsequently separated the extract into its acidic and neutral portions and, at long last, on 4 October, 1971, we obtained a non-toxic, neutral extract that was 100% effective against parasitemia in mice infected with Plasmodium berghei(伯氏疟原虫) and in monkeys infected with Plasmodium cynomolgi(食蟹猴疟原虫). This finding represented the breakthrough in the discovery of artemisinin.

...

Other gifts from Chinese medicine

Artemisinin, with its unique sesquiterpene lactone created by phytochemical evolution, is a true gift from old Chinese medicine. The route to the discovery of artemisinin was short compared with those of many other phytochemical discoveries in drug development. But this is not the only instance in which the wisdom of Chinese medicine has borne fruit. Clinical studies in China have shown that arsenic, an ancient drug used in Chinese medicine, is an effective and relatively safe drug in the treatment of acute promyelocytic leukemia(APL). Arsenic trioxide now is considered the first —line treatment for APL, exerting its therapeutic effect by promoting the degradation of promyelocytic leukemia protein(PML), which drives the growth of APL cells. Huperzine A(石杉碱甲), an effective agent for treatment of memory dysfunction, is a novel acetylcholinesterase inhibitor derived from the Chinese medicinal herb Huperzia serrata, and a derivative of huperzine A is now undergoing clinical trails in Europe and the United States for the treatment of Alzheimer's disease.

However, the use of a single herb for the treatment of a specific disease is rare in Chinese medicine. Generally, the treatment is determined by a holistic characterization of the patient's syndrome, and a prescription comprises a group of herbs specifically tailored to the syndrome. The rich correlations between syndromes and prescriptions have fueled the advancement of Chinese medicine for thousands of years.

Progress in the therapy of cardiovascular(心血管) and cerebrovascular (脑血管)diseases has also received gifts from Chinese medicine. A key therapeutic concern for Chinese medicine is the principle of activating blood circulation to remove blood stasis, and there are several examples of this principle in action in Western medicine. Compounds derived from Chinese medicinal products—the molecules chuangxiongol and paeoniflorin—have been tested for their efficacy in preventing restenosis after percutaneous coronary intervention (PCI). A multi-center, randomized, double-blind, placebo-controlled trial (335 patients, 6 months) showed that restenosis rates were significantly reduced by the medicine as compared with the placebo(26.0% versus 47.2%). Evidence supporting the therapeutic value of related strategies from Chinese medicine aimed at activating blood circulation has been obtained in the treatment of ischemic diseases and in the management of myocardial ischemiareperfusion injury.

Also in relation to cardiovascular disease, a new discipline called biomechanopharmacology(生物力药理学) aims at combining the pharmacological effects of Chinese medicine with the biomechanical properties of flowing blood. The joint application of exercise (to increase the shear stress of blood flow) with extracts from shenlian, another Chinese medicine, shows promise for the prevention of atherosclerosis. And recent reports have begun to provide a glimpse into the molecular mechanisms that account for the effects of Chinese remedies. For example, a recent study identified a potential mechanism to account for the effect of salvianolic acid B, a compound from the root of Salvia miltiorrhiza(丹参), in combination with increased shear stress, on the functions of endothelial cells.

The examples cited here represent only a sliver of the gifts or potential gifts Chinese medicine has to offer. It is my dream that Chinese medicine will help us conquer life-threatening diseases worldwide, and that people across the globe will enjoy its benefits for health promotion.

➤ 注释

Joseph Goldstein:约瑟夫 · 戈尔斯坦教授是世界第一流的<u>生物学家</u>和

医学家,诺贝尔生物医学奖得主,美国科学院院士。因在血脂生成和调控机理上的突出贡献,他获得了 1985 年诺贝尔生物医学奖。

Phytochemist　n. 植物化学家

Malaria　n. 疟疾

Parasites　n. 寄生虫

Sliver　n. 裂片,薄片

> 练习

1. What is the author's attitude toward Traditional Chinese Medicine?

三、阅读与比较

> 背景知识

中国传统医药在近两千年的时间里为中国人民的生存和发展做出了巨大的贡献,然而自明末清初西学东渐,西方医学渐渐进入中国人的视野,鸦片战争之后,震惊于西方船坚炮利的中国人痛定思痛,开始学习西方文化,反思传统文化之不足,许多中国文化遗产遭到否定,中医便是其中之一。中医存废几度成为政府和民众的议题,关于中医之效用至今仍争论不休,各种网络平台上的中医黑和中医粉势同水火。本部分选取了三段材料供读者阅读,了解中医的历史,思考中国传统医药的价值。

本部分第一篇文章来自 1935 年 7 月的《北华捷报和最高法庭与领事公报》。《北华捷报》是上海第一份英文报纸,被誉为在华的"英国官报",创办于 1851 年,1951 年停刊,是上海出版时间最长、影响最大的英文报纸,也是近代中国历史最长、影响最大的英文报纸。该报馆关注中国局势和上海发展,对中国社会对方方面面都有很多报道。这里选取的报道主要聚焦于雷士德医学研究院关于中医的研究发现,这座建立于 1932 年的研究院以英国旅沪著名建筑师、地产商和慈善家亨利·雷士德的遗产建造并命名,设备和理念在当时都遥遥领先,曾有很多著名的生理学家、病理学家和营养学家在那里工作。1954 年被上海市人民政府接管。该院原址被上海市人民政府列为上海市优秀历史建筑,现为上海医药工业研究院即中国医药工业研究总院所在地。这篇报道介绍了该研究院对于中医所做的大量科学研究,并指出传统中医药中作为药材使用的驴皮、动物器官以及植物的叶子和果实等的确包含有益人类身心的成分,建立于数千年对于自然界动植物的观察经验基础上的传统医药值得学习和研究,因为我们和古人一样要面对疾病带来的生死考验。

第二篇材料的作者为已故中医泰斗邓铁涛 2000 年发表于《新中医》上的论文节选。邓铁涛出身中医世家,生于 1916 年,逝于 2019 年,这位百岁老人见证了近代以来中医的沉浮,对于中医的理论和临床实践都作出了杰出的贡献。此文是他关于中医面临的困境及未来发展的思考。

第三篇材料来自德国慕尼黑大学医学史教授 Paul U. Unschuld,中文名文树德,他对中医学和中医史皆有独到的研究,1984 年以来一直担任东方医学国际研究会主席,他翻译了《黄帝内经》等很多中医典籍,对于中医的过去和未来有很多思考,并形诸文字。此处选取的材料来自他的著作《何为医药:中西的疗愈路径》(What Is Medicine——Western and Eastern Approaches to Healing),这段材料讲述了中医在近代以来没落和重新振兴的历史轨迹。

➢ 素材 1. Ancient Chinese Medicine Studied

It may seem to many that the healing use made of donkey skin, sheep eyes, deer's horn, dog's brain, odd herbs, etc. , all interwoven as they are in folk-lore and demonology, is just so much empty Chinese superstition, and that it is unfortunate that such great faith is placed in such absurd remedies.

However, an extensive survey now being undertaken by Dr. Bernard Read,head of the Division of Physiological Sciences and his associates at the Henry Lester Institute of Medical Research may greatly diminish popular skepticism.

It is the attitude of the Lester Institute that before today's medical science of the western world can be imposed on the Chinese people, due regard must be given to the empirical observations which form the basis of the old Chinese medical practice.

Reason has suggested that when certain therapeutic practices have been in constant use for a great many centuries not only in China but in India and with no apparent relationship in the still more ancient civilizations, as revealed in old manuscripts, it is at least likely that some real benefit is derived.

Seek Rational Basis

The work of Dr. Bernard Read with his associates and staff is to put such empirical practices upon a rational basis by employing the highly technical skill of modern workers and a more fundamental knowledge of the principle involved, to evaluate them, by new standards which emphasize improper balances, deficiencies, and faulty assimilation, and thereby to find fresh avenues for research, which may yield results of value in modern medicine.

Dr. Read has been working this field for thirty years in China, and has been rewarded by his success in chaulmoogra oil and ephedrine first produced in his laboratories in Peking, among his other important contributions to medical science. Now working under the excellent faculties of the Lester Institute in Shanghai where he came two years ago to head the division of physiological sciences, more valuable data on Chinese Materia Medica is being contributed to modern medicine. There is now in progress an investigation into the chemical composition and vitamin content of a tremendous variety of local Chinese drugs and foods.

Boiled Donkey Skin

The phenomenally widespread use in China of boiled down donkey skin, called"Ah-Chiao", as a blood regenerator, and internal styptic, and a general nutritive for weak people, especially who suffer from tuberculosis, has led to an investigation into its particular character both chemical and physiological. Dr. T. G. Ni finds that it contains a large amount of glycine(甘氨酸), cystine(胱氨酸), lysine(赖氨酸), argenine(银氨酸) and histidine(组氨酸). Administered orally it improves the calcium nitrogen absorption and raises the calcium level of the blood. This Ah-Chiao used intravenously was found to be effective in restoring a depressed circulation after hemorrhage(出血) and shock. Further work is proceeding on its beneficial effects in muscular atrophy. In Hangchow last year there was a quarter-million dollars trade of the donkey skin in one store alone.

It has been shown by dietary surveys that large numbers of people live on deficient diet such as may lead to latent or subacute scurvy. In old medical practice, such symptoms as weakness of the knees and general lassitude were treated with numerous remedies which may depend for their action upon the presence of vitamin C. Hence one hundred and twenty Chinese foods and drugs purchased in Shanghai market as they appeared for sale in ripe condition and also collected in the country close to Shanghai, have been subjected to a chemical study with a view to ascertaining the vitamin C content. The results are given in value of Pumels report written by Yuoh-Fong Chi and Dr. Bernard Read.

Among the citrus fruits, pumelo was found to have the highest vitamin C content, being superior to grapefruit and all of the various types of oranges. Many sorts of leaves which are eaten regularly and used medically such as dandelion, mulberry, nasturtium, popular, shepherd's purse and amaranth, yielded interesting data. Green amaranth, little known by foreigners, grows in great profusion in the country, and has been found to have a very high vitamin C content and to be superior to spinach in its content of iron and calcium. The high vitamin content of willow and popular leaves and shepherd's purse suggests good reason for their use in ancient medicine.

For the past 18 months the problem of preparing a substitute for cow's milk has engaged the attention of Dr Eric Reid. He has successfully prepared a spray-dried powder from soy beans and egg yolk supplemented with sugars and salts, which is free from the objectionable taste and odour of the soya bean. It has satisfactory keeping properties and is perfectly miscible with water. Its effect on growth was compared with that of cow's milk powder, and in general soy-egg powder milk produced a more favorable growth response. When fed to animals it produced the bones free from all signs of rickets and containing a normal percentage of ash. This soy bean egg milk is very inexpensive to produce and promises to be of much use especially in China infant diet.

Ancient Medicine

Professor Burnard Read states that ancient medicine in China needs considerable clarification before forward or backward-looking people are able to estimate it at its true worth. As an historical record it is of worth to anthropologist, the naturalist and the physiologist. Dissected from its folklore, demonology and outworn philosophic theories, it has a vast amount of honest observation of Chinese fauna and flora, their habitat preparation and uses as foods and remedies in treatment of disease, suggesting important path of research.

In China's great classic the Pen T'sao Kang Mu, common food staffs include such extremely toxic seeds as the bastard anise and poisonous tetrodent fish, and drugs include oranges, gelatin and liquorice. Thus for practical purposes no distinction need be made between foods and drugs. They all require scientific identification before the usual laboratory studies are undertaken. This function is performed by the materia medica labora-tory where records accumulated during the past twenty five years are kept, aided by the works of an experienced translator of old Chinese medi-cal literature. These old volumes embrace the whole field of Chinese natu-ral history, a remarkable record of observation for thousands of years. With the development of natural history workers and museums in China and the Lester Institute plans to have this laboratory act as a clearing house, when the identification of crude materials can be made more readily than at present.

Investigation Procedure

Dr. Read feels that apart from its applied value, Chinese medicine needs a more intelligent and sympathetic understanding on the part of modern medicine. It's universally believed in and followed by the Chinese country folk. There is need in Asia for a widespread application of scien-tific methods to enable people to evaluate ancient medicine at its true worth, and to heighten appreciation of modern ideas in medicine in all of its relationships.

The procedure adopted follows the general plan of (a)finding the sci-entific identity of the material, (b)chemical extraction for the study of pure principles, (c)physiological studies of the action of these pure prod-ucts, (d)toxicity values and untoward effects. (e)graduation of the dose, particularly for human consumption and (f)trial in the clinic.

Nutrition as a subject is being developed as a study from infancy to full development and sustenance of the adult. Using Chinese materials, an infant food is being prepared. The natural food staffs are being studied for their vitamin content to show their ability to promote growth and protect against disease.

Ordinary and special dietary are being studied for their caloric content, proportions of fats, carbohydrates and proteins, and essential salts. Apart from the knowledge to be gained of the requirements of the normal individual, there should be a flood or light upon some of China's deficiency diseases and nutritional problems which arise in times of farming blood and other national disasters.

Use of Animal Tissues

"It is of interest to note," states Dr Bernard Read in his report on "The Newer Pharmacology and Ancient Medicine", "that the modern medicine of the 1909 British Pharmacopoeia only included nine substances of animal origin. And those nearly all, quite innocuous things like lard and wax. While modern science is turning to liver, stomach, vitamin A from the eye, adrenalin etc. , it's remarkable to find the use of so many animal tissues in ancient medicine.

In his recently published report mentioned above, Dr. Read presents a table showing twenty-six parts of six domestic animals used in old Chinese medicine. These animals include the cow, horse, pig, chicken, sheep and dog.

When bitten by a mad dog, the brain of the same animal is applied to the wound. This suggests a connection with modern Pasteur treatment and is worthy of investigation.

The velvet horn of the Skia deer and other species is taken as a drug in powder form and is very highly regarded by the Chinese. Recent studies by Russian scientists show that the male sex hormone is present.

The iris and lens of the ship's eyes were given for dimness of vision and conjunctivitis. The eyes of the hawk, parrott and mackerel were administered for night blindness. Recently Wald has isolated vitamin A from the iris of sheep, pigs, cattle, and frogs.

In old Chinese medicine, pig's liver was recommended for night blindness, beri-beri, emancipation etc. , and has fairly recently been found to be rich in vitamin A, B, C, D and E. A great many instances of this sort are cited. Shepherd's purse is given as an excellent example of a medical herb cast aside for its apparent lack of potential principals, which has been shown to be moderately rich in three of the vitamins and well justifies the old Chinese use of it for a number of maladies.

Old Remedies Efficacious

Native remedies claiming to have power to increase human fertility are often associated with magical ideas. But Dr. Read believes that in view of the increasing volume of recent scientific work in this field there is hope that information may be forthcoming whereby these claims can be properly evaluated.

Some people suffer from a deficiency of iodine. Many centuries ago in China seaweeds were used in the treatment of goiter. It is now believed that these old remedies were often quite efficacious.

Dr. Read concluded by saying that further extensive reference might be made to a host of other remedies but that enough has been cited to show that science may progress by looking backward as well as forward, that probably the most suggestive parts of progress may be gained by studying the records of old empirical medicine, that the scientists needs more than any other to keep an open mind regarding the claims of ancient medicine, so that with the aid of modern knowledge and modern technique an unprejudiced study may be made of the customs of our forefathers, who however much they may have believed in demonology and false philosophical theories, were engaged in the same life and death struggle against disease.

In China there has been preserved for something between 30 and 50 centuries remarkably accurate records of human experience in the field of medicine. These records are not accumulations of divine intuitions but empirical findings, which up to the present have only been sifted with the very coarse sieve of last century science.

➤ 素材 2. 人类不能没有中医

中医中药是中华文化的瑰宝,是几千年来中华民族同疾病作斗争的伟大成就。中医药不仅是中华民族的宝贵文化,也是世界人民文化的精华。但这并不是所有中国人、甚至身为中医者所共识! 21 世纪已向我们走来,展望未来,我认为——人类不能没有中医。

最近美国洛杉矶加州大学东西医学中心许家杰教授在《99 澳门国际中医药学术大会论文集》上发表了《美国医学现状及发展的概况和若干思考》一文。读该文后深受启发,认为我的看法是符合世界医学的发展规律的,人类不能没有中医。

美国是当今世界医学的前沿代表,它的发展趋向值得我们研究。许氏文章认为,15 年来医学发生了很大的变化,称之为一场革命毫不为过。他说目前美国社会约有一亿人罹患各种慢性病,……大量的事实表明,仅采用封闭式的医院为主的生物医学模式来防治这些疾病,是难以减低其发病率和死亡率的。这些因素促使美国医学从过去以急性病,传染病,以住院开刀为主,正在转变为慢性病、身心疾病和老年病、退行性病,以诊治和预防保健为主。医院数量不断减少,以住院手术为主的医疗模式也正在向社会化的网络模式,包括家庭病房和家庭护理方面转变,医学的主要任务已不是诊治患病个体,而是转向保护健康群体,防患于未然。美国医学的这一变革,正是中医所长,中医药学、气功、保健运动(太极拳、八段锦、五禽戏之类)将是美国人民所最需要的医疗保健服务。可见钱学森所说世界医学要走中医之路是正确的推断。

许氏又说美国医疗费用的暴涨是引发医疗制度变革的主要原因。据统计 1996 年的全美医疗费用高达 1035.1 亿美元,占国民总产值的 14% 以上,预计到 2007 年的全美医疗费用高达 2 万亿元。……高涨的医疗费用虽然对促进现代医学模式的深入认识疾病的机理,提高疾病的诊治能力等方面起到重要作用,但也不能不看到昂贵的医疗费用并未有效地解决临床上存在的许多实际问题,尤其是对某些慢性病、老年疾病仍然一筹莫展。又说:"医疗费用的高涨,使得社会大众、国民经济和医疗保健制度和保险制度不堪重负,无医疗保险的人数超过四千多万人。"在美国无医疗保险的人,有病要自己掏钱,可不得了!

许教授的文章是世界医学最先进国家的医疗面貌的写照。反映了经济大国不堪负担,其庞大的医疗开支,值得深思。美国的出路何在?许教授说:"由于现代医学对慢性病的许多疑难病缺乏有效、简易和经济的治疗手段,以及某些西药治疗副作用多等问题,很多病人为求疗效,解除病痛,安全经济,不得不寻觅他医。……全美现有 35 个州和哥伦比亚特区批准针刺医疗活动。每年有 1 百万以上的患者接受针刺治疗,治疗人次达 1,000 万之多。目前从事针刺医师达 1 万多名,从事针刺的西医师约 3 千名。……以教授针灸和东方医学为主的学校高达 55 所。1998 年全美草药的销售额约达 35 亿美元。每年按摩的人数约 7,500 万人次,太极气功作为健身和防治疾病的运动,也越来越受到美国人的喜爱。"许教授身为美国名医,对中医有独到的认识,自学中医甚为勤奋。1992 年请我去加州大学医学院和他一起会诊疑难病人,施以中医药治法,疗效肯定,坚定了他搞中西医结合的信心,并以事实说服他的领导和同事,其后乃建成东西医学中心。该中心的求医者之多为该医院之冠。因为他是华裔,所以该中心不以中西命名,名为东西医学,亦统战之道也。该中心实行从临床医疗到预防康复,系列化和综合性治疗服务,成功地解决了许多西医棘手的疑难症和慢性病,取得了良好的社会效益和经济效益。1994 年开始,为该医学院 4 年级和 1 年级学生开展短期的试点教学,经过培训,大多数学生能应用中西医两法对病例进行思考和分析,提出治疗方案,并能进行一些简单的中医技能操作。受到学生的欢迎。许家杰教授建议设立以我的名字命名的奖学金,并由他资助,每年美金 500 元。这一奖项,在我校已颁发 7 年了,足见许教授对发展中医学的热心。

从上述可见,美国医学及其体制,是被称为当今世界最先进的,但从社会效益来衡量，并不理想，从经济角度去衡量，第一富国也叫承受不了！那么第三世界国家能走这样的路吗？世界人口已60亿，美国人口才2亿多，按美国的模式，人类的健康谁来保护呢？21世纪能有多少地方、多少人口能真正享受医疗保健的权利呢？我认为必须大力发展中医，推广中医，以简、便、廉、验的中医药造福于全人类，这是我们的职责。

> 素材 3. **What Is Medicine: Western and Eastern Approaches to Healing**

Scorn, Mockery, and Invectives for Chinese Medicine

In 1835, Peter Parker(1804—1888), an American missionary and physician, opened an ophthalmologic practice in Canton. The American Board of Commissioners for Foreign Missions had sent Peter Parker to save the souls of the Chinese. After a short introduction to his host country, he preferred to concentrate on saving their bodies, especially their eyes. There was a lot to do. Peter Parker did not have many practical tools in his bag that were superior to the healing of the Chinese. But his surgery was vastly different from anything in China. His interventions in the eye were extremely impressive. People lined up to see him. Peter Parker gave out numbers in an attempt to order the crowds. Soon, more medically trained missionaries came and lured the Chinese into their practices with the prospect of treatment of physical ills. They hoped to reroute them from there into their churches. Soon, the first Chinese were venturing to the United States to study this new medicine at its source. In the mid—1850s, the Briton Benjamin Hobson wrote a multi-volume introduction to Western science and medicine. Guan Maocai helped him translate it into Chinese. Hobson depicted a steam locomotive for the first time. He was the first to offer views into the interior of the body, never seen by the Chinese in such distinctness. He explained operations and the related instruments. All of this was previously unknown in China, yet it was immediately convincing. The medicine that used modern technology must be just as successful as modern technology. Putting airplanes into the sky was still to come. But military technology on land and sea had already made a great impression. And the locomotive was visible to all. Even if some peasants in the villages opposed the railroad, the medicine that appeared with this technology had to be just as successful. Hobson saw a fundamental difference and described it in his introduction for the Chinese readers: In Europe, research is done, because true knowledge lies in the future. In China, no research is done, because perfect knowledge is already available in ancient books. This was not completely true, but it captured the general tendencies. Europe's unbelievable enthusiasm in the nineteenth and early twentieth century to gain new knowledge by doing research and experiments had no parallel in China's own tradition. The cage of systematic correspondences had not yet opened up. And within that cage, no research could be established. Something had to change: this was clear to Chinese intellectuals by the end of the nineteenth century. The early attempt to buy certain Western technologies and use them for defense against the West failed miserably. The imperial system had reached its end. Two millennia of Chinese cultural tradition had reached their end. Thus, an ever greater number of Chinese reformers emerged. The Middle Kingdom was no longer a kingdom, nor was it in the middle. Countless associations of worried patriots were founded, where people thought about things, invited the most important Western thinkers, and asked them and themselves about the reasons for Western strength. The peak of this search came during and after World War I, when the imperial powers humiliated China. The decision to now uncompromisingly accept Western science and technology was brutal, but unavoidable. There was no difference of opinion on this between nationalists and communists. Western medicine went along with Western science. What scorn, what mockery, what invectives poured out of the reformers onto the Chinese healing tradition. Several authors and filmmakers at this time of awakening used Chinese medicine as a symbol of their fathers' and grandfathers' most decadent ways of thinking and put Chinese medicine at the center of their attacks on the structures that were now to be overcome. At the end of the 1920's, an impetuous and Chinese petition for a referendum was introduced to completely forbid tradition, effective immediately. It failed due to the resistance of vested interests, the chaotic domestic political situation during the civil war, and the Japanese invasion, but that did not help much. The decision makers, the reformers, trusted solely in modern Western medicine. They accused their own tradition of being partly responsible for China's illness.

Traditional Medicine in the PRC: Faith in Science

With the victory of the People's Liberation Army and the founding of the People's Republic of China(PRC)in 1949, Marxists made a decision about the future of medicine—adapted to the situation in China according to the thoughts of Mao. Since then, authorities have proceeded skillfully. The heritage of traditional medicine is cited, praised as the legacy of the people, and then undermined from the inside out. The roots and earth from which the tradition once pulled its strength were long since taken from the tree. But what was to be done with all that wood? Healers were still carving successful therapies out of it! But the interpretation was missing, which is not an easy thing to provide. Compromises had to be made. Memories of the old doctrines of yin-yang and the five agents were kept alive—— but from a distance! They were relativized as attempts of the ancestors to master the powers of nature with materialistic thinking. These were primitive attempts, but still attempts to leave behind the numinous and metaphysical, and to open oneself to materialism. The time of these attempts has passed. Marxism, regardless of its strain, trusts only modern science, pointing to the future. If science cannot explain everything today, then tomorrow or someday later it will. But that is still the goal one must aim for and slowly steer toward. And this is precisely the policy of the People's Republic of China. The old cage has opened up. From 1950 to 1975, commissions gutted the theoretical edifice and tally rebuilt it from the inside: set pieces from the past were put together carefully so that they no longer clashed with the new knowledge, with the reality of the new Western medicine. " The new building corresponds to modern thinking in its internal logic. The old, typically Chinese inductive thinking was exchanged for modern logic, the Western way of thinking. The great, multi-roomed, confusing, two-millennia-old cage of ideas was now turned into a cute little playpen, where nobody could get lost anymore. It was easy to handle. Tens of thousands of book chapters of heterogeneous contents, millions of knowledge-filled pages, now condensed into "overviews"—— booklets barely one or two centimeters thick. This is what remains of the theories of Chinese traditional medicine, after the lights that had conferred plausibility to them for two millennia were extinguished.

➢ 注释

demonology　n. 鬼神学

empirical　adj. 经验主义的,实证的

assimilation　n. 同化,吸收

chaulmoogra oil　大风子油

ephedrine　n. 麻黄素

styptic　adj. &n. 止血的;止血剂

atrophy　n. &v. 萎缩,虚脱

invective　n. &adj. 谩骂(的)

edifice　n. 大厦,大建筑物

tally　n. &v. 计算,记录

heterogeneous　adj. 混杂的,多种多样的

relativize　vt. 使相对化

Plausibility　n. 善辩,似真性

➢ 练习

1. Give a brief account of the history of TCM.

2. Compared with the West Medicine, what's the advantage and disadvantage of TCM?

四、拓展阅读

➢ 背景知识

本部分选取了两篇材料供读者作比较阅读。第一篇选自《史记·扁鹊仓公列传》中的扁鹊部分,司马迁在《史记》中为医者立传,可见其对于医者的看重,而扁鹊则是他所推崇的第一医家,《史记》中扁鹊的学医之路以及诸多医案反映了古代中国人对于医术以及医者的很多观念,对于今人了解中国医药的历史有不可低估的价值。第二篇英文材料选自耶鲁大学医学院舍温·努兰(Sherwin B. Nuland)的著作《西方名医列传》(Doctors—— The Biography of Medicine)第一章,是西方医学奠基人希波克拉底的传记,其中也提及了西方古代的医疗理念以及希波克拉底之前以及同时代的整体医疗状况。两传对照,读者可以细细品味中西方医术之源流,并思考中西医的不同发展路径及其背后原因。

➢ 素材 1.

扁鹊者,勃海郡郑人也,姓秦氏,名越人。少时为人舍长,舍客长桑君过,扁鹊独奇之,常谨遇之,长桑君亦知扁鹊非常人也。出入十余年,乃呼扁

鹊私坐，间与语曰："我有禁方，年老，欲传与公，公毋泄。"扁鹊曰："敬诺。"乃出其怀中药与扁鹊："饮是以上池之水三十日，当知物矣。"乃悉取其禁方书尽与扁鹊，忽然不见，殆非人也。扁鹊以其言饮药三十日，视见垣一方人。以此视病，尽见五藏症结，特以诊脉为名耳。为医或在齐，或在赵，在赵者名扁鹊。

当晋昭公时，诸大夫强而公族弱。赵简子为大夫，专国事。简子疾，五日不知人，大夫皆惧，于是召扁鹊。扁鹊入，视病，出。董安于问扁鹊，扁鹊曰："血脉治也，而何怪！昔秦穆公尝如此，七日而寤。今主君之病与之同，不出三日必见。"居二日半，简子寤。

其后扁鹊过虢，虢太子死。扁鹊至虢宫门下，问中庶子喜方者曰："太子何病，国中治穰过于众事？"中庶子曰："太子病血气不时，交错而不得泄，暴发于外，则为中害。精神不能止邪气，邪气畜积而不得泄，是以阳缓而阴急，故暴蹶而死。"扁鹊曰："其死何如时？"曰："鸡鸣至今。"曰："收乎？"曰："未也，其死未能半日也。""言臣齐勃海秦越人也，家在于郑，未尝得望精光，侍谒于前也。闻太子不幸而死，臣能生之。"中庶子曰："先生得无诞之乎？何以言太子可生也？臣闻上古之时，医有俞跗，治病不以汤液醴酒、镵石挢引、案扤毒熨，一拨见病之应，因五藏之输，乃割皮解肌，诀脉结筋，搦髓脑，揲荒爪幕，湔浣肠胃，漱涤五藏，练精易形。先生之方能若是，则太子可生也；不能若是，而欲生之，曾不可以告咳婴之儿。"终日，扁鹊仰天叹曰："夫子之为方也，若以管窥天，以郄视文。越人之为方也，不待切脉、望色、听声、写形，言病之所在。闻病之阳，论得其阴；闻病之阴，论得其阳。病应见于大表，不出千里，决者至众，不可曲止也。子以吾言为不诚，试入诊太子，当闻其耳鸣而鼻张，循其两股，以至于阴，当尚温也。"中庶子闻扁鹊言，目眩然而不瞚，舌挢然而不下，乃以扁鹊言入报虢君。

虢君闻之大惊，出见扁鹊于中阙，曰："窃闻高义之日久矣，然未尝得拜谒于前也。先生过小国，幸而举之，偏国寡臣幸甚。有先生则活，无先生则弃捐填沟壑，长终而不得反。"言未卒，因嘘唏服臆，魂精泄横，流涕长潸，忽忽承目夹，悲不能自止，容貌变更。扁鹊曰："若太子病，所谓尸厥者也。夫以阳入阴中,动胃缠缘,中经维络,别下于三焦、膀胱,是以阳脉下遂,阴脉上争,会气闭而不通,阴上而阳内行,下内鼓而不起,上外绝而不为使,上有绝阳之络,下有破阴之纽,破阴绝阳,色废脉乱,故形静如死状。太子未死也。夫以阳入阴支阑藏者生,以阴入阳支阑藏者死。凡此数事,皆五脏蹶中之时暴作也。良公取之,拙者疑殆。"扁鹊乃使弟子子阳砺针砥石,以取外三阳五会。有间太子苏。乃使子豹为五分之熨,以八减之齐和煮之,以更熨两胁下。太子起坐。更适阴阳,但服汤二旬而复故。故天下尽以扁鹊为能生死人。扁鹊曰:"越人非能生死人也。此自当生者,越人能使之起耳。"

扁鹊过齐,齐桓侯客之。入朝见,曰:"君有疾在腠理,不治将深。"桓侯曰:"寡人无疾。"扁鹊出,桓侯谓左右曰:"医之好利也,欲以不疾者为功。"后五日,扁鹊复见,曰:"君有疾在血脉,不治恐深。"桓侯曰:"寡人无疾。"扁鹊出,桓侯不悦。后五日,扁鹊复见,曰:"君有疾在肠胃闲,不治将深。"桓侯不应。扁鹊出,桓侯不悦。后五日,扁鹊复见,望见桓侯而退走。桓侯使人问其故。扁鹊曰:"疾之居腠理也,汤熨之所及也;在血脉,针石之所及也;其在肠胃,酒醪之所及也;其在骨髓,虽司命无奈之何!今在骨髓,臣是以无请也。"后五日,桓侯体病,使人召扁鹊,扁鹊已逃去,桓侯遂死。

使圣人预知微,能使良医得蚤从事,则疾可已,身可活也。人之所病,病疾多;而医之所病,病道少。故病有六不治:骄恣不论于理,一不治也;轻身重财,二不治也;衣食不能适,三不治也;阴阳并,藏气不定,四不治也;形羸不能服药,五不治也;信巫不信医,六不治也。有此一者,则重难治也。

扁鹊名闻天下。过邯郸,闻贵妇人,即为带下医;过雒阳,闻周人爱老人,即为耳目痹医;来入咸阳,闻秦人爱小儿,即为小儿医:随俗为变。秦太医令李醯自知伎不如扁鹊也,使人刺杀之。至今天下言脉者,由扁鹊也。

➤ 素材 2. The Totem of Medicine：Hippocrates

There are those who believe that the Jesus of the New Testament never existed. They dispute the deeds attributed to him, and doubt that his scriptural words were ever spoken. Much the same suspicion has been expressed concerning the founders of many of the other major religions and sects of the world. Even when seemingly solid evidence of sacred lives is available, some thinkers remain unconvinced.

In spite of personal commitments that each of us may have to either rationalism or religion, we possess no indisputable knowledge of where the reality lies. Those with deep traditional faith see a certainty that requires no documentation. History is for them illuminated by the light of God, which shines gloriously over precisely the same area that appears as an obscure emptiness to the skeptics. And so debates will go on as long as our successors survive to inhabit this earth, between those who pursue the truth and those who pursue the Truth.

On a strictly practical level, it makes not an iota of difference which group of pursuers is right. Investigating the shrouded origins of the modern ethical religions is far less important than understanding what the various groups have grown to be, and what effects each has had upon the history of the world and upon its moral vision. Most meaningful of all may be the question of their collective impact upon the thinking of contemporary man.

It is much the same with Hippocrates, the Greek physician whom we call the Father of Medicine. We think we know a few facts about his life that are separable from legend, and we think also that we have good reason to honor him in the parareligious way that has been taught us by the keepers of our medical lore. But beyond that, there is certainty about nothing except the existence of his scripture. Tradition is a persuasive teacher, even when what it teaches is erroneous. It tells us that all of the Hippocratic writings are the work of one author; it says the same of the Pentateuch of the Old Testament, and yet hard literary evidence denies such a claim as forcefully for the former as it does for the latter.

As with the books of the Bible, different Hippocratic writings seem to have been composed by different scribes at different times, setting down a permanent record of what had previously been an oral tradition of belief and practice.

Although to a lesser extent than the Biblical writ with which we make analogy, the Hippocratic Collection(or, as it is often called, the Hippocratic Corpus)contains some eternal truths and some soaring literature. The whole is united by a theology, and it is the theology, rather than the author,which makes it Hippocratic. Both the Bible and the Corpus deal with man's relationship to man and to another power outside himself In the Greek writings, however,that power is Nature; God and other forces that can be seen only when supernatural sight are excluded.

This injunction to turn a blind eye to the possibility of a deity or mystical influence in the causes and treatment of disease was the greatest contribution made by the school of Hippocrates. The Swiss medical historian Erwin Ackerknecht has called it "Medicine's Declaration of Independence"

There is not, in the entire Corpus, the slightest hint that disease is traceable to causes beyond the powers of the physician to understand. Each set of symptoms has a specific cause or causes,and treatment must be directed toward correcting the circumstances in which they appear, and not only the consequences of their presence. Thus, the setting in which the illness takes place should be considered as important a factor as the manifestations of sickness themselves. The Greeks were the first to believe that the universe functions by rational,reasonable rules. They gave us the concept of cause and effect, and thereby laid the groundwork for science. Even before Aristotle, there was Hippocrates; what we have in the Corpus is a treasure house containing the earliest extant scientific treatises in any language.

Though our debt is not so much to the Father of Medicine himself as it is to the philosophy and practice that bear his name, Hippocrates nevertheless did live, and he seems to have been a distinguished physician of his day. But before telling what little is known of his life, it is necessary to describe something of his mythical antecedents and contemporary counterparts, and most specifically the system of belief whose practitioners were known collectively as the cult of Aesculapius.

In post-Homeric times, the healing powers originally attributed to several of the principal gods, Apollo, Artemis, and Athena, were gradually transferred in large measure to a lesser deity, Aesculapius, son of Apollo by the nymph Coronis. The Aesculapian myth is polymorphous, arising, as did Greek culture itself, from a confluence of many earlier civilizations and traditions. Legend ascribes numerous miraculous cures to the god, carried out primarily by means of visions attained in dreams which the faithful sick experienced while sleeping in temples dedicated to him.

The sites of Aesculapius' shrines had qualities which all cultures have recognized as ideal for the purpose of restoring health: they were often on breeze-touched hills in the vicinity of clear flowing streams or springs, whose waters were of high mineral content. The salubrious air, the visual comfort of the surrounding forests, the beautifully cultivated gardens, and the spiritually nurturing presence of the robed priests combined to create a reassuring atmosphere in which health could be expected to reenter the body of the suffering pilgrim. Of course, the stricken petitioners had come to beg the help of a divinity, and so there were also prayers, animal sacrifices, and the diligent carving of votive tablets. Sacred serpents anointed injured limbs, licking and slithering their silent restorative way from one raw wound to another. While all of this inspirational theotherapy was in progress, the sonorous voices of the priests could be heard intoning solemn incantations and magical formulas. Surrounded by their eagerly devout supplicants, they recounted the wondrous cures that had been brought about by the power of Aesculapius and his legendary children, among whom were his daughters, Hygeia and Panacea. The god himself was present in effigy bearing a long staff around which was entwined the famous sacred snake; from this otherworldly origin comes the symbol of the modern scientific medical profession.

The focus of the cure was the god-given dream, in which Aesculapius conveyed to the sleeping patient, either directly or in symbols, the means by which recovery might be attained. Having been brought to the proper level of emotional readiness by the mystical ceremonies and the supernal atmosphere of the shrine, the patient spent several nights sleeping in the awesome temple itself until the oracular vision made its appearance. The spectral message was then interpreted by the priests in ways that were consistent with their system of therapeutics, which meant that they were likely to see in it such treatments as might be obtained through diet, exercise, or what we nowadays call recreational or music therapy. Sometimes the cure required bloodletting or purging, or even an occasional quite fanciful directive that instant restoration of health occur, probably meant to invoke the power of suggestion. If the priestly treatment was successful, the credit went to Aesculapius and to his agents, who accepted the prayers and the money of their patients with equal piety. If the treatment failed, the petitioner himself was to blame.

➤ 注释

pararetigious　adj. 半宗教性的

writ　n. 令状,文书

injunction　n. 禁令,命令,劝告

antecedent　n. 祖先,前情

Aesculapius　n. 医神,医师

oracular　adj. 神谕的,玄奥的

purge　v. 清洗,净化,通便,催吐

➢ 练习

1. Concerning the narration of the life stories of the two doctors,do you noticed any difference? What are they?

2. When talking about Hippocrates, Sherwin B. Nuland said:"We think we know a few facts about his life that are separable from legend, and we think also that we have good reason to honor him in the parareligious way that has been taught us by the keepers of our medical lore. "According to you,what reason do we Chinese have to honor Bian Que?

五、现代回声
➢ 背景知识

2019 年末出现的新冠疫情是人类进入现代社会以来席卷全球的流行病,其传染性之高,传染范围之广,流行之间之长,传播方式之多样可谓空前,面对来势汹汹的疫情,中国政府和医疗工作者调动一切社会资源,发挥我国传统中医药预防和控制疫病的特长,在短时间内迅速控制了武汉的疫情,中医在这场战疫中再立新功。本部分选取了 2020 年 5 月 27 日《环球时报》的一篇文章,该文数据可靠翔实,观点客观明确,用事实证明了中国传统医药的安全有效性,反驳了诋毁中医者的言论。

Clinical trial results prove efficacy and safety of TCM capsules on mild COVID-19 patients

By Leng Shumei and Liu Caiyu

Chinese experts and doctors have provided clinical trial data on the efficacy and safety of traditional Chinese medicine(TCM)Lianhua Qingwen

(LH)capsules on COVID-19 patients, which show that the capsules can apparently relieve symptoms and increase the cure rate of patients exhibiting mild symptoms.

Trial data showed after 14 days of regular treatment, assisted with LH capsules, the resolution rate of main clinical symptoms(fever, fatigue and cough)hit 57. 7 percent on the 7th day of treatment. It reached 80. 3 percent on the 10th day, and 91. 5 percent on the 14th day, according to a document that LH capsules producer Yiling Pharmaceutical sent to the Global Times on Wednesday.

Overall, the treatment with LH capsules for 14 days resulted in a significantly higher rate and a shorter time of symptom recovery than the control group(usual treatment), according to a paper published online by Phytomedicine, a monthly peer-reviewed medical journal.

LH is a TCM containing 13 herbs, including Lonicera japonica(金银花), Forsythia(连翘) suspense and Rhodiola rosea(红景天). It has been marketed since the SARS crisis in 2003 in China and has been widely used in the country to treat various infectious diseases, like SARS, H1N1 and COVID-19.

Trial data showed that Lonicera japonica and Forsythia suspense in the capsules could block the binding of the coronavirus with human blood vessels; and Rhodiola rosea could inhibit the inflammatory response in lung tissue, according to the paper.

The rate of viral assay results from positive to negative and the rate of conversion in patients from mild to severe, however, did not show any significant differences between patients accepting LH capsules and those who did not, according to the paper.

Yang Zhanqiu, a deputy director of the Pathogen Biology Department at Wuhan University, told the Global Times on Wednesday that the results indicate that LH capsules don't have antiviral effects.

But Cui Yongqiang, a chief physician at a hospital affiliated with the Chinese Academy of Chinese Medical Sciences in Beijing, noted that the results conform to previous observations that TCM can improve clinical symptoms of COVID-19 but cannot cure COVID-19 patients or kill the novel coronavirus directly.

The results don't overturn the fact that LH capsules are effective in treating novel coronavirus pneumonia presenting light symptoms ,Cui told the Global Times on Wednesday.

The trial was conducted jointly by more than 20 COVID-19 designated hospitals across the country under the leadership of top respiratory disease expert Zhong Nanshan, renowned epidemiologist Li Lanjuan and China's top medical adviser Zhang Boli,according to Yiling's document.

A total of 284 COVID -19 patients engaged in the trial and were equally separated into two teams: One team received LH capsules while the other did not.

This is the first multi-centered randomized clinical trials that demonstrate the safety and efficacy of LH capsules in COVID-19 patients, according to the paper.

Future double-blind,prospective and randomized controlled trials are needed to fully evaluate the efficacy of LH capsules in a larger patient population, read the paper.

By the end of April,more than 70,000 out of 80,000 confirmed COVID-19 cases in China have been treated by TCM, and more than 90 percent of patients in the hard-hit Hubei Province have taken TCM, according to media reports.

➤ **注释：**

efficacy n. 功效，效力

pharmaceutical a. 制药学的；n. 药物

phytomedicine n. 植物药

coronavirus n. 冠状病毒

Inflammatory a. 炎症性的，激动的

assay n. &v. 化验

respiratory a. 呼吸的

➤ **练习**

1. How do you think the application of double-blind, prospective and randomized controlled trials to evaluate the efficacy of TCM?

2. Translate and comment on the following paragraphs：

Dr. Read concluded by saying that further extensive reference might be made to a host of other remedies but that enough has been cited to show that science may progress by looking backward as well as forward, that probably the most suggestive parts of progress may be gained by studying the records of old empirical medicine, that the scientists needs more than any other to keep an open mind regarding the claims of ancient medicine, so that with the aid of modern knowledge and modern technique an unprejudiced study may be made of the customs of our forefathers, who however much they may have believed in demonology and false philosophical theories. , were engaged in the same life and death struggle against disease.

In China there has been preserved for something between 30 and 50 centuries remarkably accurate records of human experience in the field of medicine. These records are not accumulations of divine intuitions but empirical findings, which up to the present have only been sifted with the very coarse sieve of last century science.

第九章 科　　举
Civil Service Exam System

一、词源梳理

据《说文解字》:"科,程也。𥝲,从禾𥝲,从斗𣁬。斗者,量也"。因此科的本义为动词,即用标准容器测量谷物。后逐渐引申出三重意思:其一为标准,规定,法规;其二为品类,等级;其三为以标准测试与训练。又据《说文解字》:"举,对举也"。举字的金文字形"𦥑"中"𠆤"表示建筑顶部,"𠀟"表示房梁,"𠆢"表示两人合手用力。可见举字的本义表示众人将房梁托起,架在房柱上,后逐渐衍生出多重意思。其一延续本义作动词使用,意为抬,提,拿;其二为大规模发动或进行,此义进一步引申为大作为之意;其三为众人认同,推选,此义亦发展出"全部,全面"之意。科举一词,从语义上概括了全国统一的标准考试用以推选不同等级公职人员的制度之核心所在。中国被普遍认为是世界上最早以考试方式取录公职人员的国家,也就是说"科举"一词是中国首创的。

西方社会在很长历史过程中并没有与科举对应的以"择优录取"为原则的人才选拔考试制度,而是依赖世袭和推荐。英语中科举有时被译成 imperial examination,有时被译成 civil service examination。显然前一种译法中的 imperial 一词突出了科举考试制度的权威性。而后一种译法最早是指英国在印度殖民地东印度公司选拔文官官员时借鉴中国科举制度而举行的考试。1854 年,英国财政部常务次官查理斯·屈维廉(Charles Edward Trevelyan)与史丹福·诺斯科特(Stannford Northcote)在考察东印度公司书院后提交了著名的《诺斯科特-屈维廉报告》(*Northcote-Trevelyan Report*)。该报告首次以官方文件形式将政府公职人员统称为"文官"(*Civil Service*),号召改革公职任用制度,借鉴中国采用统一考试来任命文官,提高行政效率。

二、引导阅读

➤ 背景知识

关于科举制度的定义,有广义和狭义之争。广义讨论包含了科举制度的目的和规则,狭义讨论的是科举制度的形式和主要内容。北京大学历史系张希清教授出版了《中国科举考试制度》一书,总结道:"科举制度的实质和目的乃是一种选拔官员的制度,是国家规定的统一考试;士人可以自由报考",主要以考试成绩决定取舍。"中国的科举考试曾经深刻地影响了欧洲的人才选拔制度,近年来西方汉学界对中国科举考试制度的认识逐步摆脱了过去的全盘否定。美国普林斯顿大学历史系本杰明·爱尔曼(Benjamin Elman)教授在 Berkshire Encyclopedia of China (Berkshire Publishing Group LLC 2009 出版)一书中对于中国科举制度给予了中肯的评价。

> "The civil service examination system, a method of recruiting civil officials based on merit rather than family or political connections, played an especially central role in Chinese social and intellectual life。"

以下部分节选自本杰明·爱尔曼(Benjamin Elman)在权威杂志 Journal of Asian Studies 发表于 1991 年第 50 卷上的论文 *Political, Social, and Cultural Reproduction via Civil Service Examinations in Late Imperial China*. 在文章中爱尔曼教授充分肯定了科举制度的历史贡献和作用。

Despite centuries of repeated criticism and constant efforts at reform, the "examination life," like death and taxes, became one of the fixtures of elite society and popular culture. The examinations represented the focal point through which state interests, family strategies, and individual hopes and aspirations were directed. Civil service examinations connected various aspects of premodern politics, society, economy, and intellectual life in imperial China. Local elites and the imperial court continually influenced the dynastic government to reexamine and adjust the classical curriculum and to entertain new ways to improve the institutional system for selecting civil officials. As a result, civil examinations, as a test of educational merit, also served to tie the dynasty and literati culture together bureaucratically.

The civil service recruitment system achieved for education a degree of national standardization and local importance unprecedented in the premodern world. The civil service system engendered a national school system down to the prefectural level during the Sung and further down to counties in the Ming and Ch'ing dynasties. These high-level public schools initially prepared candidates for the written tests devised by state-appointed examiners. Fully seven centuries before Europe, the imperial Chinese state committed itself financially to support an empire-wide school network.

Although it has become sinological cant to dismiss the examination system as an institutional obstacle to modernization in China, a more comprehensive view reveals that there are no a priori reasons the gentry-official managerial elite reproduced by the system were by definition inefficient as "power managers" in a preindustrial society. In fact, a classical education based on "nontechnical" Confucian moral and political theory may have been as suitable in China for the selection of elites to serve the imperial state at its highest echelons of power as humanism and a classical education were in the nation-states of early modern Europe. If we evaluate

Confucian education solely in light of modern goals of academic specialization and economic productivity, then the social and political dynamics of this cultural and institutional enterprise are misrepresented.

Establishment of a process for institutionalizing the transmission of Confucian cultural values through the civil service, which was initiated by Sung rulers and officials tied to social and political structures peculiar to the Sung dynasty, in turn helped to reproduce those structures among Confucians during the Ming and Ch'ing. The examinations were a fundamental factor in determining cultural consensus and conditioned the forms of reasoning and rhetoric that prevailed in elite society.

Unwittingly, a brilliant piece of educational and social engineering had been achieved. Despite shortcomings in fairness due to special facilitated degrees for licentiates, hereditary privileges for some officials, purchase of degrees by merchants, and disparities in the geography of success, whether regional or rural-urban in form. The civil service examinations remained the main avenue to wealth and power in late imperial China until the nineteenth century.

> ➤ 注释:

　　fixture　v. 固定装置

　　elite society　n. 精英社会

　　prefecture　n. 县,地级市

　　dismiss　v. 摈斥,黜免

　　a priori　adj. & adv. 先天的,先验的

　　echelon　n. 梯队 v. 排成梯队

　　institutionalize　v. 使……制度化,机构化

　　consensus　n. 一致同意,共识

➤ **练习**

1. What is the common criticism against the civil examination system in Sinological studies?

2. According to Elman, what practical benefits has the civil examination system contributed to the state and the individual respectively?

3. What is the main argument in comparing the Chinese civil examination system to humanism and classical education in Europe?

三、阅读与比较

➤ **背景知识：**

科举制度建立了"唯才是举"的进步观念，在合理用人和阶层流动诸方面发挥了积极的作用。但至明清，科举制度进入衰亡期，科考内容由诗赋策论转向八股文，制度日趋僵化，逐渐蜕变为压制和摧残人才、阻碍社会发展的桎梏。

本部分节选自《聊斋志异—王子安》，作者蒲松龄大半生参加科考，却怀才不遇。这种经历和际遇使他对"三场辛苦磨成鬼，两字功名误煞人"的仕途科场有深切的感受和认识。后两种译本亦出自名家之手，供读者鉴赏分析。

The above photo shows an alley of civil examination cells used during late Qing dynasty.

➢ **素材 1. 节选自《聊斋志异—王子安》**

秀才入闱,有七似焉:初入时,白足提篮,似丐。唱名时,官呵隶骂,似囚。其归号舍也,孔孔伸头,房房露脚,似秋末之冷蜂。其出场也,神情惝恍,天地异色,似出笼之病鸟。迨望报也,草木皆惊,梦想亦幻。时作一得志想,则顷刻而楼阁俱成;作一失志想,则瞬息而骸骨已朽。此际行坐难安,则似被絷之猱。忽然而飞骑传人,报条无我,此时神色猝变,嗒然若死,则似饵毒之蝇,弄之亦不觉也。初失志,心灰意败,大骂司衡无目,笔墨无灵,势必举案头物而尽炬之;炬之不已,而碎踏之;踏之不已,而投之浊流。从此披发入山,面向石壁,再有以'且夫'、'尝谓'之文进我者,定当操戈逐之。无何,日渐远,气渐平,技又渐痒,遂似破卵之鸠,只得衔木营巢,从新另抱矣。

➢ **素材 2. "The Seven Likenesses of a Candidate" from Pu Songling's *Strange Tales of a Chinese Studio***

——by Benjamin A. Elman

A licentiate taking the provincial examination may be likened to seven things. When entering the examination hall, bare-footed and carrying a basket, he is like a beggar. At roll-call time, being shouted at by officials and abused by their subordinates, he is like a prisoner. When writing in his cell, with his head and feet sticking out of the booth, he is like a cold bee late in autumn. Upon leaving the examination hall, being in a daze and seeing a changed universe, he is like a sick bird out of a cage. When anticipating the results, he is on pins and needles; one moment he fantasizes success and magnificent mansions are instantly built; another moment he fears failure and his body is deduced to a corpse. At this point he is like a chimpanzee in captivity. Finally, the messengers come on galloping horses and confirm the absence of his name on the list of successful candidates. His complexion becomes ashen and his body stiffen s like a poisoned fly no longer able to move. Disappointed and discouraged, he vilifies the examiners for their blindness and blames the unfairness of the system. Thereupon he collects all his books and papers from his desk and sets them on fire; unsatisfied, he tramples over the ashes; still unsatisfied, he throws the ashes into a filthy gutter. He is determined to abandon the world by going into the mountains, and he is resolved to drive away any person who dares speak to him about examination essays. With the passage of time, his anger subsides and his aspiration rises. Like a turtle dove just hatched, he rebuilds his nest and starts the process once again.

> ➤ 素材 3. "The Seven Likeness of a Candidate" from Pu Song Ling's *Strange Tales of a Chinese Studio*

——by Denis C. & Victor H. Mair

Bachelors of letters who go into the examination cells have seven resemblances. When they first go in, barefoot and carrying their baskets, they resemble beggars. At roll call, when monitors shout and lictors curse, they resemble prisoners going to their own numbered cells, they resemble sluggish wasps at the end of autumn in the way their heads poke out of the openings and their feet stick out from the rooms. When they come out of the arenas, wearing every imaginable sort of dispirited expression, they resemble ailing birds just released from a cage. Then, as they are waiting for news of their results, they start at shapes they see in grass and trees, and their daydreams become full-blown fantasies. Now they see their hopes realized, and in a matter of moments a mansion and pavilions take shape; now they see themselves stymied, and in a blink and a breath their bones have decayed. At this juncture the restlessness of their movements makes them resemble an orangutan on a leash. Suddenly messengers come on flying steeds, but the expected names are not on the list. Their color pales dramatically, and they lapse into deathlike despondence. At this time, they resemble poisoned flies that are insensible even when handled. When first defeated, their hearts are like dead ashes and their spirits are broken. They rant and rave at the blindness of the examiners and uselessness of their writing brushes and ink, and inevitably come to such a pass that they gather up all the things on their desk and commit them to the flames. Burning them isn't enough, so they stomp them to pieces. Stomping isn't enough, so they throw them into the gutter. After this they let their long hair down and go to live like hermits in the mountains, where they turn their faces toward a stone wall. Anyone who brings them essays with words like 'moreover that which' and 'previously opined' will assuredly be chased away at spearpoint. But before long, as the day of their humiliation recedes into the past and their anger fades, there gradually comes again an itch to exercise unused skills. In this they resemble a pigeon whose eggs have been smashed. The only thing it can do is fly about with twigs in its beak fashioning a nest, and then sit hatching a new clutch of eggs.

> **注释:**

1. licentiate   n. 持有开业执照者,文中指秀才

2. ashen   adj. 灰色的,苍白的

3. stiffen   v. 变僵硬

4. vilify   v. 诽谤,辱骂

5. trample   v. 践踏,蔑视

6. subside   v. 平息,减弱

7. lictor   n. 官吏

8. sluggish　adj. 行动迟缓的,呆滞的

9. dispirited　adj. 意志消沉的,没有精神的

10. stymie　v. 从中作梗,妨碍

11. orangutan　n. 猩猩

12. steed　n. 战马,骏马

13. despondence　n. 沮丧,泄气

> **练习**

1. At which moment of the examination is the test taker compared to a beggar? Could you think of why is the test taker required to be bare-footed?

2. How devastating it could be to the test taker upon knowing that he had failed the examination?

3. What, according to your understanding, makes the test taker want to redo the entire process of the examination?

4. Please cite and compare the translations of the following ideas:

a. 似丐

①_____

②_____

b. 似囚

①_____

②_____

c. 似秋末之冷蜂

①_____

②_____

d. 似出笼之病鸟

①_____

②_____

e. 似被絷之猱

①_____

②_____

f. 则似饵毒之蝇

①_____

②_____

g. 似破卵之鸠

①_____

②_____

四、拓展阅读

➤ 背景知识

　　科举是隋朝之后中国历代王朝选拔官员的重要制度,但是清末科举弊端日显,抨击者日众,导致 1905 年 9 月 2 日,光绪帝颁布上谕,宣布"所有乡、会试一律停止,各省岁科考试亦即停止",在中国实行了 1300 年的科举自此终结。但是关于科举利弊的争论几乎从未停止。本部分选取的第一篇文章节选自日本学者宫崎市定的著作《科举史》,作为日本知名历史学家,京都学派集大成的代表,本书是宫崎关于科举的扛鼎之作。书中梳理了科举的历史,尤其详细考察了清朝的科举。本部分节选了《科举史》的最后一章《科举制度崩溃的意义》之结尾部分,读者可以从中看出宫崎对于科举存废及利弊的态度。

　　本部分第二篇文章是梁启超的《官制与官规》。梁启超在戊戌变法时曾主笔上呈朝廷的《请变通科举折》,自己也有《论科举》之文,与众多人反科举者站在了一起。但是 1910 年,在广泛游历西方诸国之后,他却另撰《官规与官制》一文,检点废科举后的官员选拔之混乱,对照借鉴科举的西方文官考试制度之利,悻然提出"复科举便"。梁启超对于科举的态度是前后矛盾还是始终如一,其中原因为何,科举对于中国及世界之影响如何,读者若认真品读日本学者宫崎市定和梁启超的文章,应该会有一理性的结论。

> **素材 1.《科举制度崩溃的意义》节选**

　　尽管如此,我们也不能过分夸大科举的阴暗面。科举的理想是儒教主义的贤人政治,虽然方法上存在不完善的地方,但在期待绝对公正公平的各种措施上,仍有值得采纳的地方。关于科举的是非,古今东西都有议论,评价也各种各样。在东方,特别是中国本土,科举经常是负面的,但在西洋却多半是好意的、同情的倾向,这一点不失为有趣的现象。也许是西欧人听说科举的理想后,夸大了它的效果,而亲身蒙受科举弊害的中国有识者则不禁为其流毒未尽而愤慨,甚至面对将科举复杂化、困难化并加以奖励的明太祖,做出了"其心术有过于秦始皇焚书坑儒"的辛辣评价。不过,科举之所以在西洋获得好评,应当归结为科举制首次传入时,十七至十八世纪西洋社会的落后性。定论一旦建立,就会给后世留下深刻的影响,在这一点上我们应该倾听已故的原胜郎博士(原文注:原胜郎(1871—1924):日本近代历史学家,京都帝国大学文科大学教授,专攻西洋史、日本史,通过西洋史研究提出日本同样存在中世的观点,代表作有《南海一见》《日本中世史》等。)的看法。

　　　人都说,中国的衰落是因为科举。呜呼,科举真的有罪吗? 议论者动不动就说科举祸国。清朝大厦将倾时,首先废除科举制度救国,结果科举废除没多久国家就灭亡了。如果将科举作为中国衰落的主因,那真是天大的冤枉。中国从一千多年前开始实行科举制度,其间请托勾结不断,无能之辈屡屡获得重用,但若由此论定科举效果微小,那就是夸大考试效果引发的歪论。近来文明各国任用文武官员之际,几乎都要进行考试,任用晋升必定依照能力,这很难不招来嗟怨之声。为什么唯独责难中国的科举制呢? 科举制值得采纳的点在于原则,官吏任用以公平为第一要义,最崇尚自由竞争。欧美各国在所谓旧时代的十八世纪无须赘言,进入十九世纪后,前半叶也未实行考试任用制度。即便在欧洲各国中号称先进且最民主的英国,以自由竞争为原则的文官考试制度也是在 1870 年以后才广泛采用;至于武官任用,则长期采用买官制,直到 1871 年。当时反对废除买官制的人说,考试任用法虽然多少能够期待公平,但恐怕公平的美名之下,不世出的人才只能老死于空山了,卖官制度固然有其弊害,但俊杰一跃就能到达合适的位置,不应该遽尔更改采用考试法……如果将采用考试法引起的人才拥塞之弊,与选拔俊才名下的嬖幸宠进之祸相比,两者的利害得失洞若观火。况且初任之际采用考试法,何以必然妨碍以后选拔新颖的人才呢? 非议这样的考试法,是因为预设了考试不合格的人中一定有很多人才,这难免沦为脱离实际的空谈。欧洲各国如今多采用考试法,北美合众国也吸取滥任的教训,自 1883 年起实行文官任用考试,这无疑是进步的大势所趋。中国自千年以前实行科举考试,历代逐渐加以改良,最终出现了南京贡院般巨大的建筑,这是最值得肯定的,而不应当嗤之以鼻。主义透彻与否姑且不论,通过考试广泛选拔人才,这一点远远领先欧美各国,这也是中国成为先进国的原因。中国的文明已经达到了发达的顶点,而且长期免于解体,得以维持权威性,这主要是科举的成就,它防止了阶级制带来的腐败。如果中国没有科举,其文明的末路无疑从数世纪前就开始了。

议论者又说,科举的原则很好,但实际考试的方法不得当,考的不是经世济用的学术,而是拘泥为诗文为主的八股旧套,这一点最值得讨论。此说看似有理,然而,所谓恶税使征收便利,能够保障财源,而所谓良税使征收繁杂,经常不能适应征税的目的,这是管税人经常叹息的地方。如果可以不征税则无须多论,但国家是必须收税的,税法的好坏只能是第二义的问题。就像我们应当同情收税者的苦衷一样,如果国家门户开放,为了公平任用人才,采用怎样的考试方式都是必要的,那么考试科目的是非就只是枝叶问题了。实行科目考试,总比什么都不实行要好,从这一点上来说,考试科目的好坏显然不应该成为影响科举评价的累赘。

进一步而言,即便论及科举的考试科目是否妥当,我们也不应一概斥为迂腐。如果因为科目中没有包含近期西洋盛行的政治、法律等学科,就将科举视为无用之物,那是巨大的错误。除了裁判官、技术官、翻译官等不得不将重点放在特殊技能知识上的职务,其他一般文官候补者的第一必需条件,在于高等的常识、明晰的理解力和绅士必须具备的素养,其次是记诵法律规定等。在 1876 年制定的英国高等文官考试科目中,除了罗马法、英吉利法、政治学、经济学、经济史,还有近世语的德、意、法、荷、西等外国语言和文学,古典有希腊语、拉丁语、梵语、阿拉伯语,以及理论数学、应用数学、博物学、英国史、希腊史、罗马史、近世史、哲学和伦理学等。这颇令我们满意,理解力暂且不谈,尽管常识和修养很难通过一场考试就判断孰优孰劣,但努力尝试比什么都不尝试强一万倍。从这一点来看,中国的科举以经学和诗文作为考试科目反而可谓得当。如果说中国的考试中没有常识和修养,除此以外还有复查的办法。特别是虽然没有设立历史科,但策问时需要论及时务,可以补足这一缺点……

　　总之,科举不应当是一概加以排斥的坏制度,反而有足以大加称赞的地方。就如各民族的盛衰荣辱一样,各民族创造的文明也自有定数……中国文明在几个世纪前已经极尽完善,换言之,就是到了发展的终点,其停滞不是因为科举,只是运数已尽而已。(《贡院之春》)

以上是科举制创立以来未曾有过的卓越学说,只有思路明晰、学贯古今的博士才能得出这样的论断。由此看来,评价科举的功过并非易事。科举的考察不仅无法脱离中国社会,也无法脱离天下大势。科举的功过是养育它的中国社会的功过,其功过程度必须与世界的进步相对照,才能得出公平的判断。如果科举有功,那应当是一千三百多年前就树立了如此卓越的理想;如果科举有过,应该责备的是它将各界事物全都包含在儒教的氛围之中,后来不能进行本质性的改善,并且一直延续了一千三百多年。在这种无法超越的体制之内,有人肃清科举,有人将科举浑浊化,他们作为个人都无法逃脱史家的评判。我在解说科举的同时,也尝触及与之相关的中国社会,可惜说不尽、道不详的地方还有很多。关于天下大势,我从一开始就认为自已不堪其任,所以只能抄写恩师原胜郎博士的高论作为结尾了。

> 素材 2.

《官制与官规》

全世界行官僚政治之国有四:曰德意志、曰日本、曰俄罗斯、曰我中国。德意志之所以有今日,惟官僚政治实严有功。德意志者,盖官僚政治之模范,抑亦自今以往法治国之模范也。日本者,效法德意志具体而微者也。俄罗斯官僚政治之腐败闻于天下,其人民怨讟,内乱岁闻,弊皆坐是。虽然,多数人民虽不蒙其泽,而犹能以其国竞于外。独中国之官僚政治,则上为蠹于国,而下为虱于民。此之不忧,则虽百变其政体,终无术以致人民之乐利,而厝国家于安荣。于是识者肃然忧之,咸谓改革官制为图治之本原,而宪政九年筹备案中,亦有于宣统二年厘定中外官制之条,可谓深探其本矣。虽然,吾以为本之中更有本焉,则官规是。

官制者何? 规定各种行政机关之组织也;官规者何? 规定所以运用此机关之程式也。官制则譬诸机器;官规则示运用机器之人所当有事也。苟机器缺损锈涩,虽有良工不能以运行,固也。然使运用者不得人,或虽有人而不善其用,则其究也与无机器等。今日之中国,则官制与官规两俱极敝者也。以现行之官制,虽使管葛为宰相,陶温为方镇,杜召为守令,而国终不能蒙其福,民终不能沐其泽。改弦而更张之宜也。然使徒改官制而不思所以整饬官规,则吾敢决其虽千百改,而效果卒无以异于今日。今政府所厘定之官制,仆未审其内容何如,将于他日更有所论,今且先论官规。

日本之编集法令者以官规别为一门,其项目则官等俸给也、试验也,任用、补充、进级、分限也,服务观律及惩戒赏罚也,恩给扶助也,办公费也,服制及诸仪式也,此皆整饬官僚政治之要具。吾中国未始无之,然疏漏而不适于用,久已成为具文。今绎其意而揆诸本国所能行者,著于篇,冀吾国立法家一省览焉。

一曰试验官吏法不可不改良也。畴昔以八股试帖卷折课士,一切官吏,皆自兹出。行之千年,末流极敝,识时之士,晓音瘏口,以鸣其非,仅乃去之。

夫去之诚是也。虽然，官吏新陈代谢，终不可不为新进者开其途。果何途之从而可以得适当之人才乎？此最不可不审也。畴昔也科举为之，而恩荫保举捐例辅之，恩荫为数不多甚少，保举则便于在官者之升转，而不甚便于无官者之释褐，可勿深论。其途之广者，实惟科举与捐例，今则皆废也。盖欲举天下之仕者，尽由学校，意诚善也。然以今日教育现象论之，欲求完全之大学卒业生以为用，未知期以何年，藉曰有之。然以现在教科之卤莽灭裂，因循敷衍，其所养成之人才若何，盖可相见矣，姑勿深论。按诸现行制度，则除廷试留学生外，全国人盖无复登仕之途。吾对于此制度，其欲商榷之问题有三焉：一曰留学生果尽适于为官吏乎？二曰举国官吏所需之员数，仅恃留学生足以给之乎？三曰留学生以外之人才遂无适于为官吏者乎？请逐一检点之。

第一问题，欲办新政，必赖新智识。留学生为新智识之渊薮，举行政机关以托之，宜也。然留学生非皆为仕而学也。三年以来，应试验者，其法政科不及半数。夫以治理工农医者，而官以翰林、主事、中书、小京官、知县诸职。其间惟主事一项，尚视其所分之部何如，或可得一割之用，然已仅矣。若翰林、中书、知县等职，则何待乎有理工农医之学识，而理工农医之学识，纵极奥粹，何益于为翰林、中书、知县？是则学非所用，用非所学，与前此科举时代无异，且更甚焉。夫畴昔科举时代之思想，凡学者必求仕，不求仕则不学，此实为中国致弱之大原。科举既废，谓庶几有以易之矣。今也以试验留学生制度不完故，乃益助长此风，令莘莘学子，皆以所学为敲门砖，门甫辟而砖遽弃，此非徒官规之梗，抑亦学风之扰也。且靡论他科也，即治政法学者，岂必其尽能作吏，又岂宜悉驱以作吏？世固有学极优而不能事事者矣。且使各国惟有从政家司法家而无政法家，则斯学不岂绝于天壤矣乎？学优且然，而滥竽者更何论矣？是故谓留学生果尽适于为官吏，无有是处。

第二问题，欲察留学生足以给全国官吏之员数与否，则有其先决之问题焉：曰举国官吏员数几何是也。自顷新编之京外官制未颁出，其内容如何，不敢臆断。即就现制论之，外而州县以上，内而朗主以上，官差合计，其所需有普通新学识之官吏，总须在五万员以上。若仿各国官制，其州县官厅，总须设辅助官五六员以上，其高级之地方官厅称是，如是则当骤增五六万员。

若会计官吏独立,则当增数千员乃至万员。又据新颁之法院编制法,其各审判厅管辖区域之大小,虽未有明文,然欲求周备,则初级审判厅,计平均每县应有两所;地方审判厅,计平均每府应有两所。以此推算,则全国之厅丞、厅长、推事、检察官等,当在五万员以上。大约全国行政官吏司法官吏合计,最少须得十五万员乃至二十万员,虽不中不远矣。然各级地方团体自治职,尚不知此数。今留学生每年应试验者几何? 最多数百人至千人极矣,而所学之学科,其性质不合作吏者,尚居泰半,是故谓仅恃留学生足以给全国官吏之员数,无有是处。

第三问题,今后之官吏,必以有新智识为期,固也。然不能谓仅有新智识而已足已。苟于本国历史上社会上之旧智识一无所有,则新智识又安所施? 欲求新智识,当于学校,尤当于外国学校,固也。然不能谓舍此遂无求之之途也。苟其如此,吾恐虽将国家之岁入,奉其半供留学费,而所养之才犹虞不给也。大抵人之能任事者,由于学识者半,由于阅历者半。而今日所谓之学识者,属于世界之智识者半,属于本国之智识者半。欲求世界之智识,其得于学校者半,其得于学校以外者半。留学生之资格,所以优于非留学生者,谓其能有从学校中得有世界之智识。然所优者,六分之一也。留学生之能具有彼六分之五者,固不乏人。然其得之已非恃留学生矣。若举国中未尝留学之人,其能具有彼六分之五者,抑当不少,具四者则更多焉,具三者则又更多焉,以之比普通留学生,其孰为适用,盖已未易轩轾矣。又况乎挟三以求四,挟四以求五,挟五以求六。"谓有阅历之人而求学识,有旧智识之人而求新智识,有普通新智识而求专门之新智识也",其道又非甚难也。是故国家欲得人以为理,一方面当取有新智识之人,进之以旧智识,又进之以阅历,然后用之。此用留学生之法也。一方面当取有阅历切=且有旧智识之人,进之以新智识,然后用之,此用留学生以外之人之法也。之二法者,缺一不可,而用前法则效缓,用后法则效速;用前法则途隘,用后法则途广。盖旧智识与阅历,非假以岁月,不能有功。朝出黉序,夕司民社,虽有圣智,犹将偾使,此无可如何者也。而其人既已稍有阅历,有旧智识,必其已在壮年,使之自由,以求新智识,尚或可几,必责以留学外国,以博一卒业文凭,则能者什不得一矣。而语于官吏之资格，则与其取无阅历无旧智识之留学生，毋宁取此辈也。是故谓留学生以外之人才，皆不适于为官吏，无有是处。

使吾之所以解决此三问题而不谬也，则夫现行制度以试验留学生为官吏出身惟一之途径者，其不足以应时势之要求，从可断矣。夫既以美锦学制贼夫人之子矣，以捷径干禄挠败学风矣，而其究也所得之人终不足以弥所阙之事势，固不得不横溢于此途径之外。于是有买旧昭信股票以求移奖者，有捐虚衔而求调部调省再求保实职者，今之无官而欲得官者，岂不尽趋于此两途哉？夫既趋于此两途，则试验法一无所得施而惟视苞苴奔竞之能力如何以为荣悴。凡所谓若何若何而始合于官吏之资格者，徒虚语耳。畴昔悬帖括楷法以为资格，诚属可笑。然以视并此资格而豁免之者。抑如何哉？其受试验之留学生资格，洵可谓严重矣。然以数年负笈海外之功，其结果亦不过与买一移奖，捐一虚衔者相等。欲竞争以求优胜，仍视苞苴奔竞之能力如何，人间能得几屈子，安得不汨泥而啜醨也哉？而笃学守节之士，畴昔遵功令以得一第，释褐阶进，雍容得以自效于国家者，今此途则湮矣。进之既不能逐少年以就塾，退之复不欲为赀郎以自污，则惟有槁死岩穴间已耳。夫今日宦场风习，所以流失败坏，视十年前更一落千丈者，虽其原因孔多，而官吏之制度不完全，亦其一也。循此不变，行将举国衣冠，悉为禽兽，而更何立宪专制之可言也哉？

然则当如之何？曰：法当采各国试验文官之制，标举政治、法律、生计诸科学若干种，岁集天下之士而试之于京师。其应试者，不必留学生，不必本国大学或高等学校之卒业生，不必有旧时之举贡等科第。凡国中人士有相当之学力者，皆得与。惟留学生卒业生等，则直以咨达京师，其他则先试于本省提学使，及格然后以咨达京师。其试之之科目，则一曰国家学（宪法未布以此代之），二曰大清新刑律，三曰大清民法（未颁定以前暂阙之），四曰比较行政学，五曰生计学，六曰国际法。以上六者，不许规避（民法未布前则为五，）七曰财政学，八曰大清商律，九曰民事诉讼法，十曰刑事诉讼法，以上四者，任择其一。都凡每人所试者七事，中程者赐以出身（以上科目采日本高等高等文官试验章程，彼所定实完善也）。若行此法，则中年人士不能入学校者,但试有相当之学力,即可释褐,不致终老岩穴以成弃才,一利也。国人可以多得成熟稳练之人物以从政,不致专委国事于少不更事之人,二利也。顽固老朽者,不得滥竽期间,三利也。人人争自濯磨于新学,政治智识法律智识,不期而自普及,养成立宪国民资格于无形中,四利也。老辈与新进,国学与外学缘此调和,不致相倾相轧,五利也。有此五利,行之宜也。

问者曰:子所举之十种科学,苟非入学校,则何从治之? 是所谓尽人许应试者,徒虚语耳。应之曰:不然。政府诚欲养成立宪国民资格,即微试验之举,固宜博聘通儒,将此诸学遍为简明完善之专书,俾举国士民资以诵习。其诵习而会通之者,则国家所欲得以为官吏者也。夫此诸学者,非如孔子春秋有微言大义,不可著诸竹帛,而必赖口说传授者也。欲求有此学力,岂必定由学校哉?况国家既悬此以为禄利之路,则正不劳政府之代为谋。而绩学之士固必有发箧呪笔以为之者,不旋踵而新著将阗肆矣。岂患独学者之无藉也哉。

问者曰,如子所言,是直议复科举耳,甚矣子之顽陋也。应之曰:此诚无以异于复科举,若云顽陋,则未之敢承。夫科举非恶制也,所恶乎畴昔之科举者,徒以其所试之科不足致用耳。昔美国用选举官吏之制,不胜其弊,及1893年始改用此种试验,美人颂为政治上一新纪元,而德国日本行之大效果,益更章章也。世界万国中行此法最早者莫如我,此法实我先民千年前之一大发明也。自此法行,而我国贵族寒门之阶级永消失(自唐以后,中国无复门第限人,科举之赐也,吾别著论。)自此法行,我国民不待劝而竞于学,此法之造于我国也大矣。人方拾吾之唾余以自夸耀,我乃惩末流之弊,而因噎废食,其不智抑甚矣。吾故悍然曰:复科举便。

问者曰,所恶乎科举者,谓其不按验平日学业之成绩,而争得失于一日之短长,与教育之旨相刺谬也。且尽人皆可应试,与学校卒业者无择,人亦孰更就学,学校不其湮乎? 应之曰:不然。以八股楷则为试,而争得失于一日之短长,则其弊诚不可胜穷,以美恶太无标准也。若试以所列之十科,则非相当之学力,岂易及格,此非可以一日短长言也。若云作弊,则今日学校之成绩表与卒业文凭,其弊又岂少也哉? 亦视其人与其法何如耳。至虑以此而沮学校之发达,尤属无理。彼日本行之,而观私立大学无一不以人满为忧。非其反对之显证耶？盖自修虽勤，终不如听受之易有所获，尽人能知也。固为此数年内劝中年人士求学起见不可不用此法，为将来奖励国中私立大学起见，亦不可不用此法。

据九年筹备案，应以去年编定文官考试章程，其所编者如何，今未得见。吾深望其采此主义耳，勿以其形迹近科举而讳言之也。

> **练习**

1. What do you know about the history of Imperial Civil Service Examination?

2. How do you interpret Liang Qichao's attitude towards Imperial Civil Service Examination? Do your think it inconsistent or not?.

五、现代回声

> **背景知识**

晚清科举的腐败到了触目惊心的地步，不少有志少年怀揣着远大的志向，期望一举成名，登入仕途，晋身上流。然而一年复一年的名落孙山，造成的巨大心理压力极具破坏力和报复性，最终成为影响历史的不安因素。本部分所引是华盛顿邮报专栏作家 Valerie Strauss 对于考试和战争之间的偶然个体联系的思考，从跨文化的角度，借古喻今，警示了制度僵化的消极作用。文中所说的主人公即洪秀全，在发起太平天国运动成为叱咤一时的洪天王之前，他也曾醉心科举。洪秀全少时天资聪颖，7 岁入私塾，15 岁第一次参加科举考试，但直到 31 岁，依然是童生，连个秀才也未考取，科场的屡次失利使洪秀全倍感屈辱，刺激他走上了反清之路。

How the First Standardized Tests
Helped Start a War — Really!

ByValerie Strauss, the Washington Post, December 3,2012

People who think standardized tests are ***wreak*** ing ***havoc*** in education today may be interested to take a look back at a different kind of trouble they sparked many years ago.

The first standardized tests, any world history student can tell you, were created in ancient China, during the Han Dynasty (206 BC—220 AD), when officials designed civil service exams to choose people to work in the government based on merit rather than on family status. The goal was to create an intellectual ***meritocracy*** based on Confucian learning. The system of exams was ***consolidated*** during later dynasties; through the centuries until the late 18th century, the core material was hardly altered.

Rote learning of Confucian texts was ***imperative*** to do well on the tests, and — like today — that created some dissent. During the Song Dynasty(960 and 1279), according to the website of the Society for Anglo-Chinese Understanding, Ye Shi, a well-known neo-Confucian educator, argued that learning by rote was wrong and that students learned best when Confucian principles were applied to the real world. He wrote:

"A healthy society cannot come about when people study not for the purpose of gainingwisdom and knowledge but for the purpose of becoming government officials."

He was ***prescient*** . The civil service exams actually played a part in the Taiping Rebellion, which left about 20 million people dead in the 19th century. How? In the mid-1800s, a lower middle class man named Hong Houxiu, who was only partly educated, wanted to join the Qing bureaucracy. Here's how the society's website explains what happened:

*"Hong Xiuquan as he became, failed the shengyuan examinations on four separate occasions. Nursing a **grievance** against the Confucian state system, Hong's frustration found an outlet when he read a Christian tract condemning the examinations. Prompted by visions and dreams, he went on to found the Taiping Tianguo, "The Kingdom of Heavenly Peace"*

and to launch a savage **crusade** *against the Qing* "*demon devils.*" *It is surely significant that Hong's first followers were, like him, village schoolmasters whose civil service ambitions had been dashed by their failure in the second round of state examinations.*"

"The Imperial examinations were not the sole factor in the Taiping Rebellion; *resentment of Qing rule and the humiliation China suffered in the First Opium War clearly loomed large in Hung Xiuquan's thought, while his mystic inspiration remains inexplicable. Nevertheless, the* **tantalizing** *frustration that the examination system caused in many aspiring intellectuals was certainly an* **integral** *part of Hong's motivation, and a root cause of the tragic ambition that led to slaughter then unprecedented in history.*"

Interesting history.

➤ **注释:**

wreak havoc　肆虐,造成严重破坏

meritocracy　n. 优才制度,精英管理

consolidate　v. 巩固,加强

imperative　adj. 必要的,不可避免的

prescient　adj. 预知的,有先见之明的

crusade　n. 十字军东侵,改革运动,

resentment　n. 愤恨,不满

tantalizing　adj. 难熬的,令人着急的,挑逗的

integral　adj. 完整的,整体必需的

➤ **练习**

1. How do you agree or disagree with the author's drawing connection between Hong Xiuquan's civil examination experience with his political

ambitions?

2. Read and investigate on your own about the common criticisms of the civil examination system during late Qingdynasty. Combine your own testing experiences to discuss the precautions we should beware of in modern education designs and reforms.

第十章　食　　物

一、词源梳理

　　Food 在中古英语写作"foode,fode"源于古英语"foda",其含义为"食物、营养、燃料",其比喻意义,分别源于原始日耳曼语的"fodon",日耳曼语的"fod-",和原始印欧语中词根"pa-"的扩展形式"pat-",具有"趋势,保持,过去,保护,守卫,喂养"等含义。

　　中文的"食"字源于甲骨文之🍱,由亼和皀构形。"亼",像屋顶呈三角之形,音(jí),义为屋顶,在此引申作"集"解。"皀",是古代盛黍稷的器皿,是"簋"字的初文。其字形象一个有盖有底座的容器。二字都据具体的实像造字,在六书中属于象形。二者结合成"🍱",有"进食"的意思。金文、战国文字、篆文之"食",都承甲骨文之形而来,下方的字形稍有不同而已。但经过隶书,字形大变,成了今天的"食"。

二、引导阅读

➤ 背景知识

　　古人云:民以食为天;俗话说:开门七件事,柴米油盐酱醋茶。由此可见,饮食确实是中国人生活中的重要内容。饮食本是人们生存的基本需求,它与纯粹精神领域的文化有什么样的关系呢? 在中国漫长的封建社会中,完备的农耕文明为饮食的发展提供了物质基础,那么在饮食中又能看出中国人对社会和人生怎样的态度? 在中国的饮食习惯里,是否具体而微地体现出中国文化的某些特性？

　　本文摘自《光明日报》刊登的一篇题为《中华饮食文化精神》的演讲稿。演讲者为中国社科院的王学泰研究员。他从饮食在中国文化中的地位、中国饮食的文化特征、中国饮食中的思想精神等三个方面对中国饮食文化进行梳理。在收录时，因篇幅问题，有部分删减和调整。

http://www.gmw.cn/01gmrb/2006-11/30/content_514905.htm

中华饮食文化精神

　　谈到传统文化时，我有时称"中国"，有时称"华夏"，华夏是汉族的前身。汉族的观念产生于"五胡十六国"，固定下来更晚，因此书中常用"华夏"以代汉族。"中国"这个词最早出自周代的"何尊"（六十年代出土于宝鸡）。中国，或缩小一些说，华夏的饮食文化可以看成是具体而微的传统文化。传统文化中的许多特征都在饮食文化中有所反映，如"天人合一"说，"阴阳五行"说，"中和为美"说以及重"道"轻"器"、注重领悟、忽视实证、不确定性等等都渗透在饮食心态、进食习俗、烹饪原则之中。

饮食在中国文化中的地位

　　在华夏文明中，饮食有其独特的地位。中国精神文化的许多方面都与饮食有着千丝万缕的联系，大到治国之道，小到人际往来，举凡哲学、政治学、伦理学、军事学、医学以至艺术理论、文学批评，无不向饮食学、烹饪学认同，从那里借用概念、词汇，甚至获得灵感。古人云："国以民为天，民以食为天"。"天"者，至高之尊称，也就是说"悠悠万事，惟此为大"。这是传统政治哲学精粹之所在。儒家认为民食问题关系着国家的稳定，孟子的"仁政"理想在于让人们吃饱穿暖，以尽"仰事俯畜"之责（也就是上可以侍奉父母，向父母尽孝；下可以养活妻儿），甚至儒者所梦想的"大同"社会的标志也不过是使普天下之人"皆有所养"。

　　中国传统文化注重从饮食角度看待社会与人生。老百姓日常生活中的第一件事就是吃喝，固有"开了大门七件事，柴米油盐酱醋茶"之说。食前方丈、钟鸣鼎食之家把吃饭看作一种享受，读《红楼梦》有人厌烦里面老写吃饭宴会,实际上这不仅就是贵族生活本身,而且也反映作者对生活的理解。即使普通人的日常饭菜也会使食者体会到无穷乐趣。唐代诗人杜甫在贫病之中受到穷朋友王倚并不丰盛的酒食款待后兴奋写道:

> 长安冬菹酸且绿,金城土酥静如练。兼求畜豪且割鲜,密沽斗酒谐终宴。故人情谊晚谁似,令我手足轻欲旋。

其实吃的不过是"泡菜"(冬菹)、萝卜(土酥)、猪肉(畜豪)之类,竟令诗人如此开心,手脚轻便,简直要翩翩起舞了,从中感受到生活的趣味和动力。清人郑燮(板桥)在其家书中描写了一种更为简朴的饮食生活:

> 天寒冰冻时,穷亲戚朋友到门,先泡一大碗炒米送手中,佐以酱姜一小碟,最是暖老温贫之具。暇日咽碎米饼,煮糊涂粥,双手捧碗,缩颈而啜之,霜晨雪早,得此周身俱暖。嗟乎! 嗟乎! 吾其长为农夫以没世乎!

开水泡炒米、煮糊涂粥是再寒酸不过的早餐,可是它们竟被郑板桥写得如此富于情趣和具有人情味,其实这正是他寒士生活的体验。这些与普通人的生活最接近,其感动力也最大。杜甫、郑燮都是注重写实的艺术家,长期生活在社会底层,其饮食心态代表了寒士阶层对饮食生活的感受。郑板桥写的是南方人寒士的早餐:北京的"霜晨雪早,得此周身俱暖"的"暖老温贫之具"则是豆汁。"棒打薄情郎"改做京剧也叫《豆汁记》,那个冻饿濒死的秀才就是被金玉奴的热豆汁救活的。我们在很寒俭的饮食中也能得到满足。

传统的文人士大夫最追求饮食情趣,如果有了点较为罕见的食品,那便会给他带来无穷的乐趣。近人林语堂在《中国人》中写道:

> 在我们得到某种特殊的食品之前,便早就在想念它,在心里盘算个

不停,盼望着同我们最亲近的朋友一起享受这种神秘的食品。我们这样写请柬:"我侄子从镇江带来了一些香醋和一只老尤家的正宗南京板鸭。"或者这样写:"已是六月底了,如果你不来,那就要等明年五月才能吃到另一条鲥鱼了。"秋月远未升起之前,像李笠翁这样的风雅之士,就会像他自己所说的那样,开始节省开支,准备选择一个名胜古迹,邀请几个友人在中秋朗月之下,或菊花丛中持蟹对饮。他将与知友商讨如何弄到端方太守窖藏之酒。他将细细琢磨这些事情,好像英国人琢磨中彩的号码一样。

"细细琢磨"用的真实传神。那时,文人聚会(相当于现在的沙龙)许多都是得到某种食品为由头的。《红楼梦》中写的几次小型宴集的起因都是得到了奇异食品。以这种审美的态度对待饮食生活便是生活的艺术了,它是以生活富裕为前提的。

中国人善于在极普通的饮食生活中咀嚼人生的美好与意义,哲学家更是如此。庄子认为上古社会最美好,最值得人们回忆与追求,其最重要的原因就是人们可以"含哺而嘻,鼓腹而游",也就是说吃饱了,嘴里还含着点剩余食物无忧无虑地游逛,这才能充分享受人生的乐趣。先秦哲学家中最富于悲观色彩的庄子尚且如此,那么积极入世的孔子、孟子、墨子、商鞅、韩非等人就更不待言了。尽管这些思想家的政治主张、社会理想存在很大分歧,但他们哲学的出发点却都执着于现实人生,追求的理想不是五彩缤纷的未来世界或光怪陆离的奇思幻想,而是现实的、衣食饱暖的小康生活。所以,《论语》《孟子》《墨子》才用了那么多的篇幅讨论饮食生活。饮食欲望,一般说来容易满足,"啜菽饮水",所费无几,即可果腹,所以人易处于快乐之中,李泽厚说中国古代文化传统是乐感文化,是有理由的。

当然不能说先民没有过痛苦的追求,古代无数抒情诗篇中充满了感伤情绪。屈原就曾感慨:"日月忽其不掩兮,春与秋其代序。惟草木之零落兮,恐美人之迟暮";也表示过:"吾令羲和弭节兮,望崦嵫而勿迫。路漫漫其修远兮,吾将上下而求索"(并见《离骚》)。他感到时光急迫,自己要做的事情很多,奋斗的路也很长,可是人生短促,时不我待。这种痛苦和感伤在一些浪漫主义色彩很浓或十分真诚的诗人身上表现得十分明显,但也应看到在相当多的诗人身上也有浓重的"为赋新诗强说愁"的意味。但不管是谁,当他们离开了诗人情绪的时候,在日常生活中还是奉行中国人的生活准则的。像苏东坡在《前赤壁赋》刚刚感慨完"寄蜉蝣于天地,渺沧海之一粟。哀吾生之须臾,羡长江之无穷",对于人生短暂寄予了无穷的悲慨,可是诗人善于自解,用相对主义,抹杀了长短寿夭、盈虚消长的差别,后面马上就是"客喜而笑,洗盏更酌。肴核既尽,杯盘狼藉。相与枕藉乎舟中,不知东方之既白"。吃喝解决人生的苦闷,因此在春秋时代人们就说"惟食无忧"。

至于指导人们生活与思想的哲人也只是密切地关注着现实人生,教导人们以微小的现实满足为追求目的。孔子说:"饭蔬食饮水,曲肱而枕之,乐亦在其中矣。""一箪食,一瓢饮,在陋巷之中,人不堪其忧,回也不改其乐。"(皆见《论语》)孔子或表达自己的志趣,或赞美弟子颜回都是为人们作示范楷模,这里简单的、粗糙的食品就是道德高尚的象征。虽然这些都打着"安贫乐道"、"忧道不忧贫"的幌子,但这个"道"究竟是什么呢? 把它放大到最高倍数,也不过就是实现"大同社会"。而大同社会的标志仍是人人吃饱穿暖,所以后世有些道学家把"道"解释为"穿衣吃饭",也无大谬。

中国饮食文化的特征

吃饭分主食副食、用"炒"的烹饪方法、有自己命名菜肴的方式……这些有形的特征,使中国饮食形成了一种独特的文化。

中国的饮食有它自己的特征,也就是说我们的饮食文化与外国的、特别是欧美——也就是西洋的饮食文化有不同的地方。其实这些特征从一些最表面现象中都可以看得见,往往是"形而下"的,停留在"器"的层面东西,所以大家习见而不鲜。

比如我们吃饭分主食副食,连食品店也分成"主食厨房"、"副食商店"。我们这个主副食观念还不是现在有的,早在先秦就有了。《黄帝内经》就有这样的句子"五谷为养,五果为助,五畜为益,五菜为充"。粮食被视为主食,而"果"(水果、干果)"畜"(肉类)"菜"是副食。而且主食的地位高于副食,这

虽然从名称上就可以看出来,有个故事更能说明问题:

> 《孔子家语》中说有一次孔子陪着鲁哀公吃饭,侍者端上了桃子和
> 黍米饭。孔子先吃了米饭,再吃桃子,结果左右侍者皆吃吃掩口而笑。
> 鲁哀公对孔子说:先生,黍米饭是用来擦拭桃毛的,不是吃的。孔子说,
> 我知道,但黍米是"五谷之长",是可以用来祭祀祖先的上等祭品,而常
> 用的果品共有六种,桃子的地位最低,祭祀也用不着它。我听说只能用
> 低贱的东西擦洗高贵的东西,没听过用高贵的擦洗低贱的东西。可见
> 饮食不仅有主副食之分,而且主食高贵,副食低贱(不是指价格,而是指
> 地位),这是西洋饮食文化中不能想象的。这种观念不仅在统治者头脑
> 中有,就是一般老百姓也有。解放前北京人如果吃窝头炖肉,就会有人
> 说:"啊,这是奴欺主"! 北京食谚中就有"宁教主欺奴,莫教奴欺主"的
> 说法。

还有一个明显差别,这就是"炒菜",或者说是烹饪方法中"炒"。不仅欧
美没有"炒"(西洋烹饪中 saute 实际上是指"煎",有的译作"炒"是不准确
的),就是日、韩这些汉文化圈中的民族也没有"炒"。炒最初的含义是"焙之
使干"(其声音如"吵",故名),后来才专指一种烹饪法。它的特点大体有三:
一是在锅中加上少量的油,用油与锅底来作加热介质,"油"不能多,如果多
了就变成"煎"了;二是食物原料一定要切碎,或末、或块、或丝、或条、或球,
然后把切成碎块的各种食物原料按照一定的顺序倒入锅中,不停搅动;第三
才是根据需要把调料陆续投入,再不断翻搅至熟,也就是说食物是在熟的过
程中入味的。"炒菜"包括清炒、熬炒、煸炒、抓炒、大炒、小炒、生炒、熟炒、干
炒、软炒、老炒、熘炒、爆炒等等细别。其他如烧、焖、烩、炖等都是"炒"的延
长或发展。

炒滥觞于南北朝,最早记载于《齐民要术》,成熟于两宋,普及于明清。
明清以后炒菜成为老百姓日常生活中用以下饭的肴馔,人们把多种食品、不
论荤素、软硬、大小一律切碎混合在一起加热,并在加热至熟中调味。这种

混合多种食物成为一菜的烹饪方法在西洋是不多见的,只有法式烩菜类才有把荤素合为一锅的做法(这有些像我们古代的羹)。炒菜的发明使得我们这个以农业为主、基本素食的民族得以营养均衡。

在炒菜以前,人们下饭主要靠"羹"。古代烹饪中谈到调味肴馔首要是"羹"。先秦、特别是战国以前,人们常用的烹饪法就是蒸煮炸烤。用这些烹饪法制作出的大块肉食大多是不入味的。孔子有两句最著名的话"食不厌精,脍不厌细"。"食不厌精"好理解,米舂得越细越好吃;"脍不厌细"就不好理解,为什么肉切得越薄就越好呢?历来注家很少说清楚的。原来那时煮熟的大块肉(脍)没味,要蘸酱吃,那时酱的品种有上百种之多,不同的肉还要蘸不同的酱,所以孔子说"不得其酱不食"。因为要蘸酱,所以只有切得薄才能入味。羹是要调味的,测验一个人的烹饪技巧首先也是看他会不会调制羹汤。因此唐代诗人王建咏《新嫁娘》的诗"三日入厨下,洗手作羹汤。未谙姑食性,先遣小姑尝"。结婚三天后婆家要测验新娘子的手艺了,可是对"味"的理解的主观性很强,所以才要拉拢一下小姑子,婆婆爱吃咸,还是爱吃甜?了解了婆婆的食性才好把握调味的分寸。有了炒菜,羹在中国人饮食中的地位大大降低了(粤菜除外)。现在炒菜是测验烹饪技术的主要依据了。而且现在的"汤"要比古代的羹稀了好多。

另外,我们的饮食文化中在食物的命名中很有特点。清代美食家李渔曾说:"食以人传者,'东坡肉'是也。卒急听之,似非豕之肉,而为东坡之肉矣。噫!东坡何罪而割其肉,以实千古馋人之腹哉。""东坡肉",乍一听仿佛是苏东坡的肉一样,其实是指苏轼所发明的对猪肉的加工方法。这类的例子很多。如以元代大画家倪瓒传的"云林鹤",以清代学人潘祖荫传的"潘先生鱼",以解放初教育部长马叙伦传的有"马先生汤"等等。而西洋就不会有"华兹华斯肉饼"、"丘吉尔布丁"之类。

中国饮食中的思想精神

古代所说的"天人关系"不能简单地理解为只是讲"天道"与"人道",从而把"天人合一"看作是讲人类与大自然相互依存道理的。实际上古人说的天人合一往往是指"天"有意志,它通过天子支配人事,人要顺"天"以感动天意。祭祀是人感动天的手段之一。"天"包括极其广泛,神鬼也是"天"的一部分。神源自天,这是不证自明的道理,所以神又可称作"天神",人死为鬼,鬼者,归也,所以死也称作"归天"。

古代祭祀鬼神都有食物,而且根据鬼神的贵贱及祭祀者与鬼神的亲疏关系和对他企盼的大小决定祭祀食品的丰俭。战国时齐国的淳于髡见一农夫拿着一只猪脚、一杯清水祭天,祈求五谷丰登、积谷满仓。淳于髡加以嘲笑,认为农夫企望太高,而供奉太薄。祭祀中人们感到祭品(主要是食物)是人和天的联系物、甚至认为它是鬼神曾经光顾过的(鬼神食后的剩余),因而把祭祀食品神圣化。直到清代,满人仍然把"祭于寝"的白煮猪肉称之为"福肉",亲贵大臣以能分到一块而荣耀(叫做"吃克食")。当然这只体现了浅层次的饮食生活中的天人关系。

古代的中国人还特别强调进食与宇宙节律协调同步,春夏秋冬、朝夕晦明要吃不同性质的食物,甚至加工烹饪食物也要考虑到季节、气候等因素。这些思想早在先秦就已经形成,在《礼记·月令》就有明确的记载,而且反对颠倒季节,如春"行夏令""行秋令""行冬令"必有天殃;当然也反对食用反季节食品,孔子说的"不食不时",包含有两重意思一是定时吃饭,二是不吃反季节食品。西汉时,皇宫中便开始用温室种植"葱韭菜茹",西晋富翁石崇家也有暖棚。这种强调适应宇宙节律的思想意识的确是华夏饮食文化所独有的。

　　"阴阳五行"说是传统思想所设定的世界模式,也被认为是宇宙规律。人是"三才"之一,饮食是人类生活所不可少的、制作饮食的烹饪必然也要循此规律。"凡饮,养阳气也;凡食,养阴气也"(《礼记·郊特牲》)。只有饮和食与天地阴阳互相协调,这样才能"交与神明",上通于天,从而达到"天人合一"的效果。

中和之美是中国传统文化的最高的审美理想。"中也者,天下之大本也;和也者,天下之达者也。至中和,天地位焉,万物育焉"(《礼记·中庸》)。

什么叫"中"？不能简单地用"中间"来概括它。这个"中"指恰到好处,合乎度。"和"也是烹饪概念。《古文尚书·说命》中就有"若作和羹,惟尔盐梅"的名句,意思是要做好羹汤,关键是调和好咸(盐)酸(梅)二味,以此比喻治国。《左传》中晏婴(齐国贤相)也与齐景公谈论过什么是"和",指出"和"不是"同",和是要建立不同意见的协调的基础上的。因此中国哲人认为天地万物都在"中和"的状态下找到自己的位置以繁衍发育。这种审美理想建筑在个体与社会、人与自然的和谐统一之上。这种通过调谐而实现"中和之美"的想法是在上古烹调实践与理论的启发和影响下产生的,而反过来又影响了人们的整个的饮食生活,对于追求艺术生活化、生活艺术化的古代文人士大夫,尤其如此。

如上所述,华夏民族的饮食生活体现了传统文化的特性,尽管有些特性对于现代人来说是不可理解、或者说不太科学,但饮食生活难道仅仅是"科学"二字所能说尽的吗？如果我们再关注一下"文化",那么研究中国人的饮食生活不仅是研究中国文化的必要的组成部分,甚至可以成为研究中国文化的一把钥匙。

➤ 练习

1. Please comment on the importance offoodin the Chinese culture.

2. Please describe the characteristics of Chinese food

3. Please comment on the spirits of Chinese food.

三、阅读与比较:孔子的饮食观
➤ 背景知识

在中国古代,准备食物用以供奉祭祀与圣贤倡导的修身养性思想密切相关。"夫礼之初,始诸饮食"(《礼记·礼运》)"礼必本于天,动而之地,列而之事,变而从时,协于分艺。其居人也曰养,其行之以货力辞让:饮食、冠、婚、丧、祭、射、御、朝聘"。(《礼记·礼运》)古人的观念认为人要生存就需要脱离通过竞争抢夺资源的状况,以"货力辞让"来安排分配之,此即礼之所由起也。觅食求生是古时最基本的问题,故礼亦起于会餐分食之顷。有饮食乃有生命;有生命乃能长大成人,而遂有冠有婚有丧;有个人而后才有群体,群体间才需要有祭射御朝聘等礼以"协于分艺",才能形成一个彬彬有礼的社会。

本节选取了三篇文章。第一篇文章选自教授、英国皇家科学院院士胡司德(Roel Sterckx)的著作" *Sages,Cooks,and Flavours in Warring States and Han China* "。胡司德的书探讨了充满活力的中国文化如何影响早期中国人对解释人类感官运作的方式,以及感官经验在与精神世界交流中的作用。全书不仅对周至汉代饮食文化进行了考察,还介绍了准备食物的一些有趣的仪式,以及祭祀礼仪本身。这部作品定位于思想史学科,对战国至汉代中国食物的文化和社会政治意义进行了最深入的解读。

第二篇文章选自" *Food and Environment in Early and Medieval China* ",作者是加州大学河滨分校人类学荣誉退休教授 E. N. 安德森(E. N. Anderson)。该书追溯了中国食物体系的发展历程,将中国的饮食方式置于一个广泛的比较框架之中。安德森考察了中世纪前中国的基本地理、气候和地形的优劣势、人类对自然环境的保护和掠夺,以及所有这些对饮食习惯的影响。

第三篇文章的题目为"Chinese Food and Medicine",摘自《生活的艺术》,作者是林语堂。林语堂"两脚踏东西文化,一心评宇宙文章",用多元整合的思维方式对中西文化进行融会贯通,是现代文学史上较为健全地对待中西文化的代表人物之一。而"饮食"在他的心目中无疑是生活的"第一享受"。他说:"如若一个人能在清晨未起身时,很清醒地屈指算一算,一生中究竟有几件东西使他得到真正的享受,则他一定将以食品为第一。"故而他推断:"倘要试验一个人是否聪明,只要去看他家中的食品是否精美,便能知道了。"

由于篇幅所限,本部分对文章的正文和注解做了节取和删减,这里所选取的三篇文章或多或少、或详或略、或直接或间接地描述了孔子的饮食观,读者可以详细进行鉴赏比较。

> ➢ 素材 1 **An extract from *Sages, Cooks, and Flavours in Warring States and Han China* by Roel Sterckx**

Perhaps more than in the case of any other figure in early China, narratives associated with the historical or eponymous Confucius emphasize how attitudes toward the secular and ritual consumption of food and drink served to exemplify human morality. According to the Master a gentleman does not crave a full stomach. Confucius could find pleasure in coarse food and plain water, would not eat to the full in the presence of someone in mourning and, on repeated occasions, lauds the sages of antiquity and virtuous individuals for having adopted a coarse diet. Confucius would never fail to alter his diet during periods of fasting, would not keep or eat sacrificial meats two or three days after a sacrifice, and would always make an offering even if he only had the most simple of meals. He never fails to demonstrate propriety in receiving food and tasting it:

When his lord made a gift of raw meat, he [Confucius] would invariably cook it and offer some of it up to his ancestors. When his lord made a gift of livestock, he would rear it. In attendance of his lord during dinner and when his lord was offering sacrifice, he would begin from the rice.

During periods of intensive sacrificial activity such as funerals, he would avoid being overcome by drink, and when attending a sumptuous feast he would in variably take on a formal appearance and rise to his feet.

In addition to praising Confucius's sense for propriety and occasion when dealing with food, the Lunyu also presents the Master as someone with a sensitive palate who insists on the nutritional value of his diet, hygiene, the care with which food was served, and the correct proportioning of sauces or condiments. Yet underneath Confucius' outward appearance as a distinguished gourmet, it appears that his sense for the worldly presentation and consumption of food are motivated by a desire for balance: cooking, serving, and partaking of a meal in essence represent the art of combination and proportioning.

He did not object to having his grain finely cleaned, nor to having his minced meat cut up fine. He did not eat grain that had been injured by heat or damp and turned sour, nor fish or flesh that was gone. He would eat nothing that was discoloured or smelled strange, nor anything that was not properly cooked or out of season. He did not eat meat that was not cut properly, nor what was served without its proper sauce. Even when there was meat in abundance he would not eat it in disproportionate amount over grain foods. Only in his wine he knew no measure although he never got drunk(disorderly). [127] He did not partake of wine and dried meat purchased from the market. Although he would not clear the ginger dish from the table, he would not eat it in excess.

Abundant indirect testimony of Confucius's attitude toward food occurs in sources that emerged during the centuries following the collation of the Analects. The following exemplary story is preserved in the Kong Congzi:

While Zisi dwelt in poverty, a friend gave him a present of millet from which he accepted two cartloads. Yet when someone else presented him a jar of wine and ten pieces of dried meat he considered it unacceptable. That man said: "You accepted your friend's millet and declined my wine and meat. That is, you declined the lesser quantity and took the greater. This is entirely contrary to righteousness, and what you took to be your due indicates a failure to be satisfied. What was the basis for your action?" Zisi replied: "This is true, but I was unfortunate that my poverty reached the point that my property was nearly destroyed and I was afraid I might have to cut off the sacrifices to my forefathers. Accepting the millet meant alleviating the situation. Wine and preserved meat provide the means for feasting. With respect to my present lack of food, feasting would be contrary to righteousness. How could I have been thinking of the matter in terms of portions? My action was based on righteousness." The man put his wine and meat on his shoulders and left.

In accepting plain millet instead of meat and wine, Confucius's disciple is presented here as taking the moral high ground: food, especially when received as a gift, ought never solely serve the purpose of sustaining and feeding oneself. The intake of food is by definition a communal endeavor that includes both the living and the dead who deserve to receive a portion of the meal in sacrifice. For the duty-bound gentleman, righteousness, it appears, ought to prevail over the instinctive desire to fill the belly. A famous episode in Confucius's purported biography was the moment when he was enduring hardship between Chen and Cai and forced to eat a vegetable broth without rice for seven days. According to one version of the story, this forced him to have to lie down during daylight. When Yan Hui 颜回 finally obtained some rice and cooked it for him, Confucius saw his disciple reaching for some charcoal dusted rice in the pot, which he ate. Despite the rice being spoiled by ash, Confucius still insisted to offer some of it to his former lord. Several other narratives in which Confucius is faced with the moral choice of accepting or presenting food offerings are preserved in apocryphal tales. The Kongzi jiayu records:

In Lu there was a prudent man, who once cooked food in an earthen boiler. Having eaten from it he found it good, and filling an earthen dish with it, he brought it to Confucius. Confucius accepted it and was joyously pleased as if he had received a food-present of a tai lao. Zi Lu said: "An earthen platter is a rustic vessel, and the cooked food is poor nourishment. Master, why then are you so glad with it?" The Master said: "Now he who loves to rebuke thinks of his ruler, and he who eats good food remembers his parents. I am so glad not because I consider the ingredients and implements lavish, but because, when he considers his food lavish, it is me he thinks of. "

In another story in the same chapter Confucius is presented with a rotten fish from a fisherman, which he accepts with reverence intending to perform a sacrifice with it. When one of his disciples objected to the idea of performing a sacrifice with a fish thrown away by a fisherman, Confucius replied:

I have heard that one who, thinking it a pity that the food would otherwise be rotten and superfluous, wishes thus to apply himself to giving it away, is the counter part of a good man. How could there be one who, on receiving a food-present from a good man, would not perform a sacrifice with it?

In addition to insisting on sacrifice, Confucius also used the ritual causeries that surround a dinner or banquet to make clear his judgments about others. When dining as guest of the Ji 季 clan, he does not decline any of the dishes, but refuses to eat meat and finishes his meal with the rice and liquid. By refusing to eat meat, Confucius expressed his dissatisfaction with the ritual propriety shown by his host. On another occasion Confucius praises the deference of his host by eating to the full:

When I dined as guest of the Shaoshi 少施 clan I ate to the full since they fed me with ritual propriety. When I was about to offer some food in sacrifice, my host got up and said, "My food is only coarse and insufficient to be offered in sacrifice. " When I was about to take the concluding portions, he got up saying, "My provisions are only poor and I would not dare to injure you with them. "

A passage in the Lüshi chunqiu suggests that the Master could also be

persistent in his gastronomic dislikes: "King Wen enjoyed pickled calamus. When Confucius learned this, he wrinkled his nose and tried them. It
took him three years to be able to endure them. "

In sum, despite the diverse circumstances in which these narratives
situate the historical oreponymous Confucius, the underlying message is
clear: attitudes toward food are a reflection on the Confucian gentleman's
sense for hierarchy, ritual propriety, altruism and above all, his moral integrity. While falling short of advocating persistent fasting or starvation
to achieve moral or spiritual goals, in taking or exchanging food, a respect
for the social context and role of the parties involved is made to prevail
over the physical imperative to feed the body. In the Confucian perspective
nourishing the body was seen as a form of moral nourishment.

Mencius likewise presents the acceptance of food as a question of morality in his account of Chen Zhongzi 陈仲子, who allegedly spat out the
goose stew his mother had given him because he thought it was ill-gotten.
He ate what his wife cooked for him but refused to accept food from his
mother. Mencius frequently argues that the overindulgence in food or full-
y stocked granaries at the court during periods of hardship should be taken
as a sign of moral decay and the incompetence to govern. He also con-
demns the neglect of sacrificial duties and the use as food of victims des-
tined for sacrifice.

Whereas in the stories presented so far food hygiene may have been
no more than the subject of the mood swings of fretful philosophers, for
cooks and kitchen staff cooking hygiene could be a matter of life and
death. The Han Feizi reports a case in which a cook is reprimanded for
leaving a slice of raw liver in his master's soup. In another case a member
of the kitchen staff is executed when a hair was found entangled in his
lord's skewered roast. A similar incident is the subject of a Han legal pro-

ceeding. Among a catalogue of judicial records excavated in 1983—1984 at Zhangjiashan 张家山(2nd c. B. C. E. ;Jiangling,Hubei)is a case of a couple wishing to impeach a maid servant for dropping a hair in their broiled meat and leaving a piece of grass in their rice. A detailed investigation follows which concludes that neither the person chopping nor the person broiling the meat could be guilty. The magistrate concludes that the hair was blown into the food by a fan,and the so-called grass turned out to be a fibre from the maid's worn out shirt. In the end the plaintiff is ordered to buy the maid a new shirt instead.

SAGES,COOKS,AND FLAVOURS IN WARRING STATES AND HAN CHINA Author(s): Roel Sterckx Source: Monumenta Serica ,Vol. 54(2006),pp. 1—46 Published by: Taylor & Francis,Ltd. Stable URL: http://www. jstor. org/stable/40727531 Accessed: 13-09-2016 11: 02 UTC

> **素材 2. An extract from "*Food and Environment in Early and Medieval China*" by E. N. Anderson**

Recent work on the Zhou Li— theoretically the government manual of the Zhou Dynasty but actually a Han reconstruction— promises to add to our understanding of food and nutrition. It was the Zhou Li that first established nutrition as the highest branch of medicine. The Zhou Li claims that the court had— along with shamans,dream interpreters,and so on— special officers in charge of aromatic plants, wines, chickens, and other food items. The idealized Zhou court should have two court nutritionists overseeing all. They were the most important medical officials in Zhou. A proper court should also have 152 feast masters, supervising some 70 butchers,128 cooks for the inner court,128 more for the outer offices and functions, 62 assistant cooks, 335 masters of the royal domain who(among other things)oversaw collecting the foodstuffs, 62 game hunters, 24 turtle catchers, 28 meat driers, 110 butlers, 340 winemakers, 170 other beverage makers, 94 icehouse attendants, 31 people to manage serving baskets, 61 meat picklers, 62 other picklers, and 62 salt makers—some 2,263, or 55 percent of the 4,133 officers of the royal household(Knechtges 1986: 49). Of course, it is more than doubtful that the Zhou ever had anything close to so many. One finds it hard to believe that they had any specialized turtle catchers, let alone 24. Still, these figures confirm historical testimony that feasting was extremely important, being, among other things, owed to the ancestors(K. - c. Chang 1977).

Food in those days was, as always in China, based on boiled grain. The relish eaten with it ran heavily to geng, stews and thick soups. The poor ate vegetable geng, with pigweed or lambs quarters(li, Chenopodium spp.)a particular marker of poverty food; Confucius was reduced to it in his poorer days(Sterckx 2011: 15- 16). A "meal of plain vegetables" became symbolic of rustic virtue. Of course, the geng of the rich involved various kinds of meat, fish, game, and turtles. Status was clearly shown by food: "In the retinue of the Lord of Mengchang, 'Senior Retainers ate meat, Regular Retainers ate fish, Junior Retainers ate vegetables' " (A. Meyer 2011: 79, quoting a fragment preserved in later works). One hopes that the suffering juniors got occasional meat!

With Zhou, we first find occasion to refer to the superb and encyclopedic history of Chinese food technology by H. T. Huang(2000), one of the greatest food historians. This book, the life work of Dr. Huang, sets a new standard for Chinese food research. Although it begins with the Neolithic, it really comes into its own with Zhou food. Among other things, Huang identifies the ritual vessels and shows some of the superb archaeological relics.

Roel Sterckx has recently taken up the task of seriously considering Warring States and Han food. He points out in The Animal and the Daemon in Early China(2002)that different regions had different animals,people,and customs and there seemed to be a mystic resonance here. His book Food,Sacrifice and Sagehood in Early China(2011;and see Sterckx 2005 and Lo 2005)goes into great detail not only about the food itself but also about the meanings it had during a time when rites and rituals changed from being genuine religious practices to being political gestures— no doubt having some sacred functions,but also serving to show off wealth,bond courtiers together,train the young in their obligations, and allow ritualists and organizers of ceremonies full play.

These sociological functions led Confucius and his followers to see rituals as critically important not only to statecraft but also to personal development. The proper gentleman(junzi)is trained in self-control and develops self-respect and a properly thoughtful,considerate,mindful attitude from following rituals to the letter,as the great founders of Zhou did in ancient times. Thus food took on a mystical importance: religiously important as sacrifice to the gods and ancestors,politically important as marker of status and solidarity,and personally important as part of a regimen of personal training and improvement. As I pointed out(E. Anderson 1988),this prevented puritanism from getting a foothold in China. That sour and mean philosophy was not without advocates(such as Mozi),but reverence for elders and ancestors meant that they had to be given the best of everything,and puritanism could not survive that imperative. It is a strange fact about humans that excuses for innocent enjoyment always seem necessary;puritanism is rampantly persuasive otherwise. It was to surface again in China when Buddhism became influential and became one of the reasons that Confucians condemned Buddhists for not caring about ancestors.

Sterckx provides a meticulous and fascinating account of the food of the era. A highly varied and complex cuisine(even including things like wolf's breast;Sterckx 2011:17)is attested in the records. In general,it is confirmed by food residues in cooking vessels. The five flavors—the four of Western food studies,plus hot spiciness—were well organized and balanced in cooking. (There is now known to be yet another flavor,umami—the savoriness of fermented soy products. The Chinese did not pick up on this one because they did not yet have soy ferments;those came in late Warring States or Han times. Hotness is not a flavor but a feeling;the various chemicals in question actually stimulate the heat receptors,or the pain receptors,in the mouth.)The five flavors distinguished by Chinese thought were associated with the many other"fives"of Chinese correspondence theory. These were well described in countless sources,most of which date back to the Yellow Emperor's Classic,of Han Dynasty vintage (see below).

Food preservation became a major need and an important art. Preservation included not only salting,drying,smoking,pickling,and so on,but also icing;snow and ice were collected in winter and stored in pits under insulating material. (Many Americans did the same within my memory).

Literature,including the Li Ji(Chapter 6),attests the technique later used for"beggars' chicken"—baking an animal in clay without removing the fur or feathers,which would stick to the clay and come off by themselves. "Fragments of a Han gastronomic treatise recovered in 1999 from the tomb of Wu Ying... include recipes for boiled deer,boiled lamb,and boiled horse"(Sterckx 2011:16). Sterckx does not find much else about eating horses,but several famous stories mention eating them,and frequent careful directions to avoid the liver indicate that the rest of the horse was a popular thing to eat. Horse liver was believed to be poisonous. I suspect that the liver accumulated toxins from vegetation the horses ate.

An enormously complex etiquette governed eating, feasting, and food-ways. Norbert Elias's"civilizing mission"had already been completed long ago, except for those"barbarians. "Barbarians, of course, ate as barbarians do — at least according to Chinese records. In fact, of course, those records reflect biased stereotypes rather than reality. The Chinese began to use the term"raw barbarians"for those who had not learned Chinese cultural behavior; those who had were"cooked barbarians. "The raw were the ones who supposedly ate their food raw; the civilized ones cooked it(Sterckx 2011: 20— 21). Of course, it is highly doubtful whether anyone really ate food raw. Grain and meat would not be very digestible, and raw pork would be downright dangerous. The point is that the more civilized the ethnic groups were, the more they ate like the Chinese of the central plains. The distinction between"raw"and"cooked"barbarians persisted in government records throughout the history of imperial China.

Sterckx provides a wonderful account. One can go to the Li Ji and Zhou Li for more; the rules go on and on, and the slightest infringement could get a servant killed or a lord assassinated. Confucius and his disciples and followers, known as ru, often made their living as ritual experts, planning and overseeing great rituals for local courts. Death and mourning had their own rules; the three -year mourning period for a parent involved moving from near fasting to an eventual full return to normal life. A large number of odd beliefs about food presage the ones that still exist in Chinese society. Avoidances, magical beliefs, and other ideas were current, including the idea that eating a rabbit's kneecap could doom you to having your kneecap cut off in punishment(Sterckx 2011: 23).

One point made by Sterckx concerns Zhuangzi's famous parable of the expert butcher. The butcher could keep his knife sharp forever by cutting only between the joints, where there was no resistance(anyone used to cutting up chickens is familiar with this concept). Zhuangzi has him advising the lord to govern accordingly— with a minimum of effort and bloodshed. But the brilliant and outspoken statesman Jia Yi(201- 169 BCE)— martyred for his"fearless speech"in the early Han Dynasty— put a new spin on this recommendation by maintaining that even the best butcher could not cut up big thighbones and hipbones without a hatchet and axe, and thus the emperor should deal with restive feudal lords by the direct approach(Sterckx 2011: 53). Unfortunately, the emperor took the advice all too much to heart; Jia was later executed himself.

Then as now, meat could be boiled, roasted, grilled, or left raw. Sacrifices were eventually buried and hidden, supposedly, but surely people ate the meat, as they did at other times in history. Many spirits, then as now, preferred sacrifices of raw meat, often with the hair still on. Sterckx argues that such spirits liked things pure and tasteless, but in modern China the spirits that prefer raw and hairy meat are often wild, savage, and intimidating spirits.

Spirits in Zhou and Han times liked their water pure and cold; it was called"dark mysterious liquor"(Sterckx 2011: 89ff.). Sometimes moonlight was reflected into it by mirrors. The cosmological history of the times associated the Xia Dynasty with bright pure water, the Shang with unfermented grain drink(presumably a sort of near -beer), the Zhou with fermented ale(92). As now, spirits had varied taste in ales, waters, and liquors in general, but, unlike today, they never got tea; it had not yet come to China. Of course, since the spirits got only the qi of the offerings while the humans got the material remains, this led to a serious danger of drunkenness, discussed and condemned at great length in documents quoted by Sterckx (101ff.). Recall Lothar von Falkhenhausen's observations (see above) on the reduced numbers of wine vessels in late Western Zhou.

The documents go into incredible detail on the sacrifices and the construction of altars. An altar could be desacralized: " ' When a state has ceased to exist, its altar of the soil is roofed above and fenced with wood below to indicate that its connection with Heaven and Earth has been cut off' " (Sterckx 2011: 117, quoting Wang Chong, ca. 1 CE).

Such sacrifices were a major economic activity. We read of offerings of "nearly 3,000 sheep and boar" at one time, of "more than 12,000 specialists... to oversee...more than 24,000 offerings" at another, and 37,000 shrines constructed in one year around 1 BCE (Sterckx 2011: 134). Of course, this created a huge demand, both for meat and for ru. The Chinese economists of the time— who were perfectly aware of Keynesian theory long before John Maynard Keynes himself— celebrated the major stimulant effect it had on the economy. A huge pottery workshop in Chang'an, the Han capital city (now Xi'an), could turn out 8,000 sacrificial figurines at one time (Sterckx 2011: 146). Even the humble bulrush supported a major industry, since it was used to manufacture mats and also strainers for ale (156). These were "jing reeds," described as having three ribs running the length of the stem, that is, bulrushes. The accounts tell us that demand for them led to a huge flow of wealth into the otherwise impoverished marsh districts and to an increase in economic activity generally, all described in terms that would delight Keynes and his recent followers. Ancient Chinese economists were no fools.

E. N. Anderson "Food and Environment in Early and Medieval China" University of Pennsylvania Press Philadelphia

> ➤ 素材 3. *An extract from Chinese Food and Medicine by* Lin Yutang

A broader view of food should regard it essentially as including all things that go to nourish us, just as a broader view of house should include everything pertaining to living conditions. As we are all animals, it is but common sense to say that we are what we eat. (If a man will be sensible and one fine morning, when he is lying in bed, count at the tips of his fingers how many things in this life truly give him enjoyment, invariably he will find food is the first one. For him "rice could never be white enough and mince meat could never be chopped fine enough." He refused to eat "when meat was not served with its proper sauce,""when it was not cut square,""when its colour was not right," and "when its flavour was not right." I am quite sure that even then his wife could have stood it, but when one day, unable to find fresh food, she sent her son Li to buy wine and cold meat from some delicatessen and be through with it, and he announced that he "would not drink wine that was not homemade, nor taste meat that was bought from the shops," what else could she do except pack up and run away? Sun Ssemiao(sixth century A. D.)says, "A true doctor first finds out the cause of the disease, and having found that out, he tries to cure it first by food. When food fails, then he prescribes medicine." Thus we find the earliest existing Chinese book on food, written by an Imperial physician at the Mongol Court in 1330, regards food essentially as a matter of regimen for health, and makes the introductory remarks: "He who would take good care of his health should be sparing in his tastes, banish his worries, temper his desires, restrain his emotions, take good care of his vital force, spare his words, regard lightly success and failure, ignore sorrows and difficulties drive away foolish ambitions, avoid great likes and dislikes, calm his vision and his hearing, and be faithful in his internal regimen. How can one have sickness if he does not tire his spirits and worry his soul? Therefore he who would nourish his nature should eat only when he is hungry and not fill himself with food, and he should drink only when he is thirsty and not fill himself with too much drink. He should eat little and between long intervals, and not too much and too constantly. He should aim at being a little hungry when well-filled and being a little well-filled when hungry. Being well-filled hurts the lungs and being hungry hurts the flow of vital energy. "

This cook book, like all Chinese cook books, therefore reads like a pharmacopoeia. For me, the philosophy of food seems to boil down to three things: freshness, flavour and texture. The best cook in the world cannot make a savoury dish unless he has fresh things to cook with, and any good cook can tell you that half the art of cooking lies in buying, and that it is always better to depend upon nature than upon culture to furnish us with the greatest epicurean delights. The texture of food, as regards tenderness, elasticity, crispness and softness, is largely a matter of timing and adjusting the heat of the fire. Chinese restaurants can produce dishes not possible in the home because they are equipped with a fine oven. As for flavour, there are clearly two classes of food, those that are best served in their own juice, without adulteration except salt or soya-bean sauce, and those that taste best when they are combined with the flavour of another food. And there is a large class of food, most valued by the Chinese, which have no flavour of their own, and depend entirely on borrowing from others. The three necessary characteristics of the most expensive Chinese delicacies are that they must be colourless, odourless, and flavourless. These articles are shark-fin, bird's nest and the "silver fungus". All of them are gelatinous in quality and all have no colour, taste or smell. The reason why they taste so wonderful is because they are always prepared in the most expensive soup possible.

Chinese Food and Medicine by Lin Yutang

➢ **注释**

eponymous   adj. 齐名的;使得名的

laud   v. 称赞,赞美

invariablyad   v. 总是;不变地;一贯地

sumptuous   adj. 豪华的;奢侈的;腆;美轮美奂

hygiene   n. 卫生,卫生学;保健法

broth   n. 肉汤

apocryphal   adj. 伪造的;真实性可疑的;作者不明的;

deference   n. 顺从;依从;尊重;敬重

gastronomic   adj. 美食(烹饪)法的,烹饪学的

calamus   n. 省藤属植物,菖蒲,羽根

eponymous   adj. 齐名的;使得名的

altruism   n. 利他主义,无私;爱他主义;利人主义

granary   n. 谷仓,粮仓

reprimand   v. 谴责;惩戒;责难

skewer   vt. 用串肉扦串起来;刺穿;串住

excavate   v. 挖掘;开凿;挖出;发掘

shaman   n. 萨满教的道士,僧人或巫师

retinue   n. 一批随员

courtier   n. 侍臣,廷臣

statecraft   n. 管理国家的本领;经纶

puritanism   n. 清教徒的行为和教义,清教主义

reverence   n. 尊敬,敬畏;敬礼;受尊敬;尊严

gastronomic   adj. 美食(烹饪)法的,烹饪学的

treatise   n. 论文;论述;专著

infringement　n. 侵权；违反；违背

presage　vt. 预示，预兆

desacralize　vt. 使非神圣化，使世俗化

regimen　n. (为病人规定的)生活规则，养生法；养生之道

pharmacopoeia　n. 药典，一批备用药品

epicurean　adj. 好美食的，爱奢侈享受的

adulteration　n. 掺假；掺杂，掺假货

gelatinous　adj. 胶状的

> 练习

1. Please read Passage 1, and then comment on "Despite the diverse circumstances in which these narratives situate the historical or eponymous Confucius, the underlying message is clear: attitudes toward food are a reflection on the Confucian gentleman's sense for hierarchy, ritual propriety, altruism and above all, his moral integrity."

2. Please read Passage 2, and then comment on "Thus food took on a mystical importance: religiously important as sacrifice to the gods and ancestors, politically important as marker of status and solidarity, and personally important as part of a regimen of personal training and improvement."

3. Please read Passage 3, and then comment on " A true doctor first finds out the cause of the disease, and having found that out, he tries to cure it first by food. When food fails, then he prescribes medicine."

4. Please read the translation of the following passage adopted from the Analects of Confucius. And write out the English expressions of the following words.

> 食不厌精，脍不厌细。食饐而餲，鱼馁而肉败，不食。色恶，不食，臭恶，不食。失饪，不食。不时，不食。割不正，不食。不得其酱，不食。肉虽

多,不使胜食气。惟酒无量,不及乱。沽酒市脯不食。不撤姜食。不多食。

    脍(kuai4):细切的肉＿＿＿＿＿＿＿＿＿

    饐(yì):陈旧。食物放置时间长了,陈旧,霉烂变质。＿＿＿＿＿＿＿＿

    餲(ài):变味了。＿＿＿＿＿＿＿＿＿

    馁(něi):鱼腐烂,这里指鱼不新鲜。＿＿＿＿＿＿＿＿＿

    败:肉腐烂,这里指肉不新鲜。＿＿＿＿＿＿＿＿＿

    饪(ren4):烹调制作饭菜。＿＿＿＿＿＿＿＿＿

    时:应时,时鲜。＿＿＿＿＿＿＿＿＿

    割不正:肉切得不方正。＿＿＿＿＿＿＿＿＿

    气:同"饩"(xi4),即粮食。＿＿＿＿＿＿＿＿＿

《论语》

Version for Reference

The master did not indulge in refined cereal or delicious meat. He did not eat long-exposed, sour food, nor did he eat rotten fish or meat. He did not eat what looked or smelt bad, nor did he eat anything not properly prepared or not served at meal time. He did not eat meat which was not rightly butchered. He did not eat food without its appropriate sauce. Plenty of meat as there was, he did not take it to exceed the due proportion for the rice. What he did not limit himself was only wine, but he did not allow himself to get drunk. He did not help himself to wine and dried meat that were bought in the market. He rejected no ginger, but did not take too much. Wu Guozhen

"The Analects of Confucius" Trans lated by

四、拓展阅读

➤ 背景知识

    色香味是衡量食物好坏的基本标准。如何可以烹饪出具有色香味的食物呢? 食物的制作有哪些秘诀呢? 本部分对比点为中国食物的制作工艺。第一篇选自新加坡的 Periplus Editions(HK)Ltd 出版的 Food of Asia 一书。第二篇来自胡适对 TO HOW TO COOK AND EAT IN CHINESE 一书所作的序言。请读者鉴赏比较。

➢ 素材 1.

From a country whose usual greeting is "Chi fan le mei you?"-Have you eaten? -you can expect nothing less than a passionate devotion to food. Chinese food is known the world over,thanks to the peripatetic nature of its people, but the success of its food hinges on much the same things: fresh ingredients and the balance of flavors. The next time you go to an Asian market, observe: the Chinese shoppers are likely to be the ones who prod the fish, inspect entire bunches of vegetables, and accept and reject a batch of shrimp based on the kick in their legs.

While the array of seasonings and sauces used by Chinese cooks is not vast, every dish must meet three major criteria: appearance, fragrance and flavor. The Chinese also prize texture and the health-giving properties of food.

An old Chinese proverb says, "To the ruler, people are heaven; to the people, food is heaven. " This is no truer than in China, where gastronomy is a part of everyday life.

The Making of a Cuisine

So large is China, and the geographic and climatic variations so diverse, that you can travel through the country and never have the same dish served in exactly the same way twice. The paradox of Chinese food is that it is one borne of hardship and frequent poverty: this is, after all, a country that houses 22 percent of the world's population and has only seven percent of the world's arable land.

There is much debate and confusion about how many regional cuisines there are, but most gourmets agree that at least four major Chinese regional styles exist: Cantonese, centered on southern Guangdong province and Hong Kong; Sichuan, based on the cooking of this western province's two largest cities, Chengdu and Chongqing; Hunan, the cooking of eastern China-Jiangsu, Zhejiang, and Shanghai; and Beijing or 'Northern' food, with its major inspiration from the coastal province of Shandong. Some would add a fifth cuisine from the southeastern coastal province of Fujian.

All regions use various forms of ginger, garlic, scallions, soy sauce, vinegar, sugar, sesame oil, and bean paste, but combine them in highly distinctive ways. What distinguishes these regional styles is not only their cooking methods but also the particular types and combinations of basic ingredients.

The southern school of cooking was the cuisine taken to the West by Chinese migrants-egg rolls, *dim sum*, *chow mein*, sweet and sour pork, *chop suey*, and fortune cookies. With the exception of the last two, which were American inventions, the other dishes are orthodox Cantonese creations.

Cantonese food is characterized by its extraordinary range and the freshness of its ingredients, a light touch with sauces, and the readiness of its cooks to incorporate "exotic" imported flavorings such as lemon, curry, and Worcester shire sauce. Cantonese chefs excel in preparing roasted and barbecued meats (duck, goose, chicken, and pork), and *dim sum*, snacks taken with tea for either breakfast or lunch. *Dim sum* can be sweet, salty, steamed, fried, baked, boiled or stewed, each served in their own individual bamboo steamer or plate. To eat *dim sum* is to "*yum cha*" or drink tea. In traditional *yum cha* establishments, restaurant staff walk around the room pushing a cart or carrying a tray offering their tasty morsels. Dim sum restaurants are important institutions where the locals go to discuss business, read newspapers and socialize.

The home of spicy food, Sichuan, is a landlocked province with remarkably fertile soil and a population of over 100 million. The taste for piquant food is sometimes explained by Sichuan's climate. The fertile agricultural basin is covered with clouds much of the year and there is enough rain to permit two crops of rice in many places.

Strong spices provide a pick-me-up in cold and humid weather, and make a useful preservative. The most popular spices are chilies and Sichuan peppercorns (prickly ash), tempered with sugar, salt, and vinegar. Despite the province's incendiary reputation, many of the famous dishes are not spicy at all, for example, the famous camphor-and tea-smoked duck, made by smoking a steamed duck over a mixture of tea and camphor leaves. But it is the mouth burners that have made Sichuan's name known all over the world, dishes like *ma po dou fu* -stewed bean curd and ground meat in a hot sauce; *hui guo rou* -twice-cooked (boiled and stir-fried) pork with cabbage in a piquant bean sauce; *yu xiang qiezi* , eggplant in "fish flavor" sauce; and *dou ban yu* -fish in hot bean sauce. When the Grand Canal was built in the Sui dynasty AD 581—618, it gave rise to several great commercial cities at its southern terminus, including Huaian and Yangzhou, after which this regional cuisine (Hunan) is named. Its location on the lower reaches of the Yangtze River in China's "land of fish and rice" gave it an advantage in terms of agricultural products, and it was renowned for seafood such as fish, shrimp, eel, and crab, which were shipped up the canal to the imperial court in Beijing. Hunan cuisine is not well known outside of China, perhaps because it rejects all extremes and strives for the "Middle Way". Freshness (xian) is a very important concept in the food of this region, but xian means more than just fresh. For a dish of steamed fish to be described as xian, the fish must have been swimming in the tank one hour ago, it must exude its own natural flavor, and must be tender yet slightly chewy. Xian also implies that the natural flavor of the original ingredients should always take precedence over the sauce. Some of the best known dishes from this region are steamed or stewed and require less heat and a longer cooking time, for instance chicken with chestnuts, the glorious pork steamed in lotus leaves, duck with a stuffing made from eight ingredients, and the evocatively named "lion head" meatballs.

The cuisine of Beijing has perhaps been subjected to more outside influences than any other major cuisine in China. First came the once-nomadic Mongols, who made Beijing their capital during the Yuan dynasty (1279—1368). They brought with them mutton, the chief ingredient in Mongolian hot pot, one of Beijing's most popular dishes in the autumn and winter. The Manchus, as the rulers of the Qing dynasty(1644—1911), introduced numerous ways of cooking pork. As the capital of China for the last eight centuries, Beijing became the home of government officials who brought their chefs with them when they came from the wealthy southern provinces. But the most important influence comes from nearby Shandong province, which has apedigree that goes back to the days of Confucius C. 550 BC. Shandong cuisine features the seafood found along China's eastern seaboard: scallops and squid, both dry and fresh, sea cucumber, conch, crabs, and shark's fins, often teamed with the flavors of raw leek and garlic.

Beijing's most famous dish, Peking duck, owes as much to the culinary traditions of other parts of China as to the capital itself. The method of roasting the duck is drawn from Hunan cuisine, while the pancakes, raw leek, and salty sauce that accompany the meat are typical of Shandong.

Beijing is also famous for its steamed and boiled dumplings(*jiaozi*), which are filled with a mixture of pork and cabbage or leeks, or a combination of eggs and vegetables.

The Food of the People

The proliferation of refrigerators in China today is making inroads on an institution that for centuries has been an essential part of daily life: shopping in the local food market. Many housewives and househusbands go to the market two or three times a day. In some state-run offices in Beijing, half-hour rest periods are allotted to enable its employees to shop for fresh produce.

In addition to fresh food markets, there are shops selling a huge variety of prepared and packaged food. Along with food markets, most cities have areas where snack foods are sold in stand-up or sit-down stalls. Breakfast may be a fried egg wrapped in a pancake; an "elephant ear" plate-sized piece of fried bread; noodles; congee(rice gruel) or bean curd jelly accompanied by a deep-fried cruller(*you tiao*); or a slice of cake and a jar of milk. Lunch or dinner could be noodles from a food stall or careful preparation of the just-bought produce from the market.

Every region has its own particular snacks, very often sold on the street. Snack food is very inexpensive and includes such regional specialties as Beijing's boiled tripe with fresh cilantro, fried starch sausage with garlic, sour bean soup, and boiled pork and leek dumplings (*jiaozi*). Shanghai is known for its steamed *baozi* dumplings, sweet glutinous rice with eight sweetmeats(*babaofan*) and yeasty sweetened wine lees(the sediment of the wine left after fermentation). Sichuan is noted for spicy *dan dan* noodles, dumplings in hot sauce, and bean curd jelly(*dou hua*), while Cantonese *dim sum* is a cuisine unto itself.

The average urban family eats its main meal of the day in the evening. This meal usually consists of a staple such as rice or noodles, one or two fried dishes, at least one of which contains meat or fish, and a soup. Northerners eat more wheat than rice, in the form of steamed buns or noodles, which are fried or simmered in stock. Beer regularly accompanies meals at home; stronger spirits are reserved for special occasions. The whole family gets involved in the business of shopping and cooking, and friends or relatives may be invited to join in the feast. Western foods have made tentative inroads into the 6000-year-old bastion of Chinese cuisine, but fast-food outlets succeed mainly because of their novelty and location in Chinese tourist cities.

China's Gourmet Culture

As the Son of Heaven, the emperor of China enjoyed a status so elevated above the common mortal that it is difficult to conceive of the awe in which he was held and the power that he enjoyed. There are no dining rooms in the Forbidden City; tables would be set up before the emperor wherever he decided to eat. Every meal was a banquet of approximately 100 dishes. These included 60 or 70 dishes from the imperial kitchens, and a few dozen more served by the chief concubines from their own kitchens. Many of the dishes served to the emperor were made purely for their visual appeal. and were placed far away from the reach of the imperial chopsticks. These leftovers were spirited out of the palace to be sold to gourmets eager to "dine with the emperor."

From the palace, this gourmet culture filtered down to the private homes of the rich and powerful and to the restaurants where the privileged entertained. Banquets are important social and commercial events in China today and many high officials attend banquets five or six nights a week. Almost any event can supply the reason for a banquet: the completion(or non-completion)of a business deal, wedding, graduation, trip abroad, return from a trip abroad, promotion, moving house and so on. One can also give a banquet to save or give "face" in the case of some unpleasant situation or mishap.

Some of the best restaurants in China today are the pre-1949 enterprises that have managed to survive by virtue of the quality of their cooking and by their location. One example is Fangshan Restaurant in Beihai Park in Beijing, set in a former imperial palace on the shores of an artificial lake, where many of the recipes are taken from the late-Qing dynasty Forbidden City. Fangshan is renowned for its Manchu-Chinese Banquet, a three-day dining extravaganza that consists of over 100 different dishes, a souvenir of Qing dynasty court banquets. At another famous restaurant, listening to the Orioles Pavilion, in the gardens of the famed Summer Palace (known to the Chinese as *Yi He Yuan*), dinners for 10 at around $1000 per table are reputedly not uncommon.

The Chinese Kitchen and Table

Rice is essential to a Chinese meal. This is particularly true in South China, although this division is not hard and fast. One reason the Grand Canal was built in the sixth century was to transport rice from the fertile Yangtze delta region to the imperial granaries in the relatively dry North. And since the Ming dynasty (1368—1644), an annual crop of short-grain rice has been grown in the suburbs of Beijing, originally for the palace and today for the military leadership. Numerous varieties of rice are produced in China, supplemented by the more expensive Thai rice which is available at urban markets throughout the country. Southerners seem to prefer longgrain rice, which is less sticky than other varieties and has strong "wood" overtones when steaming hot.

The basic Chinese diet and means of food preparation were in place about 6000 years ago, although many imported ingredients entered the Chinese larder and new cooking methods were adopted. From the earliest times,the Chinese have divided their foodstuffs into two general categories: *fan* (cooked rice and staple grain dishes) and *cai* (cooked meat and vegetable dishes). A balanced mixture of grain and cooked dishes has been the ideal of a Chinese meal since time immemorial. Further balances were sought between the yin(cooling) and yang(heating) qualities of the foods served. The notion of food as both preventative and curative medicine is deeply embedded in the Chinese psyche.

The specific proportion of grain and cooked dishes on a menu depends on the economic status of the diners and the status of the occasion. The grander the occasion,the more cooked dishes and less grain. Even today, this tradition is maintained at banquets,where a small symbolic bowl of plain steamed rice is served after an extensive selection of dishes.

Rice is served steamed,fried(after boiling) or made into noodles by grinding raw rice into rice flour. It is also cooked with a lot of water to produce congee or zhou(rice gruel),a popular breakfast food and late-night snack eaten with savory side dishes. Rice is eaten by raising the bowl to the mouth and shoveling the grains in with the chopsticks in a rapid fanning motion.

The Chinese table is a shared table. The average meal would comprise three to four *cai*, *fan* ,and a soup,served at once,to be shared between the diners who help themselves. The *cai* dishes should each have a different main ingredient,perhaps one meat,one fish,and one vegetable. Each dish should complement the other in terms of taste,texture and flavor,and the total effect appeal to both the eye and the tongue.

When cooking Chinese food,prepare all the ingredients and have them ready before you start cooking as trying to juggle a hot wok and chop a chicken at the same time inevitably leads to catastrophe!

Tea is drunk before and after a meal. but rarely during a meal. The most famous of clear-spirits drunk "straight up" in small handle-less cups or glasses during a meal is Maotai, made in the south-west province of Guizhou.

Chinese meals are socially important events, and special menus are presented for weddings and birthdays; important festivals also have their traditional dishes and snacks.

Finally, some tips on etiquette. Don't point with your chopsticks and don't stick them into your rice bowl and leave them standing up or crossed. Don't use your chopsticks to explore the contents of a dish-locate the morsel you want with your eyes and go for it with your chopsticks without touching any other pieces.

If you wish to take a drink of wine at a formal dinner, you must first toast another diner, regardless of whether he or she responds by drinking. If you are toasted and don't wish to drink, simply touch your lips to the edge of the wine glass to acknowledge the courtesy.

It is incumbent upon the host to urge the guests to eat and drink to their fill. This means ordering more food than necessary and keeping an eye out for idle chopsticks. It is polite to serve the guest of honor the best morsels, such as the cheek of the fish, using a pair of serving or "public" chopsticks or with the back end of one's chopsticks. And remember, all food is communal and to be shared.

Kong Foong Ling

Food of Asia　Periplus Editions(HK)Ltd.

> **素材 2. "FOREWORD" TO HOW TO COOK AND EAT IN CHINESE by Hu Shih**

Long, long ago, Confucius made this observation: "There is no one who does not eat and drink. But few there are who can appreciate taste. "

This observation is all the more remarkable because it came from a man who elsewhere declared that he could enjoy life even though he had only coarse food to eat and water to drink and his own bended arm to pillow.

The essence of Chinese cooking lies in the traditional insistence that food must have taste or flavor even though the materials used may be the most common and inexpensive kind of fish or vegetable. It is taste which gives joy in eating. And it is the art of the housewife, the cook, or the gourmet to work out the ways and means to give taste to food.

A Chinese gourmet of the eighth century A. D. , has left us this dictum: "Every eating material can be made palatable provided that it is given the proper cooking-time (huo-bou, literally, 'fire-timing'). " Please note that this expert did not say that palatability depended upon the use of the right kind of seasoning or flavoring materials. It is the proper "fire-timing" which really counts in all good cooking.

"Good cooking, "says Mrs. Chao, "consists in making the best use of the eating material. The cooking materials should only enhance the natural taste of the eating material and not take its place. "In these words, our author has summed up the art and the philosophy of Chinese cooking. All the "twenty and one" principal methods of cooking described in this book— from the slow and time-consuming "red-cooking" and "clear-simmering" to the quick and impressionistic "stir-frying" and "plunging"—are in reality gradations in "fire -timing".

......

She has created a new terminology, a new vocabulary, without which the art of Chinese cooking cannot be adequately introduced to the Western world. Some of the new terms like "Defishers, ""Stir-frying, ""Meeting, " "Plunging, "and a host of others, I venture to predict, will come to stay as the Chaos' contributions to the English language.

Of course I am not qualified to pass judgment on her recipes, not even to praise them. But I must tell a story to testify to the accuracy of her descriptions. I happened to be at Mrs. Chao's house just before she returned the galley proofs of her book to the publisher. I picked up one sheet at random and read the tail end of the recipe. "Why", I exclaimed, "this must be the Huichou Pot!" When I found the preceding page, there it was, the title "Huichou Pot," which, I believe, Mrs. Chao had learned from my wife and which was nostalgically familiar to me.

Twenty-three years ago, I was one of the two friends who had the honor to serve as witnesses at the wedding of Dr. and Mrs. Yuen-ren Chao. The unconventional bride cooked the dinner for the four of us. Since that memorable evening, I must have partaken at least a hundred meals prepared by Mrs. Chao. She has become not only a truly excellent cook, but, as this book testifies, an analytical and scientific teacher of Chinese cooking. It is, therefore, as a family friend and an appreciative "taster" of her food that I kow have the pleasure of presenting her book to the English-speaking world.

Chinese cooking, as Mrs. Chao tells us in the introduction, is not difficult to learn. A little thinking and a little willingness to experiment will go very far. Here is what our author has to say about roasting chestnuts:

Roast chestnuts are never good in America. They crack and stay raw because of uneven and interrupted heating. In China chestnuts are roasted in sand. The hot sand, stirred all the time, surrounds the chestnuts on all sides with medium heat. In the course of time, the meat becomes soft and fragrant like well-baked sweet potatoes.

All of her hundreds of recipes, like this one on roasting chestnuts in hot sand, represent the successful results of thinking and experimentation on the part of numberless frugal and ingenious men and women. They are now precisely recorded for the benefit and enjoyment of all those who would approach them in the spirit of willingness to think and experiment.

How to Cook and Eat in Chinese by Buwei Yang Chao Publisher: The John Day Company, New York

➤ 注释

gourmet　n. 讲究吃喝的人,美食家(gourmet 的名词复数)

morsels　n. 一口(morsel 的名词复数);(尤指食物)小块,碎屑

piquant　adj. 辛辣的;开胃的;刺激的;有趣的

pedigree　n. 血统;家谱;血统表

extravaganzan. 内容狂妄的作品;盛大表演(比赛),盛事

➤ 练习

1. Do you agree that there are at least four major Chinese regional cuisines?

2. Please read the first passage and comment on "Freshness(xian)is a very important concept in the food of this region, but xian means more than just fresh. "

3. Please read the second passage and comment on "Good cooking consists in making the best use of the eating material. The cooking materials should only enhance the natural taste of the eating material and not take its place. "

五、现代回声

➤ 背景知识

随着中国移民走向海外,中餐也开始发生迁移。中国食物反映了中国移民的社会背景、生活方式和文化价值观。在美国,中餐馆的历史不仅仅是

一个食物迁移和变化的故事，它还揭示了中国移民所遇到的挑战，体现了他们在美国生存和斗争的成功经验。美国当地人对中国饮食文化有好奇，也有偏见，甚至敌意。本节文章选自刘海明的《从广州饭馆到"熊猫快餐"美国中餐的历史》，介绍了中餐馆在美国的发展历史，供读者赏鉴。

Liu, Haiming, 1953- From Canton Restaurant to Panda Express: a history of Chinese food in the United States/ Haiming Liu.

Food has followed every wave of Chinese immigrants to the United States, from the mid-nineteenth century to today. Food tradition reflects the social background, lifestyle, and cultural values of both early and contemporary Chinese immigrants. Thus Chinese restaurant history in the United States is more than a story of food migration and change. It reveals who Chinese immigrants are; what challenges they have encountered; and how they have survived, struggled, and succeeded in their American experience. The American food market is both a meeting ground for different ethnic cuisines and a field of racial politics in which Chinese food culture has met with curiosity, prejudice, and even hostility. Yet through engagement and creative adaptation, Chinese immigrants have made Chinese food a vital part of American culinary culture.

Chinese restaurant history, at least before the 1960s, reflects more Chinese adaptation to America than what Chinese eat in China. The Chinese restaurant business has a long history in the United States, and its food, cooking, and operation illustrate the constant and continuous linkage between Chinese Americans and China.[1] Departure from the old country does not mean a break from the past for Chinese immigrants but the beginning of a new life in America. Chinese American food culture and restaurant business are a transnational history and should be understood as such. The goal of this book is not to chronicle the Chinese food and restaurant business in America but to explore a deeper meaning embedded in the Chinese restaurant experience.

Restaurant and food operations were among the earliest economic activities pursued by pioneer Chinese immigrants in California. Though modest in number, early Chinese restaurants were the "best eating houses" during the gold rush. Chinese restaurants' yellow silk flags, their famous commercial mark, attracted many customers. The first Chinese restaurant was established in 1849. With 300 seats and English-speaking bartenders, Canton Restaurant was a landmark food institution in San Francisco during the gold rush. While American "forty-niners" rushed to the mining fields, Chinese pioneer immigrants foresaw other opportunities for making money.

Forty-niners from China were restaurateurs, tradesmen, or investors who migrated to California not to dig gold but to engage in trade. Equally eager to strike it rich, Chinese forty-niners seemed more rational, calculating, and patient in making money. Trade was their profession. As merchants, they established import and export companies, brought in commodities for daily needs, and ran restaurants, tool shops, warehouses, herbal pharmacies, grocery stores, lodging houses, and many other retail and service businesses in San Francisco. Then they sponsored and encouraged waves of immigrants from their home regions in Guangdong Province, South China, to join the gold rush, to become the pioneer agricultural laborers, and to build the Central Pacific Continental Railroad. [2] As the historian Kevin Starr put it: "No Asian group played a more important role in the establishment of the state [California] in the nineteenth century than the Chinese. Chinese were more than immigrants. They were founders. "[3] Rather than a desperate escape from poverty and hunger, Chinese migration to the United States began as a transplanted social network of entrepreneurs who brought with them trade, business, and people. Collectively, early Chinese immigrants were far more stable and rooted in California than most gold rush"sojourners"who came to the state merely for gold.

Food culture was an ethnic marker. Though Chinese restaurants were one of the pioneer food businesses in San Francisco, the city had only a small number of Chinese restaurants in the last three decades of the nineteenth century, when all kinds of food and restaurant businesses were thriving there. In 1882, the year that the U. S. Congress passed its first Chinese Exclusion Act, there were only fourteen Chinese restaurants in San Francisco. In comparison, there were 175 Chinese laundries. The restaurant business was one of the oldest professions in China. Chinese cuisine was one of the best in the world. However, the Chinese food business failed to carve a big niche in the city's restaurant market.

This was not a culinary failure. Anti-Chinese sentiment reached its peak during the last three decades of the nineteenth century. Several Chinese exclusion laws were passed between 1882 and 1904. Food culture in America was also tainted by racial ideology. Chinese food tradition was stereotyped. Rice became a racial symbol of Asian inferiority; beef consumption represented white American superiority. A century-long racist image of Chinese eating rats made many white Americans suspicious of the Chinese diet. Food was used as a tool in racial ideology. Eating in a Chinese restaurant could be culturally embarrassing or socially awkward for a middle-class white family. American society judged Chinese food through racial rather than culinary criteria.

The Chinese restaurant businesses made a rebound in the form of chop suey houses after Li Hongzhang's visit to the United States in 1896. Li was China's most important diplomat during that time. While racial discrimination against the Chinese was intense, American businessmen were still keenly interested in China trade and the Chinese market. American media had daily coverage about Li's visit. When the media reported that chop suey was Li's favorite food, the American public underwent a craze for Chinese food. Chop suey became an imagined authentic Chinese dish. Chinese immigrants quickly capitalized on the legend. They changed chop suey's ingredients, flavor, and method of preparation to fit the palate of Americans. They grasped the opportunity to expand their restaurant business outside of Chinatown.

Chop suey houses soon proliferated across the country. Based on chop suey, a simple rural dish, Chinese immigrants generated a series of Americanized Chinese meals such as beef chop suey, chicken chop suey, chow mein, and egg foo yong. From 1900 to the late 1960s, chop suey houses were synonymous with Chinese restaurants in the United States. Modified Chinese food became rooted in American society and constituted an important part of the American restaurant market. However, this is not an example of Chinese "assimilation" into American society. Instead, chop suey became a tool or a strategy for Chinese immigrants to create an occupational niche for themselves during the Chinese exclusion era. It represents a creative adaptation of Chinese Americans to American society.

The popularity of chop suey houses also reflected a dynamic interaction between Chinese food and American customers. While Chinese food was being transformed, reinvented, and even altered by American popular taste, Chinese restaurant businesses at the same time helped shape the American diet. It was an interesting process of cultural negotiation. Though popular, chop suey symbolized cheap exoticism in the eyes of many American customers. It succeeded mostly as a bargain ethnic food. American customers readily accepted it as a "foreign" food made in the United States. Its success reflected mainstream Americans' social expectations of Chinese cuisine. Rather than a culinary wonder, chop suey is a meaningful social construct in racial America.

Yet chop suey houses embodied not only Chinese ethnicity but also metropolitan Americanness. A Jewish man recalled his childhood in New York in the early twentieth century: "I felt about Chinese restaurants the same way I did about the Metropolitan Museum of Art—they were the two most strange and fascinating places my parents took me to, and I loved them both. "⁴ By historical chance, Chinese Americans and Americans Jews shared residential proximity in New York City at the turn of the twentieth century. Both groups explored ways to adapt to American society. Through frequenting Chinese restaurants, Jewish immigrants and their descendants became more metropolitan and more adapted to American urban life. Chinese food helped them gradually break away from their religious, restrictive, and symbolic dietary rules of the Old World. For many American Jews, eating Chinese food has become a weekly routine, a Christmas tradition, and a childhood memory. It is rare but significant that the food of one ethnic group has evolved into an expressive form of another group's identity. This meaningful episode of American ethnic history reflects how the Chinese reached out to other cultures through food and how Jewish immigrants longed for a new identity.

The Chinese restaurant business began to change after World War II following the return of the U. S. servicemen from Asia and a restaurant boom in America. But a significant new turn took place in the 1970s. After the Immigration and Nationality Act of 1965, hundreds of thousands of Chinese immigrants came to the United States from Taiwan and Hong Kong, and later mainland China. Upon their arrival, chop suey houses gradually lost their appeal. Chinese restaurants started to serve authentic Chinese food. In Chinese culinary culture, authentic food means regional cuisines. China has no national food. Different geographical areas have different food products, local flavors, and famous dishes in their culinary culture. Between eight and ten regional cuisines are best known across the country, such as Guangdong, Hunan, Sichuan, Shandong, and Shanghai. In the 1970s and 1980s, the most popular Chinese food in New York was Hunan cuisine. However, few American customers knew that those Hunan restaurants in New York, New Jersey, Washington, D. C. , or other areas on the East Coast were established by immigrants from Taiwan rather than Hunan Province in southwest China.

The popularity of Hunan restaurants in Taiwan and then in America is an interesting piece of Chinese Diaspora history. After the civil war in China ended in 1949, nearly two million Nationalists and their followers fled to Taiwan. Their arrival changed the social landscape of the island. The Nationalists and their families came from a variety of geographical regions of China. For them, food evoked memories of home and specifically the culture of their home regions. As a result, Hunan, Sichuan, Shandong, Shanghai, and many other Chinese regional cuisines were reproduced based on the collective memory of those Nationalists and their families. Though there was no political contact for decades across the Taiwan Strait, thousands of restaurants featuring Chinese regional flavors appeared in Taiwan. Cultural preservation was simultaneously a process of cultural reproduction. When Hunan cuisine spread from Taiwan to the United States, it was both a Chinese regional and a Chinese Diaspora food. Embedded in Hunan restaurants is the remigration experience of post-1965 Chinese immigrants from Taiwan.

Food represents an important aspect of contemporary Chinese American culture. Instead of wholesale assimilation, post-1965 Chinese immigrants have selectively maintained some of their native cultural traditions such as food. Food expresses ethnic solidarity and cultural traditions. The restaurant is an institution where Chinese socialize and pass on food traditions to younger generations.

Food culture of contemporary Chinese Americans reflects a seemingly paradoxical adaptation strategy. It is not only possible but also increasingly preferred for many immigrants to maintain their Chinese ethnic tradition while becoming Americans. With numerous restaurants, grocery stores, and ethnic strip malls visibly congregating and rooted in the San Gabriel Valley of Southern California, the transnational and multicultural identity of Chinese Americans is no longer an abstract idea but a solid and tangible reality. In food and restaurant operation, we see how transnational culture is deeply ingrained in the contemporary Chinese American community. Moreover, the flourishing of Chinese restaurant businesses in the metropolitan areas of the United State shows how new immigrants have enriched American culinary culture and how food choices continuously expand in the American restaurant market.

With more than 40,000 Chinese restaurants across the country in the early twenty-first century, Chinese cuisine has become an important component of the American food market. But the first and so far only full-service, sit-down Chinese restaurant that is a publicly traded stock company on Nasdaq is P. F. Chang's China Bistro, which was actually established by Paul Fleming, a white American restaurateur who used to own four Ruth's Chris Steak House franchises. As a full-service, sit-down restaurant, P. F. Chang's is in the same price range as Olive Garden, California Pizza Kitchen, or the Cheese Cake Factory. It caters mainly to middle-class mainstream American customers, and seldom locates in or close to a Chinese American community. In the shadow of its success, we ponder the question of who owns culture. Culture seems hereditary or primordial and is often considered as a genetic soft power of a community or an ethnic group. In reality, culture, especially restaurant culture, is a "public domain" in which every participating agent, organization, or corporation could have access to or even own it. Chinese Americans have no controlling power or patent rights to their own food in the American restaurant market. When food becomes a commodity, it is no longer an inherited culture. Corporate America could easily appropriate it. Food is both a culture and a commodity.

If P. F. Chang's is a case of a mainstream America food business embracing authentic Chinese culinary culture, Panda Express shows how Chinese restaurateurs have integrated American fast-food concepts into their business. It is the fastest growing and the largest fast-food Chinese restaurant chain in the United States. Established in 1983 by Andrew and Peggy Cherng, an immigrant couple from Taiwan and Hong Kong, Panda Express started in Southern California, the birthplace of the American fast-food industry. McDonald's, Carl's Jr. , and In-NOut are some of the big names that can trace their origins to this area. However, running a Chinese fast-food restaurant is far more challenging than running a McDonald's or a Burger King restaurant. As one food critic put it, "Panda Express is a real innovation. Where most attempts at Chinese fast food have settled for egg rolls, rice, and chow mein, Panda Express offers orange-flavored chicken, tofu with black mushrooms, beef with broccoli, and many other dishes conceived by Chinese chefs and prepared on site by trained cooks. "[5] Like P. F. Chang's, Panda Express caters mainly to non-Chinese customers. It has affected the contemporary American palate almost as much as chop suey did in the first half of the twentieth century. The rapid growth of Panda Express has made Chinese food a visible option for American customers in the fast-food restaurant market.

Today, Chinese restaurants can be found in almost every city in the world. Local restaurant customers in New York or Southern California probably have more options in choosing different regional flavors of Chinese cuisine than Chinese customers in any midsize city in China. But authenticity in Chinese food is a complex issue, as shown in Din Tai Fung, a Shanghai-style dumpling house that originated in Taiwan. This internationally renowned restaurant has stores in the United States, Japan, Australia, and Hong Kong, as well as in Shanghai, Beijing, Guangzhou, Shenzhen, and a number of other cities in mainland China. Settling down in Shanghai, the birthplace of Shanghai steamed dumplings, can Din Tai Fung claim its own products as more authentic than products of 100-year-old native stores like Longxiang Restaurant? Who represents the genuine Shanghai dumplings? As Din Tai Fung shows, food authenticity is a fluid and flexible concept. This is especially true considering how Chinese cuisine has become a global phenomenon. The culinary identity of Din Tai Fung and many Chinese restaurants in the United States is simultaneously local and national, Taiwanese and Chinese, Diaspora and transnational. It confirms Tu Weiming's conception of cultural China as both a unified and fractured entity. 6

Liu, Haiming, 1953- From Canton Restaurant to Panda Express: a history of Chinese food in the United States/ Haiming Liu.

> 练习

Please read and then comment on the following statements:

1. Instead, chop suey became a tool or a strategy for Chinese immigrants to create an occupational niche for themselves during the Chinese exclusion era. It represents a creative adaptation of Chinese Americans to American society.

2. After the Immigration and Nationality Act of 1965, hundreds of thousands of Chinese immigrants came to the United States from Taiwan and Hong Kong, and later mainland China. Upon their arrival, chop suey houses gradually lost their appeal. Chinese restaurants started to serve authentic Chinese food.

3. If P. F. Chang's is a case of a mainstream America food business embracing authentic Chinese culinary culture, Panda Express shows how Chinese restaurateurs have integrated American fast-food concepts into their business.

第十一章　战　术

一、词源梳理

　　"war"一词来源于"werre"，是古法语"guerre"的北方方言。"guerre"来自史前日耳曼语的"werra"（斗争，冲突）一词，它的构词基础是 wers-（也是英语词 worse 和德语的 wirren"混淆"的词源）。在古法语中"guerre"含义为"困难、争端；敌对；打仗、战斗、战争"。"war"(n.)在古英语晚期写作"wyrre"，"were"，含义为"大规模军事冲突"，其词源为古法语北方方言"were"，含义为"战争"。

　　英语中"Art"一词与"arm"，"arthritis"，和"article"等词一样，可以追溯到印欧语系中的词根"ar"，意思是"把东西放在一起，结合起来"。把东西放在一起需要某种技巧；因此拉丁语的"ars"一词解释为"技术"。它的词干"art-"产生了古法语中的"art"一词，而这个词是英语单词"art"的来源。它带来了"技巧"的概念，这一概念至今仍保留着。

　　中文的"战"字，形声。根据《说文解字》，"战"从戈，单（占）声。战，斗也。斗字本写作"鬪"。斗者，两士相对。兵杖在后也。战者、圣人所慎也。故引申为战惧。

　　"战"始见于战国晚期，当时主要有两种形体。一种是图 1 的金文，左旁是"单"，甲骨文的"单"本来是一种长柄的狩猎工具，后演变成杀敌的武器；右旁是"戈"，本义是一种用于勾割的兵器，二者结合起来，便成了图 1 的金文，意指拿着"单""戈"等武器或狩猎武器去搏斗。此外"单"与"战"音相近，

"单"也可视为声旁。另一种是图4的金文,左边部分是"嘼","嘼"就是兽;右边部分是"戈",表示持戈和野兽(或野兽般的人)拼斗,从这个意思看,"战"的本义也是战斗,也是会意字。

图9的字形是小篆。字的左旁已统一为"单",作为表音的声符;字的右旁以"戈"表意。以后便以小篆为基文,相继发展为隶书和楷书。繁体的"战"字共十六画,书写速度慢,于是新造了一个以"占"为声,以"戈"为形的"战",这个字见于明末的官府文书档案《兵科抄出》和清初的《目连记弹词》中,后作为简化汉字。

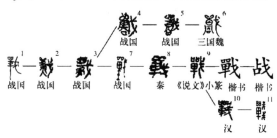

戰(战) zhàn　章纽、元部;章纽、线韵、之膳切。

1、2、3、5、7《战文编》815页。4、8《战文编》814页。6《篆文编》579页。9《说文》266页。10、11《篆隶表》898页。

"衕"字在现代汉语简化为"术"(注意,术与衕并不完全等同)读 shù。《说文解字》给的解释是:"衕,邑中道也。从行,术声。"形声字。本义是都邑中的道路;也泛指街道、道路。但"术"在《说文解字》中是"禾"部"秫"字的省写。

"衕"字在徐锴《说文系传通论》中有说:"邑中道而衕,大道之派也。""派"的本义就是水的支流,那么,衕,其实就是大路的支线。后来,"衕"也引申为途径。后来,又借指沟渠。这些基本上还是本义的引申用法。

在哲学层面,"道"是规律、是思想、是法则,是事物的本质、本源,有极强的普适性和理论性;而"术"是技术、方法,是具体、细节的东西,有可操作性。所以从概念上说,"术"小于"道"。在文字学角度说,"辵"部的"道"指的是大路,通达之路,而"術"指的邑中之道,是小路,是街巷,所以即便仅在文字学层面,"術"也不如"道"。只不过汉字简化之后,术字已经看不出"道路"的意思了。

从词源学的梳理结果可见,不论是"战"所具有的"圣人所惧",还是"术"所具有的"道"之支线的含义,都是与中国文化中止戈为武,更重视文治而非武功的态度吻合一致的。

二、引导阅读

➤ 背景知识

《孙子兵法》是中国战国时期(公元前 403—221 年)关于东方军事战略的一部极有影响的著作,拿破仑和道格拉斯·麦克阿瑟将军等西方历史伟人都声称它是灵感的源泉。

曹操在《孙子略解》的自序中曾写道:"吾观兵书战策多矣,孙子所著深矣。"南宋郑厚在《艺圃折衷》中认为:"孙子十三篇,不惟武人之根本。文士亦当尽心焉。其词约而缛,易而深,畅而可用,《论语》《易》《大传》之流,孟、荀、杨著书皆不及也。"明代人茅元仪在评价《孙子》一书时说:"前孙子者,孙子不遗;后孙子者,不能遗孙子。"唐太宗李世民评论:"朕观诸兵书,无出孙武"。孙中山说:"就中国历史来考究,二千多年的兵法,有十三篇,那十三篇兵书,便成立为中国的军事哲学。"唐太宗曾给予"观诸兵书,无出孙武"的极高评价,司马迁说:"世俗所称师旅,皆道孙子十三篇"。可见《孙子兵法》在军事领域的崇高地位。

本部分节选自"The Science of War—Sun Tzu's Art of War re-translated and re-considered",作者是 Christopher MacDonald。克里斯托弗·麦克唐纳在本书中对《孙子兵法》进行了全面的评述,所节选部分包括对《孙子兵法》的框架简介和一些术语解释,供读者赏鉴。

Art of War or science of war?

There may well be an art to war;just as there is an art to government and an art to life,a body of skills and principles typically acquired through experience and taught by example. But art is not the focus of the *Sun-tzu*.

The work's title in standard romanized Chinese is *Sunzi Bingfa* (孙子兵法), and that term *bingfa* (兵法) combines a Chinese character indicating weaponry, soldiers and armed conflict, with one connoting method, or a system of rules and principles. In classical times the pairing formed a generic term for any functional treatise on applied military matters. *Bingfa* texts explained campaign and battlefield tactics alongside the logistical, institutional and political dimensions of war. In structure and content they were designed to provide practical guidance, in the form of strategic principles governing the overall approach to war combined with specific techniques to use before and during the fight. The thinkers whose views came to be disseminated in the *bingfa* form, offered commanders a tool for prioritizing their energies and resources during the run-up to war; along with a menu of practical methods for winning war.

The Sun Tzu treatise was not the first of its kind, though it is the earliest to have survived the wholesale destruction of manuscripts that occurred in the Qin dynasty(221—206 BC). It was also the most succinct, comprehensive and best structured *bingfa* of the era, offering systematic analysis of operational tactics combined with the first-known outline theory of military strategy. In effect, Sun Tzu pioneered the science of war.

Structure

As discussed in the preceding section of Part One, analysis of the text indicates that each of the thirteen chapters in the Sun-tzu originated as a standalone tract before being integrated into the work we know today. Each chapter focuses on a particular aspect of warfare, and does so from the perspective of a commander at the head of a massive Warring States (5th century to 221 BC)army, tasked with the challenge of extracting victory from among the chaotic currents of interstate conflict. In sequence, the thirteen chapters broadly track the process of preparing for and then engaging in armed conflict, providing commanders with a programme for rational military management while also offering philosophical insight into the irrational and in many ways unmanageable nature of war.

The first seven chapters of the treatise place the events of war in their strategic context—the battle as part of a campaign, and the campaign as part of a wider pattern of confrontation. Preparation begins with early empirical analysis of the overall situation and proceeds to the shaping of a strategic landscape that favours victory for your side. The next four chapters cover a compendium of operational and tactical considerations, mostly related to maneuvers, terrain and environmental factors, while the final two chapters are specialist tutorials on incendiary attacks and intelligence operations.

Within this framework, there is a degree of overspill between chapters and plenty of digression. For example, Chapter 10 of the treatise, entitled "Terrain", begins with a classification of terrain types before digressing to list a series of circumstances, attributable to poor leadership, in which armies capitulate. After briefly returning to the topic of terrain, the chapter veers off again to discuss key character traits of a chief commander; then concludes with a short disquisition on the relationship between knowledge and victory.

Every chapter in the Sun-tzu contains off-topic statements and sections, often patched into place with the aid of conjunctive characters meaning "so...", "hence..." or "in this way...". For the purpose of this translation, sub-headings and spacing are inserted between passages to signal switches of theme and topic. Nevertheless, the liveliness which the narrative skips around can be confusing.

The sometimes indiscriminate succession of ideas in part reflects the manner, more than 2,000 years ago, in which writings were stitched together and amended, often over the course of generations. At a number of points in the text, characters from an unknown earlier edition have clearly gone astray or been wrongly transcribed, and several passages of the treatise appear to have been wrongly interpolated or loosely copied from earlier chapters.

But thematic free-association was also one of the rhetorical conventions of classical Chinese, which allowed writers to express their thinking in a non-linear fashion. Key assertions were to be circled over and presented from various angles so that readers could probe for connections and anomalies while bringing their own perspectives to bear. Moreover, a "reader" in classical times was just as likely to be a listener; with the text presented orally and construed character by character and phrase by phrase, in the presence of a tutor or in discussion with other readers.

For modern readers, in a Western language, this is an unfamiliar approach to constructing a written argument and it can be an obstacle to understanding. In China, by contrast, the Sun-tzu has generally been regarded as structurally and conceptually coherent, and well worth its reputation as the ancient world's most profound and intelligible text on the principles of warfare.

That coherence resides partly in the text's presentational tone — the tone of the commander and strategist known as Master Sun—and partly in the structural and conceptual fabric of the work. Structural, in terms of the sequence of chapters, and the ordered presentation of information within individual passages, typically involving classified lists. Conceptual, in terms of a handful of core ideas which are woven throughout the text.

Lists are used in numerous passages to organize information and simplify practical guidance. They include five sets of factors by which a commander analyses the strategic balance before war; in Chapter 1 ("Assessing the Conditions"), six categories of terrain enumerated in Chapter 10 ("Terrain"), and five types of intelligence source described in Chapter 13 ("Intelligence Operations"). Each list identifies a class of conflict-related factors or scenarios, and the reader is then offered mental blueprints by which to recognize patterns, set priorities and, where necessary, take action. For example, the list of guidance on tactics to use following an incendiary attack on the enemy position, in Chapter 12 ("Incendiary Attacks"), includes the following rule of thumb: "When a blaze breaks out but the enemy remains calm, wait and watch-do not attack. If practical, follow through as the flames peak. Otherwise stay put".

While classified lists provide structure within individual passages of the text, the work's overall conceptual consistency comes from a set of core strategic ideas. Three of the most powerful of these ideas are conveyed by paired characters carrying opposing meanings: the unconventional and the orthodox, the empty and the solid, and the oblique and the direct. Each of these pairs of complementary opposites opens a new semantic domain in the space between two familiar components. A related effect occurs in English with words like "tragicomic" or "bittersweet", or an oxymoron like "deafening silence"— twin poles of a shared axis. In classical Chinese, where allusion is preferred to direct reference, and fuzzy reasoning trumps raw logic, the use of complementary opposites helps to stretch the imagination, challenging the reader to explore for deeper patterns in the material and grasp abstractions that may be new and unusual.

Key tactical and strategic concepts

The Sun-tzu is packed with practical advice for commanders seeking tactical advantage in a range of battlefield and campaign scenarios, but it is the work's strategic dimension that sets it apart.

The message for any would-be all-conquering general is, naturally, to master campaign tactics and mass organizational skills, but also to look beyond those to the task of long-term planning for which he needs a deep understanding of the military and non-military dynamics at play when the interests of different states clash. The general who follows Sun Tzu grounds his approach to these dynamics in hard reality, immune from wishful thinking and emotionalreflex. By dint of training and experience, he develops the intuition to recognize and respond to emerging patterns in the overall strategic dynamic. Ultimately he masters that dynamic, reaching beyond conventional formulas to shape a strategic landscape tailored to his objectives.

The tension in the Sun-tzu between tactics and strategy, between convention and innovation and between prescribed and improvised responses, is part of a pattern of contrasts at the core of the work, which is highlighted in the following core pairs of complementary opposites.

Theunconventional and the orthodox

Qi-zheng(奇正—"odd/irregular"plus"regular/correct/standard"), in Sun Tzu, is a pair of opposites that alludes to the combination of left-field moves and textbook tactics by which an able commander stays unpredictable.

Until the Warring States era, when the Sun-tzu was composed, military convention demanded a degree of honourable conduct on the part of thecombatants. It was a fading echo of the chivalric code which, in earlier generations, had governed armed conflict among the nobility of the small principalities and city states of the Yellow River plain. Among other things, that code had precluded acts of outright deviousness in war. By the time of Sun Tzu, however war had largely transitioned to a new phase of large, attritional campaigns waged without scruple among massive armies directed by technocratic professionals rather than vainglorious aristo-crats. Cheating on the rules of war was widespread, though aspects of the old taboos still applied.

Zheng, in the martial context, stood for all that was traditional, cor-rect and proper; in the moral order of the universe as well as in the forma-tions and tactics of the army. Qi, by contrast, implied the unpredictable and the unorthodox, in life as in war. Sun Tzu shamelessly celebrates subversive, qi approaches("War is all about trickery and deceit"- ch. 1. 5), albeit in a context in which the army and its commanders have first es-tablished their zheng credentials("Battles generally begin with orthodox openings, but it is the unconventional move that wins the day"- ch. 5. 2). For best results, the qi has to stand on a foundation of zheng, and vice ver-sa:"Strategic dominance is built on only two types of tactic, the uncon-ventional and the orthodox, but combining them generates more variations than could ever be known. "(ch. 5. 2).

As the treatise emphasizes, commanders need to remain honourable and upright if they are to inspire confidence and earn the respect of their subordinates. Army hierarchy has to be rigid and efficient, and battalions have to be drilled to perfection in standard formations and maneuvers. These are all zheng-type qualities. Yet, according to the Sun Tzu ideal, commanders also have to be masters of subterfuge, cunning and espio-nage, and the army has to move and fight in a way that is fluid, innovative and wholly unpredictable — all very qi concepts. Where necessary, the commander-in-chief is to tear up the rulebook, keeping friends and foes guessing:"Manage the course of battle by adapting to the enemy's ap-proach rather than relying on pre-determined tactics"(ch. 11. 11).

So, the pairing of qi and zheng describes those paradoxically com-bined approaches — simultaneously novel and traditional, honourable and devious, orthodox and unconventional — that a gifted and experienced Sun Tzu-type commander brings to war; at both the tactical and strategic levels.

The empty and the solid

Xu-shi(虚实——"empty/immaterial"plus"substantive/solid"), in Sun Tzu, indicates the asymmetrical presence or absence of military forces at a given locale, by which a commander ensures he has overwhelming numerical superiority at the point of combat:"When troops take action, the impact must be that of a whetstoneflung against an egg. It is a matter of a-symmetrical force".

Rather than going head-to-head against enemies of similar or greater strength, the able commander aims to act unopposed, maneuvering to concentrate his elite or massed forces against weak points where enemy soldiers are absent, or thin on the ground, or are renderedineffective by sickness,poor leadership or lack of weapons:"To advance without being repulsed, thrust where opposing forces are most dispersed"(ch. 6. 3). Meanwhile,he lures the enemy's best forces to expend their energy striking at shadows, and ensures that the enemy's lesser units, if they attack, encounter fierce resistance from a well-prepared mass of defenders,properly led and full of zeal:

"An accomplished campaigner imposes his will on the opponent rather than being imposed upon. He entices the enemy to move of his own accord into the intended position. He deters the enemy from going where he would otherwise go"(ch. 6.1).

Mastery of the xu-shi principle means exploiting the opportunities for tactical and strategic advantage that fluctuate, as fluidly as water; between xu and shi:"Water forms channels according to the lie of the land,and armies fashion victory according to the presence of the enemy"(ch. 6. 7).

The oblique and the direct

Yu-zhi(迂直——"winding/circuitous" plus "straight/direct"), in Sun Tzu, refers to the guileful interplay of linear and non-linear movements by which a commander misdirects the enemy; while his own forces maneuver for initiative.

At an operational level, the commander applies his mastery of this principle to delay and exhaust the enemy in the run-up to battle:

"By side-tracking the opponent and distracting him with easy gains, one reaches the battlefield first despite marching later"(ch. 7. 1).

At the more strategic and philosophical levels, the commander must correctly assess the benefits of taking direct action in pursuit of a military objective, compared with those of holding off or adopting a more circuitous approach: "Weigh up the strategic benefits before making a move. The commander who best masters the interplay between oblique and direct maneuvers, will prevail"(ch. 7. 3).

As with qi-zheng (unconventional/orthodox) and xu-shi (empty/solid), the yu-zhi(winding/ straight)pairing works in both a literal and figurative sense. The enemy must be physically misdirected on the ground and mentally wrong-footed in his planning and preparations, in both cases expending valuable energy and resources before battle. And in common with those other pairings, the yu-zhi principle instils in readers a tactical and strategic approach that emphasizes mind and maneuvers over brute force.

These three key pairs of complementary opposites in Sun Tzu form part of a pattern of dual perspectives thatpermeates the treatise. Each, in its way; reproduces the tension between chaos and order that is fundamental to military action.

Order is the conventional military solution to the chaos of the fight. Hierarchies are established, discipline is imposed and maneuvers are drilled, formations are fixed and tactics are developed and honed. Lines, columns and squares are used to concentrate manpower into manageable, moving blocks, controlled through a strict regimen of command. The larger the military machine, the greater the reliance on organized systems of management and control.

But as the scale of armies expanded during the Warring States era, it was discovered that too much order in the structure of an army or the planning of a campaign hardened into brittleness and inertia. A rigid, rectilinear force can be outflanked by one that is more flexibly configured. Orthodox tactics may be rendered defunct by an opponent's unanticipatedgambit. A cautious, deliberative commander may be stunned by the audacity of a faster-thinking, more innovative rival.

The tactical and strategic guidance in the Sun-tzu plays repeatedly on this paradox. To seize victory in the fog of war; the commander needs a measure of order and control on his side, while imposing disorder and uncertainty on his opponent.

"Disorder on one side comes from order on the other" (ch. 5. 4). Yet he needs to remain seemingly chaotic enough to disrupt the ordered plans and fixed formations of the opposition, such that "the enemy does not know where to defend [and] does not know where to attack" (ch. 6. 2).

For the Sun Tzu commander; there are three grounding concepts by which to navigate the resulting jumble of possibilities. The first is "victory" itself. The sovereign and his chief commander must clarify their conception of success, whether for a one-off battle or a lengthy campaign. What will victory look like? How will it be measured? What happens afterwards? The second is "knowledge". The decisions they make and the actions they take in pursuit of victory, need to be grounded in concrete reality; as understood via the objective assessment of verifiable facts. The third is a specialist concept particular to Sun Tzu, which is translated here mostly as " strategic dominance" (shi, 势). The astute commander looks beyond immediate appearances to the shifting currents, or patterns of forces, that underlie every aspect of the conflict. To the degree that it is possible, he works to shape those currents for advantage, and ultimately to gain such an overwhelming advantage that the outcome of the conflict becomes a foregone conclusion.

Victory

It is asserted from the outset in the Sun-tzu that victory is the sole standard against which a commander benchmarks his decisions, actions, tactics and strategic considerations in the run-up to and during armed conflict. Not glory, reputation, pride, popularity; morality or political expedience — those are auxiliary or irrelevant. The objective is to win, not just to fight. What matters is to suppress or eliminate the threat that an adversary poses to one's own state, and that goal may be achieved either bloodlessly or by battle, depending on the circumstances. Sun Tzu is clear about which is better: "The military ideal is to force an opposing army to submit without battle" (ch. 3.1).

It is worth noting the contrast between the ideal of victory without destruction advocated by Sun Tzu, and the focus in Clausewitz, the West's nearest equivalent in influence, on victory as the culmination of a process in which both sides inevitably escalate towards maximum available force in the effort to destroy one another. Indeed, Clausewitz, in his book On War, dismissed the idea of victory without battle as nonsense. For Sun Tzu, however; battle is such a risky and costly component of the campaign to achieve state objectives that it is much better if a lower-risk, lower-cost alternative can be found. This explains why the "best tacticians of old" (ch. 4.2), often faded invisibly into history. Their victories were such battle-free walkovers that they failed to leave a trail of corpses and devasta-tion in their wake.

The twin objectives of victory without bloodshed where possible, and a coup de grace delivered on the battlefield where necessary, are pursued in parallel throughout the Sun-tzu. But in both cases, the commander must also grasp the point that victory, whether bloody or otherwise, is of limit-ed worth if it simply seeds the ground for another costly phase of conflict: "No state has ever profited from protracted war"(ch. 2.2).

Knowledge

Any commander applying principles from Sun Tzu, having set his sights on victory, must then assess the factors that may influence that out-come. Rational analysis is emphasized in the treatise as a source of reliable knowledge, and knowledge is key to the Sun Tzu commander's success. Indeed, the treatise begins and ends with chapters on the practical aspects of gathering accurate information by which to assess and influence the course of the conflict.

Chapter 1 opens with a five-part methodology for compiling and as-sessing comparative data on the two sides, while Chapter 13 stresses that judiciously managed intelligence operations provide the only assurance of anticipating an enemy's intentions.

As the intervening chapters make clear; knowing everything about the enemy it is not, in itself, enough. A successful commander must also thoroughly understand conditions on his own side, including the capacity; morale and readiness of his troops, as well as being able to objectively ap-praise his own personal and professional capabilities.

"When a commander understands equally well the condition of the op-position and the condition of his own side, his victory is never in doubt. " (ch. 10.5).

Sun Tzu also counsels commanders to obtain in-depth information about the terrain that must be marched, and about the battleground itself, so as to smooth progress and multiply their tactical options.

"The best generals assess the challenges of the terrain and plan for the distances involved, so as to anticipate the enemy and create conditions for victory"(ch. 10. 3).

Knowledge, in the Sun-tzu, is acquired partly in the form of empirically derived information, partly by correct analysis of that information, partly through studious preparation—the statement"It is imperative that this be studied and understood in depth" occurs five times in the treatise — and partly as a matter of judgment and experience. It is by developing his ability to acquire knowledge and objectively appraise conditions, at the operational level and in the broader strategic environment, that the Sun Tzu commander nurtures the awareness he needs to impose a necessary degree of order on the chaos of conflict.

Strategic dominance

A clear conception of victory and a solid foundation of objective knowledge together give the commander a sound footing for analysing and understanding the position he finds himself in at any point during the conflict. In order to anticipate the position, he is likely to be in tomorrow, or next month, however; he needs also to comprehend the evolving flow of events in which both he, and his adversary; are key actors. Better still, he needs to take command of that flow of events and turn it to advantage. This is where the concept of shi(势)comes into play.

"Strategic dominance,"as shi is rendered in this translation, refers to the inexorable momentum, both operational and strategic, that one side acquires when the balance of military tension tipsirreversibly in its favour. Sun Tzu offers vivid analogies for this phenomenon. Strategic dominance is "like a torrent, forceful enough to tumble boulders"(ch. 5. 3). Gaining strategic dominance is " like drawing taut a crossbow,"(ch. 5. 3). And, "For the commander who successfully exploits strategic dominance,giving battle is akin to rolling logs and boulders down a slope. "(ch. 5. 5).

The astute commander is always watching for trends and patterns among the factors that drive the strategic dynamic. Chapter 1 of the treatise groups these factors into five sets, some determined by the tactical and strategic choices of the commander himself, some dependent on the political and military institutions of the state, and some environmental, such as weather conditions and terrain. The balance among them continually shifts, sometimes subtly and sometimes dramatically. The Sun Tzu commander; who recognizes that he cannot simply impose static order on a dynamic situation,endeavours to read the currents and steer events in his side's favour:"Strategic dominance is a matter of exercising control over the situation by exploiting opportunities"(ch. 1. 4).

"Victory", "knowledge" and "strategic dominance" are foundational concepts in Sun Tzu, along with the treatise's three core pairs of complementary opposites. Together they orient readers towards what is probably the most fundamental skill of Sun Tzu-style military command—the ability to discern and act on deep patterns identified among the complex conditions of war. A useful way to contextualize these concepts,and the holistic science of war that they give rise to, is to briefly consider the dominant philosophical currents of the Warring States era.

Philosophical backdrop

An early task of Chinese philosophical thinking was tointuit deep patterns in the imagined workings of the universe, based on the rhythms in Nature that governed the lives of people in a settled, agrarian society. The methodological approach was largely holistic, seeking to relate the local to the global and the global to the local. For example, by observing natural phenomena like the flow of a stream, the phases of the moon and the cycle of life, death and renewal, one might infer cosmic principles based on currents and cycles, which could in turn inform an understanding of human affairs. In their holistic approach, Chinese philosophies differed from the methods of reductionist reasoning—analysing problems by dissecting them into their smallest constituent elements — that were coming to prevail in the Mediterranean region during that same period. Thinkers in ancient China attached greater value to ideas that conformed with direct experience and could be conveyed by analogy; than to knowledge based on an accumulation of logically linked facts.

Just as in ancient Greece, there was to begin with no sharp distinction in the Warring States world between applied knowledge and pure philosophy. The philosophical theories that endured in ancient China were those that could best be put to practical use in the realms of statecraft, medicine, ethics, military affairs and human relations. Practitioners in each of these fields shared a common recognition that the world and its diverse phenomena were subject to endless flux, some of it proceeding according to pattern and some of it incomprehensible. For example, the observation that extremes tended to be followed byreversals had the force of universal law. One way or another; good times would be followed by bad times, and then by good times again, and so on. Similarly with the observation that things that were joined together tended to break up, and later to merge again, and later still to break up again. Allies would at some point become enemies, and enemies would at some point become allies.

Whether or not there was a purpose to all thisflux, or an ideal state into which conditions might eventually subside, was another matter; and not a particularly practical one. The point was to recognize the inevitability of change, and come to know some of its patterns, and then, to the degree that one had personal control, to navigate a pathway through evolving circumstances in a manner that delivered a desired outcome-which might be a good harvest, moral virtue, political success, social harmony; or military victory.

That pathway was called the dao(道), literally a road or a way; and by implication the right road or way. Over the centuries the concept of dao became progressively more abstract and esoteric, as the practice of philosophy branched beyond its practical origins. In Warring States China, however, to write of the dao in any given field of knowledge was, in general, to apply a functional concept.

The Warring States era was philosophicallyeclectic, with numerous schools of thought attracting adherents and competing for patronage. All shared a fundamental faith in the principle of flux, and each employed, in their respective fashion, the trope of the dao. The different schools were, during this period, in the process of coalescing into the three broad ideologies that later came to be established as Taoism, Confucianism and Legalism, and traces of each can be found in the Sun-tzu.

The Science of War, Sun Tzu's Art of War re-translated and re-considered, Christopher Macdonald

➢ 注释

romanized　v.古罗马化,用罗马字书写

succinct　adj.简明的,简洁的,简练的

standalone　adj.单独的,独立的

compendium　n.摘要,纲要

incendiary　adj.引火的;燃烧的;纵火的;煽动的

digression　n. 离题，岔开

capitulate　vi. 认输，屈服；屈从，停止反抗；有条件投降；让步

disquisition　n. 专题论文，专题演讲

interpolate　v. 插入，插（话）；篡改

thematic　adj. 词干的；题目的；主题的；论题的

anomaly　n. 异常，反常；不规则；异常现象

tragicomic　adj. 悲喜剧的；又悲又喜

oxymoron　n. 矛盾形容法，逆喻

reflex　n. 反应能力；反射作用；影像，映像

dint　n. 作为（做）……的结果；凭借……

unconventional　adj. 非传统的；非常规的；不依惯例的

orthodox　adj. 规范的；公认的；普遍赞同的；正统的

combatant　n. 斗士；战士；

chivalric　adj. 有武士气概的，有武士风范的

principality　n. 公国，侯国

deviousness　n. 迂回；曲折

scruple　n. 良心上的不安；顾虑，顾忌

technocratic　adj. 由技术专家官员组成的；受技术官僚影响的

vainglorious　adj. 非常自负的，虚荣心强的；爱虚荣

whetstone　n. 磨石，油石

asymmetrical　adj. 不均匀的，不对称的；非对等

guileful　adj. 狡诈的，诡计多端的

rectilinear　adj. 直线的，形成直线的；用直线围着的，有直线的

outflank　v. 翼侧包围

gambit　n. 开局让棋法；策略，诡计

trope　n. 修辞，比喻

coalesce　v. 联合，合并

> **练习**

　　1. Please comment on"But art is not the focus of the *Sun-tzu*."

　　2. What are three pairs of the most powerful ideas carrying opposing meanings conveyed by Sun-tzu? Please comment on them.

　　3. What are the three grounding concepts for the Sun Tzu commander to navigate the resulting jumble of possibilities? Please comment on them.

三、阅读与比较:《孙子兵法》的三个版本

> **背景知识**

　　《孙子兵法》的英译历程一直到近代才得以开启,大致可以分为四个阶段。

　　萌芽期:20 世纪初期。1905 年,由英国皇家野炮兵上尉卡尔斯·罗普翻译的首部英文版《孙子兵法》在日本东京出版,开创了《孙子兵法》英译的先河。罗普的译本是在日文译本"十三篇"的基础上二度翻译得来,所以不管是准确度还是完整度都有缺失,在风格上也偏向于"日式"。1908 年,在吸取前作经验教训之后,罗普以《孙子兵法》的中文版本为原本对其进行了二次翻译,并将其命名为《兵书——远东兵学经典》。纵览全书,这部译作没有过多"日式风格",并且增加了吴起兵法和英文索引,相较前作内容更加丰富。但由于语言和理解的障碍,罗普的译作仍有不少错误之处,所以不能算是成功的译作。

　　1910 年,英国汉学家和翻译家翟林奈选择以清代《孙子十家注》为原本对其进行英译,书名为《孙子兵法——世界最古老的军事著作》。翟林奈的译本行文流畅,逻辑严谨,且比较准确地传递出原作的兵学理论和哲学思想,因而被后人奉为《孙子兵法》的经典译作,对促进《孙子兵法》在英语世界的广泛传播有不容忽视的作用。

　　发展期:20 世纪 40 年代至 70 年代是《孙子兵法》英译历程的快速发展期,先后共有 6 个英译本问世。第一部是由马切尔·考克斯于 1943 年出版的《孙子的战争原理》。跟随其后的是 1944 年萨德勒的英译本。由于质量

欠佳,这两部作品并没有引起太大反响。1945 年,郑麐翻译的名为《孙子兵法——约写成于公元前 510 年的军事指南》在重庆发表,这也是第一部由中国人自行翻译的《孙子兵法》,对促进中西方文化交流具有重大意义。1963年,葛振先翻译的《孙子兵法》在台湾出版。同年,塞缪尔·格里菲思的《孙子的战争艺术》在伦敦、牛津、纽约发售。格里菲思本身有着良好的汉语功底,且对《孙子兵法》有着透彻的研究,所以他的译本拥有极高的完整度,一经发行就获得极高赞誉。《孙子的战争艺术》在当年还被联合国教科文组织纳入《中国代表作丛书》,并成为后来转译他国文字最多的英译本,多次出版发行,是影响最为深远的《孙子兵法》英译本。1969 年,唐文长编译的《孙子重编:中英对照本》发表,这是第二部由中国人译著的《孙子兵法》英译本。

繁荣期:20 世纪 70 年代初至 90 年代中期。1972 年尼克松访华开启了中美两国关系改善和发展的新纪元。中美交流的增多使得《孙子兵法》的英译进入繁荣阶段,无论是研究人员、研究领域还是研究成果都有重大突破。1981 年,美籍英国作家詹姆斯·克拉维尔重新编辑出版了翟译本,鉴于其对《孙子兵法》颇具人文色彩的通俗解释和精心编辑,使得该书一经问世即成为发行最为广泛的《孙子兵法》普及读物。1987 年,纽约斯特林出版公司出版了陶汉章将军所著的《孙子兵法概论》英译本《孙子战争艺术》,被列为"20 世纪 80 年代最为畅销的军事理论书籍"之一。1993 年共有三部《孙子兵法》英译本问世。第一部是汉学家罗杰·埃姆斯(中文名为安乐哲)以我国西汉年间简本《孙子》为原本翻译,出版时名为《孙子兵法:第一个含有银雀山新发现竹简本的英译本》。值得一提的是,该译本是最早以汉简为原本进行翻译的译作之一。第二本是拉夫尔·索耶尔出版的《古代中国的七部军事经典》,该书的原本是《五经七书》,《孙子兵法》是其中一章。第三部是J. H. 黄翻译的《孙子兵法新译》。

鼎盛期:20 世纪 90 年代中期迄今。20 世纪 90 年代后,《孙子兵法》的英译达到高潮,除了传统意义上的文本翻译,人们还将其与军事领域之外的其他领域结合,用以指导人们的生活实践。这个时期比较重要的译作有这样几部:第一部是 1999 年加里·加利亚尔迪译著的《兵法:孙子之言》,因其译文之流畅、语言之精美,自出版后便成为各大网站的畅销书,并在 2003 年获得"独立出版商多元文化非小说类图书奖"。第二部是 2002 年著名汉学家约翰·闵福德出版的《孙子兵法》译作,由于其多年研究中国文化,所以这部译作很大程度上做到了忠实于原文。第三部是 2002 年由美国丹玛翻译小组出版的《孙子兵法》英译本,他们在翻译过程中力求保存原文的韵律格调。为弥补其内容上的缺失,他们还在文后附上注释汇总以方便读者理解。此后,汉学家梅维恒、作家卡伦·麦克里迪等人也相继出版了其作品。

文章来源:《孙子兵法》在英语世界的译介

2018 年 09 月 26 日 06:58 来源:中国社会科学网-中国社会科学报 作者:唐瑭 董晓波

http://news.cssn.cn/zx/bwyc/201809/t20180926_4569361_1.shtml

➢ 本节所节选的是《孙子兵法》的"计"篇,辅以两个英译本以借鉴比较。第一个是英国的第二代汉学家莱昂内尔·贾尔斯(Lionel Giles,1875～1958),其中文名为翟林奈的译本。第二篇则是加里·加葛里亚蒂的译文。1999 年,加里·加葛里亚蒂(Gary Gagliardi)出版了《兵法:孙子之言》(*The Art of War: In Sun Tzu's Own Words*)英译本。2003 年其更新版本 *Sun Tzu's Art of War Plus the Ancient Chinese Revealed* 获得"独立出版商多元文化非小说类图书奖",是唯一获奖的《孙子兵法》译本,也是唯一一个将《孙子兵法》翻译成其他语言的英文译本。供读者鉴赏比较。

➢ **素材 1.《孙子兵法》节选**

始计篇

孙子曰:兵者,国之大事,死生之地,存亡之道,不可不察也。

故经之以五事,校之以计,而索其情:一曰道,二曰天,三曰地,四曰将、五曰法。道者,令民与上同意也,故可以与之死,可以与之生,而不畏危。天者,阴阳、寒暑、时制也。地者,远近、险易、广狭、死生也。将者,智、信、仁、勇、严也。法者,曲制、官道、主用也。凡此五者,将莫不闻,知之者胜,不知者不胜。故校之以计,而索其情,曰:主孰有道? 将孰有能? 天地孰得? 法令孰行? 兵众孰强? 士卒孰练? 赏罚孰明? 吾以此知胜负矣。

将听吾计,用之必胜,留之;将不听吾计,用之必败,去之。计利以听,乃为之势,以佐其外。势者,因利而制权也。

兵者,诡道也。故能而示之不能,用而示之不用,近而示之远,远而示之近;利而诱之,乱而取之,实而备之,强而避之,怒而挠之,卑而骄之,佚而劳之,亲而离之。攻其无备,出其不意。此兵家之胜,不可先传也。

夫未战而庙算胜者,得算多也;未战而庙算不胜者,得算少也。多算胜,少算不胜,而况于无算乎? 吾以此观之,胜负见矣。

> **素材 2. An extract from** *The Art of War* **by Sun Tzu Translated by Lionel Giles(翟林奈)**

I. Laying Plans

1. Sun Tzu said: The art of war is of vital importance to the State.

2. It is a matter of life and death, a road either to safety or to ruin.

Hence it is a subject of inquiry which can on no account be neglected.

3. The art of war, then, is governed by five constant factors, to be taken into account in one's deliberations, when seeking to determine the conditions obtaining in the field.

4. These are:(1)The Moral Law;(2)Heaven;(3)Earth;(4)The Commander;(5)Method and discipline.

5,6. The Moral Law causes the people to be in complete accord with their ruler, so that they will follow him regardless of their lives, undismayed by any danger.

7. Heaven signifies night and day,cold and heat,times and seasons.

8. Earth comprises distances, great and small; danger and security; open ground and narrow passes;the chances of life and death.

9. The Commander stands for the virtues of wisdom,sincerely,benev-

olence,courage and strictness.

10. By method and discipline are to be understood themarshaling of the army in its proper subdivisions, the graduations of rank among the officers, the maintenance of roads by which supplies may reach the army, and the control of military expenditure.

11. These five heads should be familiar to every general: he who knows them will be victorious; he who knows them not will fail.

12. Therefore, in your deliberations, when seeking to determine the military conditions, let them be made the basis of a comparison, in this wise:

13. (1)Which of the two sovereigns is imbued with the Moral law? (2)Which of the two generals has most ability? (3)With whom lie the advantages derived from Heaven and Earth? (4)On which side is discipline most rigorously enforced? (5)Which army is stronger? (6)On which side are officers and men more highly trained? (7)In which army is there the greater constancy both in reward and punishment?

14. By means of these seven considerations I can forecast victory or defeat.

15. The general that hearkens to my counsel and acts upon it, will conquer: let such a one be retained in command! The general that hearkens not to my counsel nor acts upon it, will suffer defeat:——let such a one be dismissed!

16. While heading the profit of my counsel, avail yourself also of any helpful circumstances over and beyond the ordinary rules.

17. According as circumstances are favorable, one should modify one's plans.

18. All warfare is based on deception.

19. Hence, when able to attack, we must seem unable; when using our

forces, we must seem inactive; when we are near, we must make the enemy believe we are far away; when far away, we must make him believe we are near.

20. Hold out baits to entice the enemy. Feign disorder, and crush him.

21. If he is secure at all points, be prepared for him. If he is in superior strength, evade him.

22. If your opponent is of choleric temper, seek to irritate him. Pretend to be weak, that he may grow arrogant.

23. If he is taking his ease, give him no rest. If his forces are united, separate them.

24. Attack him where he is unprepared, appear where you are not expected.

25. These military devices, leading to victory, must not be divulged beforehand.

26. Now the general who wins a battle makes many calculations in his temple ere the battle is fought. The general who loses a battle makes but few calculations beforehand. Thus do many calculations lead to victory, and few calculations to defeat: how much more no calculation at all! It is by attention to this point that I can foresee who is likely to win or lose.

> 素材 3. An extract from *Sun Tzu's The Art of War* by Gary Gagliardi

Chapter 1: Analysis

SUNTZU SAID:

1 This is war.

It is the most important skill in the nation.

It is the basis of life and death.

It is the philosophy of survival or destruction.

You will know it well.

Your skill comes from five factors.

Study these factors when you plan war.

You must insist on knowing your situation.

1. Discuss philosophy.

2. Discuss the climate.

3. Discuss the ground.

4. Discuss leadership.

5. Discuss military methods.

It starts with your military philosophy.

Command your people in a way that gives them a higher shared purpose.

You can lead them to death.

You can lead them to life.

They must never fear danger or dishonesty.

Next, you have climate.

It can be sunny or overcast.

It can be hot or cold.

It includes the timing of the reasons.

Next is the terrain.

It can be distant or near.

It can be difficult or easy.

It can be open or narrow.

It also determines your life or death.

Next is the commander.

He must be smart,trustworthy,caring,brave,and strict.

Finally,you have your military methods.

They shape your organization.

They come from your management philosophy.

You must master their use.

All five of these factors are critical.

As a commander, you must pay attention to them.

Understanding them brings victory.

Ignoring them means defeat.

2 You must learn through planning.

You must question the situation.

You must ask:

Which government has the right philosophy?

Which commander has the skill?

Which season and place have the advantage?

Which method of command works?

Which group of forces has the strength?

Which officers and men have the training?

Which rewards and punishments make sense?

This tells when you will win and when you will lose.

Some commanders perform this analysis.

If you use these commanders, you will win.

Keep them.

Some commanders ignore this analysis.

If you use these commanders, you will lose.

Get rid of them.

3 Plan an advantage by listening.

Adjust to the situation.

Get assistance from the outside.

Influence events.

Then planning can find opportunities and give you control.

4 Warfare is one thing.

It is a philosophy of deception.

When you are ready, you try to appear incapacitated.

When active, you pretend inactivity.

When you are close to the enemy, you appear distant.

When far away, you pretend you are near.

You can have an advantage and still entice an opponent.

You can be disorganized and still be decisive.

You can be ready and still be preparing.

You can be strong and still avoid battle.

You can be angry and still stop yourself.

You can humble yourself and still be confident.

You can be relaxed and still be working.

You can be close to an ally and still part ways.

You can attack a place without planning to do so.

You can leave a place without giving away your plan.

You will find a place where you can win.

You cannot first signal your intentions.

5 Manage to avoid battle until your organization can count on certain victory.

You must calculate manage advantages.

Before you got to battle, your organization's analysis may indicate that you might not win.

You can count few advantages add up to victory.

Few advantages add up to defeat.

How can you know your advantages without analyzing them?

We can see where we are by means of our observations.

We can foresee our victory or defeat by planning.

➢ **注释**

benevolence   n. 仁慈;善行

marshal   v. 整理,排列,集结

➢ **练习**

Please compare the following English versions.

孙子曰:兵者,国之大事,死生之地,存亡之道,不可不察也。

Lionel Giles 译:Sun Tzu said: The art of war is of vital importance to the State. It is a matter of life and death, a road either to safety or to ruin. Hence it is a subject of inquiry which can on no account be neglected.

袁士槟译:War is a matter of vital importance to the state; a matter of life or death, the road either to survival or to ruin. Hence, it is imperative that it be studied thoroughly.

Gary Gagliardi 译：Sun Tzu said：This is war. It is the most important skill in the nation. It is the basis of life and death. It is the philosophy of survival or destruction. You will know it well.

林戊荪译：Sunzi said：War is a question of vital importance to the state, a matter of life and death, to road to survival or ruin. Hence, it is a subject which calls for careful study.

四、拓展阅读

➢ 背景知识

本部分旨在探究《孙子兵法》所表述的核心观点。其比较点为"战争"与"和平"。所选两篇文章分别从不同角度对这一主题进行探讨。第一篇文章节选自剑桥大学出版社出版的《中国古代和近代欧洲早期的战争与国家形成》，其中对中国古代和近代欧洲早期政权体系进行了比较。第二篇文章的作者从自身体验与经历出发探讨孙子兵法与和平的艺术。

➢ 素材 1. An extract from *War and State Formation in Ancient China and Early Modern Europe* by Victoria Tin-bor Hui

Was the Ancient Chinese System MoreHobbesian and Machiavellian Than the Early Modern European System?

Is it too counterintuitive to argue that the ancient Chinese system was more Hobbesian and more Machiavellian than the early modern European system? Constructivists, cultural relativists, and Chinese alike may find the current analysis puzzling. Chen Jian, for example, proclaims that"[t]erritorial expansionism or imperialism as known in the West was never an active part of Chinese civilization. " Roland Bleiker similarly argues that "a Confucian-oriented foreign policy is less likely to resort to violent means" because it seeks to establish in fluence "not through wars,but via nonviolent and persuasive methods such as education and indoctrination. " For those who believe that"the Chinese people are a uniquely peace-loving people," even Sunzi *bingfa* 's dictum of subduing the enemy without fighting-a coercive strategy tailored to overcome the logic of balancing-somehow becomes proof for the "pacifist bias" in China's military tradition.

True, the Chinese tradition can claim the Confucian-Mencian norm, which "assumes essentially that conflict isaberrant...When force is used, it should be applied defensively,minimally, only under unavoidable conditions,and then only in the name of the righteous tradition of a moral-political order. "Among Confucian thinkers, Mencius was "the most forthright pacifist. " The Mencius argues that *renzheng* or benevolent rule was the key to hegemony because a state with a good government will simultaneously secure its own strength and enjoy the sympathy of populations in other states. In addition to Confucians and Mencians,the Mohists treated war as an unnecessary evil;they developed the concept of justified war and engaged in the art of defensive warfare for cities under siege. These norms most likely originated from the elaborate system of li or rites codified in Western Zhou. In Zhou feudalism,honor dictated that one should not attack another *guo* of the same *ancestral* lineage,launch a surprise campaign, attack another state whose ruler recently died, take advantage of another state's internal power struggle except to help install the legitimate heir, employ a former official from the enemy camp to seek unfair advantage, injure or insult the ruler of the enemy state in combat, harm convoys sent from the enemy camp,kill prisoners of war, or cause casualties to civilians of the enemy state.

If such extensive norms about the proper conduct of war and diplomacy had been regularly followed,Chinese history would have been very different. China's classical texts produced in this era are testimonies against the "verbiage about China's pacific heritage." Various military classics take "a parabellum or hard realpolitik view of security" and "accept that war-fare and conflict are relatively constant features of interstate affairs, that conflict with an enemy tends towards zero-sum stakes, and consequently, that violence is a highly efficacious means for dealing with conflict."

In such abrutish world, international politics was "a match of fraud and deceit" in which "only the foolish and soon-to-be-defeated were burdened by the old code of ethics." The *Zhanguo ce* offers "a vivid portrait of the ruthless amorality... that characterized the... interstate relations of the period in general." Qin, in particular, could not have achieved domination had it not blatantly violated shared expectations. For scholars who are aware of Sunzian stratagems in the ancient Chinese era, there is the opposite tendency to think that the European system is exceptionally normative. Kalevi Holsti, for instance, argues that Europe was a "society of states" because "European sovereigns more or less adhered to fundamental norms that provided some semblance of order and even security." In contrast, ancient China was a "system of states" in which "insecure polities warred incessantly against each other and made conquest(and thereby obliteration) of neighboring states their ultimate political goal." Holsti adds that treaties were generally binding in modern Europe but were merely "temporary stratagems" in ancient China. It is true that there were extensive international treaties that formally codified norms about the conduct of war and diplomacy in Europe. But in early modern Europe as in ancient China, rules that interfered with *raison d'etat* were readily discarded. Machiavelli advocated fraud and deceit because he already witnessed "how treaties and promises have been rendered null and void by the dishonesty of rulers. " For instance, Francis I accepted an unfavorable treaty while under Charles V's captivity but quickly renounced it as soon as he was released. Louis XIV later ushered "an age of treachery" with little regard for tradition, religion, or loyalty. The self-strengthened Prussia and Russia further pursued a predatory foreign policy that made "a mockery of the conventions and constrictions of European statecraft. " Frederick the Great, in particular, disregarded the formalities of war declaration by attacking Austria at the death of Emperor CharlesVI in1740. Even the seemingly supreme norm about legitimate dynastic rights was either hypocritically exploited as an excuse for various wars of succession or conveniently ignored by self-strengthened states. Ultimately, it was the legacy of self-weakening expedients rather than respect for international norms that tempered both Hobbesian competition and Machiavellian stratagems in early modern Europe. Europeans were also saved by the availability of overseas colonies where nonnormative standards applied and enemies could be wiped out completely.

War and State Formation in Ancient China and Early Modern Europe, VICTORIATIN-BORHUI, University of Notre Dame, Cambridge University, Cambridge University Press.

➤ 素材 2. An extract from Sun Tzu for Success"Art of War vs. The Art of Peace"by Colin Benjamin

The writings of Sun Tzu have consistently delivered practical wisdom in my personal search for a creative approach to personal conflicts and challenging opportunities. Sun Tzu continues to offer practical advice in my daily battles to balance business survival with the desire to undertake struggles for social justice around the world.

For more than 40 years I have studied The Art of War as a source of strategic guidance. This study included the works of Niccolo Machiavelli, De Jomini, and Mao Ze Dung as I attempted to identify the differences between the mind of the military and civilian strategists.

In this extensive study, the practical wisdom of Sun Tzu shines like a beacon—the battle is not the war. The war is won in the mind of the opposing forces, not on the battleground. Peace, not war, is the key to best practices in strategy.

The works of Rudyard Kipling, Ian Fleming, Le Carre, Arthur Conan Doyle, and Tolkien proved literary ammunition for an appreciation of the genius of Chapter Thirteen on "The Employment of Secret Agents." Here, in one short chapter, is a profound insight into the Art of Peace— the means of avoiding unnecessary loss of life with practical, down-to-earth instruction on the management of people in the world of spies and secrets.

As a student participant in organizing anti-conscription for Vietnam campaigns, while also serving as a member of the volunteer Citizens Military Forces, I was in a strategic double bind.

My service was as a member of a psychology corps responsible for officer selection. As a result, I was placed in charge of a psychological warfare resource designed to understand the mind of the enemy. This led me for the first time to Sun Tzu's *The Art of War* and a lifetime interest in the mind of my opponent.

Australia entered the Vietnam War late in the campaign, much like it entered the war in Afghanistan. We adopted this position in support of the ANZUS alliance and in recognition of America's decisive role in defense against external aggression. My unit was in a psychology corps responsible for officer selection. As a clinician working in the field of mental health and clinical psychology, I was naturally interested in this field of study. I soon found the hidden genius in Sun Tzu. Here was a mother lode of wisdom, with passages such as "Therefore, the skillful leader subdues the enemy's troops without fighting," and "The supreme excellence is breaking the enemy's resistance without fighting."

Regular visits to China over the past 20 years have given me the chance to work with Chinese professors, entrepreneurs, and military leaders seeking to apply the thinking of Sun Tzu to the development of national enterprises. All have shared their view of Sun Tzu's work as a reference to the realities of commercial conflict with community goals. Sun Tzu's emphasis on winning with strategy is a counterpoint to the more action-oriented Western thinking.

It has been humbling to learn how to apply this ancient strategist's thinking to the construction of new community initiatives and government programs—all more than two centuries after *The Art of War* was written. Working for government ministers, multinational corporations, and my own firms offers a constant reminder of one of Sun Tzu's key rejoinders: "In battle, there are not more than two methods of attack—the direct and the indirect; yet these two in combination give rise to an endless series of maneuvers."

In summary, the struggle to apply Sun Tzu's wisdom has provided a valuable insight into the military and political mind. I see that every day it is necessary to survey the competitive terrain, identify the paths to success, and build a platform for achievement. The lessons learned are that peace is not just the absence of war. Peace is a measure of goodwill, personal trust, and freedom.

➤ 注释

Hobbesian adj. (英国政治哲学家)霍布斯的霍布斯哲学的

Machiavellian   adj. 马基雅弗利的,权谋术的

convoy   n. 车队,舰队

verbiage   n. 〈贬〉冗词;赘语;用语;措词

realpolitik   n. 实力政策

incessantly   adv. 不断地,不停地;接连不断;连绵不断;不已

obliteration   n. 涂去,删除;

expedients   n. 应急有效的,权宜之计

➢ 练习

1. Please read the passage 1 and comment on "the Chinese people are a uniquely peace-loving people, "even Sunzibingfa's dictum of subduing the enemy without fighting——a coercive strategy tailored to overcome the logic of balancing——somehow becomes proof for the "pacifist bias" in China's military tradition. "

2. Please read the passage 2 and comment on "the battle is not the war. The war is won in the mind of the opposing forces, not on the battle-ground. Peace, not war, is the key to best practices in strategy. "

五、现代回声

➢ 背景知识

商业中的孙子兵法

今天,孙子的魅力已经从军事领域延伸到商业领域,其原则非常适合于竞争激烈的商业环境。在美国和欧洲,关于战略、组织和竞争的书籍中广泛引用《孙子兵法》,其中许多引人注目的表述已经成为商业文章的导语。

在蓬勃发展的亚洲商业世界中,孙子的战略原则受到尊重,并被许多首席执行官用来带领公司走向繁荣。就像战争一样,商业是对意志的考验,充满活力,节奏迅速,以士气和装备为基础,处理如何高效地利用稀缺资源,它是永恒的和不断变化的,许多商人在世界各地发现了孙子的教导价值。

本部分的文章取自《孙子营销战略》一书，讲述如何在商战中运用孙子兵法。供读者鉴赏。

Passage: Extract from *Sun Tzu Strategies for Marketing* ——12 Essential Principles for Winning the War for Customers by Gerald A. Michaelson with Steven W. Michaelson

War is a matter of vital importance to the state; a matter of life and death, the road either to survival or to ruin. Hence, it is imperative that it be thoroughly studied.

Sun Tzu *The Art of War*

Why is a book written 500 years before the birth of Christ a modern-day best-seller? Why do coaches, professors, and business executives read Sun Tzu's *The Art of War*? Why does HBO's Tony Soprano quote the Master's work? What are the marketing applications of the timeless wisdom found in this ancient classic?

The Art of War is recognized as the concentrated essence of winning strategy. Within Sun Tzu's principles are the foundations for understanding the strategic principles of modem marketing. Gaining one insight will lead you to want to find more.

The Art of War is the cornerstone of Eastern military and business strategy. Today, there are more than a dozen translations of this ancient work into the English language. Dozens more apply the translations to business, sports, and personal success. Copies of The Art of War can be found in almost every language.

The basic tenet of Sun Tzu's philosophy is that if your strategy is well founded, you will win——and if you have a truly great strategy, you will win without fighting. This Eastern emphasis on overcoming your opponent with strategic wisdom differs significantly from Western strategy, which emphasizes action(fighting the big battle)as the way to win.

The strength of *The Art of War* for the contemporary manager is its simplicity. Inscribing laboriously on bamboo strips, Sun Tzu had to make every thought meaningful. There was nothing very complicated about battle in Sun Tzu's time. When battle was required, the war was won by foreknowledge, calculation, deception, and maneuver. It is the very simplicity of the ancient battle strategies that helps in making the transition from yesterday's lessons to tomorrow's plans.

Sun Tzu's maxims are simple, yet profound; brief, yet deep. The power of these concepts is overwhelming. They apply equally well to business and to everyday life. To win, we need Sun Tzu's power of the extraordinary applied in a precisely timed stroke to develop a torrent of momentum. Ask any Olympic champion about the momentum of extraordinary effort at just the right moment.

......

Over thousands of years, principles have been developed that serve as guidelines governing action. Sun Tzu lists five conditions and seven attributes as prerequisites for laying plans. Marketing's original four Ps have been expanded to eight. The American army field manual lists nine principles as the foundation of its strategies. From the armies of the world and from practical experience, we have distilled 12 principles as the cornerstone of great marketing. All principles embody these characteristics:

- Laws indicating the wisdom of certain actions
- Conditions that can lead to success
- Fundamental truths relevant to the success of the discipline

Following the principles does not guarantee victory. Ignore the principles, and you will surely lose. Perhaps a principle is most of all a guide that can sometimes be violated, but must always be considered. Principles are most often ignored by young nations and young companies. Substantial hard evidence indicates that winners adhere to principles.

Principles do not change over time. As we shall see in applying the timeless wisdom of Sun Tzu, the same basic principles have directed great leaders for centuries. Tactical doctrine is revised with every change in technology or technique.

In advice for applying principles, military strategist Edward Luttwak writes:

> Some writers attempting to use the military as a basis for business lessons have ignored the principles. No doubt, they found them frustratingly vague. But it is precisely the principles of war that best capture the essential lessons of the military experience, as opposed to mere techniques, which seem more useful at first because they can be precise, but which also turn out to be inapplicable to real-life needs in most cases.

It would be folly to believe that all principles apply in all situations. You should violate the principles only when you truly know that you are violating them. To know the principles and violate them is to take risks. The further you stray from the principles, the greater the risk. Professionals understand the subtleties of the principles; amateurs ignore the principles. Both take risks. Both win and lose. Only one has the odds in his or her favor. Only in unusual circumstances do great military and marketing generals take the risk of violating principles.

Amateurs violate principles simply because others have violated them. Principles adapted from war are a foundation for sales and marketing strategies. We shall consider these principles as a foundation for the "soft science" of marketing, where formulas are based on probabilities rather than certainties.

The application of these principles is an art. It is in this art that judgment comes into play. Application requires good judgment based on an understanding of the principles. The application to the planning function is called strategy. Their application to the execution of the plan is tactics.

Analyze the principles thoroughly. The assessment before the battle is often ignored in the rush to action.

First Principle: Honor the Customer. If the customer doesn't purchase your product or service, nothing else matters.

Second Principle: Organization of Intelligence. Know your market as well as you know yourself.

Third Principle: Maintenance of the Objective. A clear intention and a steady aim.

Fourth Principle: A Secure Position Occupy a position that cannot easily be taken by your opponents.

Fifth Principle: Offensive Action. Keep on the offensive to secure freedom of action.

Sixth Principle: Surprise. Surprise is the best way to gain psychological dominance and deny the initiative to your opponent.

Seventh Principle: Maneuver. The easiest routes are often the most heavily defended; the longest way round can be the shortest way home.

Eighth Principle: Concentration of Resources. Mass sufficiently superior force at the decisive place and time.

Ninth Principle: Economy of Force. Assess accurately where you employ your resources.

Tenth Principle: Command Structure. The management process un-leashes the power of human resources.

Eleventh Principle: Personal Leadership. It requires the leader's faith in his or her people and their faith in the leader's ability to win.

Twelfth Principle: Simplicity. Even the simplest plans are difficult to execute.

➤ 练习

1. Read the above passage and give a brief account of Gerald A. Michaelson and Steven W. Michaelson's view of Sun Tzu's *The Art of War*.

2. Please comment on"The basic tenet of Sun Tzu's philosophy is that if your strategy is well founded,you will win-and if you have a truly great strategy,you will win without fighting."

图书在版编目(CIP)数据

比较视野中的中国文化/曾新,褚颖主编. —上海:
上海三联书店,2022.

ISBN 978 - 7 - 5426 - 7818 - 8

Ⅰ.①比… Ⅱ.①曾…②褚… Ⅲ.①中华文化—研
究 Ⅳ.①K203

中国版本图书馆 CIP 数据核字(2022)第 153171 号

比较视野中的中国文化

主　　编　曾　新　褚　颖

责任编辑　钱震华
装帧设计　徐　炜

出版发行　上海三联书店

　　　　　(200030)中国上海市漕溪北路 331 号

印　　刷　上海昌鑫龙印务有限公司

版　　次　2022 年 10 月第 1 版
印　　次　2022 年 10 月第 1 次印刷
开　　本　700×1000　1/16
字　　数　330 千字
印　　张　22.5
书　　号　ISBN 978 - 7 - 5426 - 7818 - 8/K·682
定　　价　88.00 元